Off the Map

Off the Map challenges how international lawyers picture the world. While traditional scholarship continues to treat the "World Map" of states as natural, this book exposes the discipline's cartographic inheritance and its growing fatigue. Drawing on critical geography, international relations, and media theory, Nikolas M. Rajkovic reveals how global authority now operates less through contiguous territories than through infrastructures, corridors, and nodes. Introducing the concept of "juriscapes," he illuminates the legal significance of ports, data cable landings, aviation hubs, sanctions screens, and cloud regions – sites where rules bite and power circulates. He also develops the idea of pointillistic geographies, showing how law is enacted through coordinates, flows, and switches that escape the flat image of bordered states. Provocative yet accessible, *Off the Map* revisualizes international law for a fractured global order, equipping readers with the concepts to see where authority truly moves today.

NIKOLAS M. RAJKOVIC is Chair of International Law at Tilburg University, and a senior faculty member of Harvard Law School's Institute for Global Law and Policy.

"This sharp and lucidly argued book offers us powerful insights into the ways in which established perspectives have occluded our understanding of how power works in the international system. It is an indispensable guide to illuminating crucial developments in a time of crisis and bewilderment."

Antony Anghie, University of Utah

"*Off the Map* is a bold intervention that compels international lawyers to confront a dimension of their discipline that has long been taken for granted: its cartographic imagination. Nikolas M. Rajkovic shows with remarkable clarity how international law's core concepts – territory, jurisdiction, sovereignty – are products of a historically contingent visual and spatial order that continues to evolve. As Rajkovic says, to remain on the map, International Law must move beyond defending an inherited conceptual turf. This is a book that will greatly appeal to all students and scholars of International Law, but also of International Relations, Political Geography and History."

Ayşe Zarakol, University of Cambridge

"To map is to govern, to order, to comprehend – until the world outpaces your map. In this interdisciplinary tour de force, Professor Rajkovic reimagines the cartography of international law for a world of digital infrastructures, algorithmic management, informal economies, and black sites. In a series of elegant meditations, Rajkovic brilliantly challenges traditional notions of sovereignty, jurisdiction, and territory for a world truly gone, in his words, 'off the map.'"

David Kennedy, Harvard Law School

"Law and lawyers, rule and rules, maps and mapping, space and place, landscape and territory, information and infrastructure, optics and units, meaning and metaphor, worldview and world view: In this stunningly original book, familiar themes are reconfigured, concepts realigned, theory transformed. Juriscape displaces jurisdiction – definitively. All things modern melt away."

Nicholas Onuf, Florida International University

LSE International Studies

This series, published in association with the Centre for International Studies at the London School of Economics, is centred on three main themes. First, the series is oriented around work that is transdisciplinary, which challenges disciplinary conventions and develops arguments that cannot be grasped within existing disciplines. It will include work combining a wide range of fields, including international relations, international law, political theory, history, sociology and ethics. Second, it comprises books that contain an overtly international or transnational dimension, but not necessarily focused simply within the discipline of International Relations. Finally, the series will publish books that use scholarly inquiry as a means of addressing pressing political concerns. Books in the series may be predominantly theoretical, or predominantly empirical, but all will say something of significance about political issues that exceed national boundaries.

Previous books in the series:

Culture and Order in World Politics Andrew Phillips and Christian Reus-Smit (eds.)
On Cultural Diversity: International Theory in a World of Difference Christian Reus-Smit
Socioeconomic Justice: International Intervention and Transition in Post-war Bosnia and Herzegovina Daniela Lai
The World Imagined: Collective Beliefs and Political Order in the Sinocentric, Islamic and Southeast Asian International Societies Hendrik Spruyt
How the East Was Won: Barbarian Conquerors, Universal Conquest and the Making of Modern Asia Andrew Phillips
Before the West: The Rise and Fall of Eastern World Orders Ayşe Zarakol
Capitalism, Jacobinism and International Relations: Revisiting Turkish Modernity Eren Duzgun
The Counterinsurgent Imagination: A New Intellectual History Joseph MacKay
Dying Abroad: The Political Afterlives of Migration in Europe Osman Balkan

Resisting Racial Capitalism: An Antipolitical Theory of Refusal Ida Danewid
Regional Politics in Oceania: From Colonialism and Cold War to the Pacific Century Stephanie Lawson
Fueling Sovereignty Naosuke Mukoyama
Ways of Seeing International Organisations: New Perspectives for International Institutional Law Negar Mansouri and Daniel R. Quiroga-Villamarín
Representants and International Orders: The Staging of Political Authority Alena Drieschova
Global Decolonisation and Non-Sovereignty: Small Island States in the Caribbean Grace Carrington
Anticolonialism and Social Thought Anaheed Al-Hardan and Julian Go
Türkiye, Iran, and the Politics of Comparison: America's Wife, America's Concubine Perin E. Gürel
From Frontiers to Borders: How Colonial Technicians Created Modern Territoriality Kerry Goettlich
Before Recognition: How the Politics of Religion shaped the International Order Maria Birnbaum

Off the Map

A Critical Geography of International Law

NIKOLAS M. RAJKOVIC
Tilburg University

CAMBRIDGE
UNIVERSITY PRESS

CAMBRIDGE
UNIVERSITY PRESS

Shaftesbury Road, Cambridge CB2 8EA, United Kingdom

One Liberty Plaza, 20th Floor, New York, NY 10006, USA

477 Williamstown Road, Port Melbourne, VIC 3207, Australia

314–321, 3rd Floor, Plot 3, Splendor Forum, Jasola District Centre,
New Delhi – 110025, India

Cambridge University Press is part of Cambridge University Press & Assessment,
a department of the University of Cambridge.

We share the University's mission to contribute to society through the pursuit of
education, learning and research at the highest international levels of excellence.

www.cambridge.org
Information on this title: www.cambridge.org/9781009444361
DOI: 10.1017/9781009444392

When citing this work, please include a reference to the
DOI 10.1017/9781009444392

First published 2026

Cover image: brightstars/Photographer's Choice RF/Getty Images

A catalogue record for this publication is available from the British Library

*A Cataloging-in-Publication data record for this book is available from
the Library of Congress*

ISBN 978-1-009-44436-1 Hardback
ISBN 978-1-009-44438-5 Paperback

To my Family – my formative geography
For my Mentors – who taught me to see the world differently
With my Colleagues – fellow navigators of what continues to unfold
And to my Students – who shall redraw the bounds of what is possible

Contents

Figures

Preface

[T]he eye sees only what the mind is prepared to comprehend.

Robertson Davies, *Tempest-Tost*

Off the map is a colloquial expression that speaks to the fluctuating and splintering geographies of our contemporary legal globe. It conjures a range of images: atmospheric heat domes and geoengineering; contagion; Russia's occupation of eastern Ukraine; the legal crises surrounding Gaza's bombardment and blockade; the covert dynamics of shadow wars and drone strikes; climate-driven territorial claims over the Arctic and Greenland; the rise of cyberattacks and decentralized e-currencies; and tariffs targeting the geographies of global value chains. From dictionaries we learn that the phrase denotes spatial marginality, remoteness, obscurity, and exclusion from dominant mappings of the world.[1] Yet beyond this descriptive register, the phrase carries a deeper ontological charge – it points to spaces, places, and practices that exist outside prevailing frameworks of cartographic and legal intelligibility.

International lawyers encounter such dynamics whenever legal institutions struggle to *see* or engage actors and practices that do not conform to inherited cartographic coordinates of sovereignty, jurisdiction, and territory.[2] These blind spots are often framed through the language of exception or rendered obscure under categories such as black sites, extraterritorial military bases, informal economies, or digital infrastructures. But these are not mere anomalies. Rather, they reveal novel spatial grammars that disrupt the cartographic

[1] *Collins English Dictionary*, s. v. "off the map," accessed June 18, 2025, www.collinsdictionary.com/dictionary/english/off-the-map

[2] David Kennedy, *A World of Struggle: How Power, Law, and Expertise Shape Global Political Economy* (Princeton, NJ: Princeton University Press, 2016), 23–24.

rationality through which International Law has long organized its view of "the World." These disruptions challenge the assumption that International Law simply reflects an inherent geography of global order; instead, they suggest that law is deeply implicated in a cartographic ordering it purports to govern.

The observation captured in the epigraph frames this predicament at its most elementary level. What appears *off the map* is rarely absent from the world; it is more often misaligned with the visual and conceptual grammars through which International Law has *learned to see* and order planetary space. Legal vision, like cartographic vision, is structured in advance: It renders certain spatial forms legible while consigning others to obscurity. In this sense, being *off the map* signifies an ontological condition as much as a spatial one – an incapacity to read forms of authority, jurisdiction, and ordering that fall outside inherited cartographic frames.

In this light, *off the map* assumes a more critical significance: It denotes a condition of invisibility, illegibility, and unrecognizability within dominant regimes of knowledge, authority, and spatial ordering. This insight gains particular traction when considered vis-à-vis a concept we will explore across the book: *cartographization*. It is a historically consequential – yet largely overlooked – term you will struggle to find in most dictionaries. Cartographization refers to a process whereby the brute and manifold Earth has been transformed into a mapped, institutionalized, and cartographic sphere, rendered legible and governable as a tableau of geometric rationalities. Far from being a neutral or technical experience, this process functioned as a disciplinary project that inscribed the Earth's complex, relational materiality into a singular, bordered, and gridded legal globe. It engineered a cartographic world that continues to underwrite the spatial and ontological assumptions of international legal thought.

To be *on the map*, then, is to have been subjected to the conceptual and visual disciplining of cartographization – to be rendered visible within a cartographic-legal imaginary that privileges state-centric, contiguous, and planar territorialities. Conversely, to be *off the map* is not simply to reside outside geographic representation but to exist somehow disconnected from the globalized image of international legal cartography. This connotation applies to physical spaces as well as to institutional and normative formations that persist in between, beneath, or beyond cartographic world-making. It underscores the extent to which International Law depends on a particular spatial imaginary to assert authority and govern the global.

This dynamic is particularly pressing for disciplinary International Law, which has long been predicated on cartographic world-making to ground its spatial doctrines – sovereignty, jurisdiction, territorial integrity. These concepts, however, are not natural givens; they are themselves products of cartographization, which elevates specific contiguous, volumetric, and planar forms as legally self-evident. As Martti Koskenniemi has shown, international legal argument often obscures the contingency of its normative foundations beneath a veneer of technical neutrality, enabling specific spatial and political arrangements to appear inevitable and depoliticized.[3] The "World Map" of states is not a passive reflection of geo-legal reality; it is a legal text, invested with authority through repetition, institutionalization, and the erasure of alternatives.

Failing to recognize the constructed nature of cartographic world-making leads to what might be called an "ontological freeze" – a condition in which the visual grammar of legal space remains static, even as real-world practices of territorial rule become increasingly networked, pointillistic, layered, and noncontiguous – which the ensuing chapters will discuss. While international lawyers may presume that cartography reflects preexisting legal space, the inverse is true: Mapping practices have been actively used to shape and naturalize legal realities. As the renowned critical cartographer J. B. Harley underlined, maps are better understood as texts than as mirrors (see Chapter 6) – they construct narratives, project normative authority, and embed ideological claims under the guise of spatial precision.[4]

Engaging critically with the notion of being *off the map* thus offers more than rhetorical flair; it opens a conceptual and methodological entry point for rethinking geo-legal ordering on a global scale. It compels international lawyers and social scientists alike to examine how legal visibility and subjectivity are produced: whose spaces are included or excluded, which forms of authority are legitimized or denied, and

[3] Martti Koskenniemi, *From Apology to Utopia: The Structure of International Legal Argument* (Cambridge: Cambridge University Press, 2007), 5–6.

[4] See J. B. Harley, "Deconstructing the Map," *Cartographica* 26, no. 2 (1989): 1–20.

how cartographic mapping has functioned as a medium of rule. In this view, *off the map* is not a spatial aberration but a theoretical and empirical invitation – one that prompts us to examine the multiple, overlapping, and sometimes invisible legal boundaries that structure global exclusion and inclusion beyond formal, cartographic frontiers.

But the implications of being *off the map* extend beyond the perception of global space and rule – they penetrate the metaphorical ground of International Law as a discipline. Just as International Law is implicated in the cartographization of global authority, it is itself subject to mapping – by adjacent fields, institutional and nonstate actors, experts, think tanks, and evolving epistemic formations. Here, the stakes involved are not only territorial or geopolitical but also disciplinary and conceptual. The position of International Law *on the map* of global knowledge production is neither fixed nor transhistorical. For much of its history, international legal thought has drawn epistemic security from its association with a cartographic imaginary that privileges statehood, borders, and the contiguous logics of territorialization. These cartographic conventions helped secure the discipline's ontological authority – anchoring its concepts in supposedly self-evident spaces. But this reliance now faces critical challenges.[5] Scholars, from varied disciplines such as International Relations,[6] Geography,[7] Anthropology,[8] and Science and Technology Studies,[9]

[5] Gail Lythgoe, "A New Legal Geography for International Law," in *The Rebirth of Territory* (Cambridge: Cambridge University Press, 2024), 249–58.

[6] Jens Bartelson, *Becoming International* (Cambridge: Cambridge University Press, 2023); Tanja Aalberts and Thomas Gammeltoft-Hansen, "Sovereignty at Sea: The Law and Politics of Saving Lives in *Mare Liberum*," *Journal of International Relations and Development* 17 (2014): 439–68; and Sarah M. Chih and Mikael Rask Madsen, "Legal Diplomacy: Law, Politics, and the Genesis of Postwar European Human Rights," *Law and Contemporary Problems* 82, no. 1 (2019): 137–61.

[7] Nicholas Blomley, *Law, Space, and the Geographies of Power* (New York: Guilford Press, 1994); Nicholas Blomley, *Unsettling the City: Urban Land and the Politics of Property* (New York: Routledge, 2003); Stuart Elden, *The Birth of Territory* (Chicago: University of Chicago Press, 2013); and Joe Painter, "Prosaic Geographies of Statist Sovereignty," *Political Geography* 25, no. 7 (2006): 752–74.

[8] Annelise Riles, *The Network Inside Out* (Ann Arbor: University of Michigan Press, 2000); and Mark Goodale, "After International Law: Anthropology beyond the 'Age of Human Rights'," *AJIL Unbound* 115 (2021): 289–93.

[9] Bruno Latour, "*Onus Orbis Terrarum*: About a Possible Shift in the Definition of Sovereignty," *Millennium: Journal of International Studies* 44, no. 3

are increasingly interrogating law's spatial assumptions, drawing on alternative grammars – flows, networks, platforms,[10] ecologies – that defy the gridded coordinates through which International Law traditionally imagines global order.

This disciplinary remapping is not merely metaphorical; it is deeply historical and epistemic. It reflects an evolving struggle over who can authoritatively speak about space, law, and global governance. Concepts once presumed to 'belong' exclusively to International Law – sovereignty, jurisdiction, territory – are now being actively reinterpreted across other disciplines and epistemic communities.[11] To be *off the map*, in this context, does not only mean spatial illegibility; it also signals the risk of disciplinary marginalization amid shifting intellectual and social boundaries. To remain *on the map*, International Law must go beyond defending an inherited conceptual turf. It must confront the contingency of its own cartographic foundations and engage seriously with alternative spatial imaginaries now reengineering and shaping global legal ordering.

What is at stake here is not ontology in the philosophical sense of probing "being" as such, but rather the recognition that International Law is structured through particular ontological schemata that govern what can be perceived, articulated, and acted upon as "legal space." These are not neutral frameworks of description; they constitute the very conditions of intelligibility within which global order is conceived. While much of critical legal scholarship has foregrounded temporality – through genealogies, periodization, or narratives of rupture and continuity – this book instead emphasizes the spatializing work of International Law: the landscaping of global space into contiguous,

(2016): 305–20; Bruno Latour, *Down to Earth: Politics in the New Climatic Regime* (Cambridge: Polity, 2018); and Sheila Jasanoff, "Subjects of Reason: Goods, Markets, and Competing Imaginaries of Global Governance," *London Review of International Law* 4, no. 2 (2016): 361–91.

10 Giovanni de Gregorio, "The Law of the Platforms," in *Digital Constitutionalism in Europe: Reframing Rights and Powers in the Algorithmic Society*, Cambridge Studies in European Law and Policy (Cambridge: Cambridge University Press, 2022), 80–122.

11 David Kennedy, "The 'Rule of Law,' Political Choices, and Development Common Sense," in *The New Law and Economic Development: A Critical Appraisal*, ed. David M. Trubek and Alvaro Santos (Cambridge: Cambridge University Press, 2006), 95–173; and Martti Koskenniemi, "Miserable Comforters: International Relations as New Natural Law," *European Journal of International Relations* 15, no. 3 (2009): 395–422.

bordered, and standardized forms. This spatializing gesture, far from being incidental, has long been secured through a deep ontological standardization that predates contemporary debates about formal and informal "standards" in lawmaking. The legal imagination of the state as a geometric, polygonal unit – flattened, bounded, and equivalent – operates as an unspoken standard that normalizes a symmetry of sovereign equality. It is this silent regularity of the cartographic imaginary, more than any explicit treaty or institution, that has standardized the "thinkable" in international legal thought. To apprehend this is to recognize that the discipline's conceptual foundations are themselves products of a cartographic ontology – one that naturalizes its own abstractions while excluding alternative spatialities from recognition as legal ordering.

Reflexivity or Retromania?

Responding to the spatial challenges of the present requires more than doctrinal reform or institutional adaptation; it demands disciplinary and theoretical reflexivity – a critical reckoning with how International Law's dominant World Map was historically produced, by whom, and to what ends. What forms of knowledge and agency were obscured or effaced in that process?[12] Which worlds were excluded? In a moment when the very idea of a coherent global legal order appears fractured, International Law must ask whether its reigning spatial imaginary remains adequate to contemporary legal practices and global conditions. Without such engagement, the field risks clinging to a cartographic worldview in institutional decline – descending into what might be called a juridical *Retromania*.

Simon Reynolds' concept of *Retromania* – the cultural condition of compulsive recycling of the past – offers a useful lens for diagnosing such a theoretical malaise. In *Retromania*,[13] Reynolds explores how popular culture has become addicted to its own history, privileging nostalgia and repetition over innovation. Artistic creativity, he argues,

[12] See Walter D. Mignolo, "Putting the Americas on the Map: Cartography and the Colonization of Space," in *The Darker Side of the Renaissance: Literacy, Territoriality, and Colonization* (Ann Arbor: University of Michigan Press, 2003), 259–313.

[13] Simon Reynolds, *Retromania: Pop Culture's Addiction to Its Own Past* (London: Faber & Faber, 2011), 3–6.

has given way to curation and reenactment, producing a feedback loop in which the past dominates the imaginative horizon of the future.

International legal thought exhibits similar tendencies. Confronted by transboundary phenomena such as climate breakdown, cyber governance, global financial flows, and algorithmic regulation, it continues to organize itself around a spatial logic rooted in cartographic territoriality.[14] Statist jurisdiction, Euclidean geometry, and contiguous boundaries remain central axioms within International Law's inherited World Map – even as these spatial premises are increasingly outpaced by emergent modes of legal ordering. To borrow Reynolds' metaphor, international lawyers seem to be nostalgically reissuing doctrinal vinyl: reasserting territorial integrity, rehearsing sovereignty, and redrawing jurisdictional lines, as if these containers retain timeless relevance in a world marked by fluidity, networks, and trans-territorial forms of authority. This is not merely doctrinal conservatism – it may signal a deeper ontological and epistemological fatigue. Rather than envisioning new spatial forms, international legal thought tends to curate inherited ones, maintaining a cartographic orthodoxy that forecloses engagement with plural spatialities.[15] The result is a legal map that retains surface coherence while being increasingly overwhelmed by dispersed, noncontiguous, and trans-territorial configurations of authority, power, and rule.[16]

Avoiding juridical *Retromania* requires more than a critique of International Law's cartographic inheritance; it demands a reconfiguration of the discipline's spatial grammar to apprehend the legal geographies reshaping global order. As trans-territorial configurations become increasingly operative – from digital infrastructures and climate systems to global production chains and transnational

[14] See Elden, *The Birth of Territory*, 112–15; and Saskia Sassen, *Territory, Authority, Rights: From Medieval to Global Assemblages* (Princeton, NJ: Princeton University Press, 2006), 84–88.

[15] Bruno Latour, *Politics of Nature: How to Bring the Sciences into Democracy*, trans. Catherine Porter (Cambridge, MA: Harvard University Press, 2004), 62–66; and Sundhya Pahuja, *Decolonising International Law: Development, Economic Growth and the Politics of Universality* (Cambridge: Cambridge University Press, 2011), 129–34.

[16] See Mariana Valverde, "Jurisdiction and Scale: Legal 'Technicalities' as Resources for Theory," *Social & Legal Studies* 18, no. 2 (2009): 139–57; and Anna Lowenhaupt Tsing, *Friction: An Ethnography of Global Connection* (Princeton, NJ: Princeton University Press, 2005), 38–42.

enforcement regimes – the institutional architectures of International Law are being stretched, reoriented, and, in some cases, fractured. Legal authority now circulates through modalities that defy conventional metrics of territorial presence: via drone operations,[17] algorithmic governance, extraterritorial sanctions, and the infrastructural regulation of flows.[18] In such contexts, foundational coordinates such as sovereign consent, jurisdictional exclusivity, and fixed borders lose normative traction – not merely as tools of enforcement but also as frameworks of legal legibility.

To navigate this shifting terrain, International Law must cultivate a renewed spatial imagination – one capable of theorizing and tracing alternative spatial forms that more accurately reflect contemporary juridical realities.[19] These may include imaginaries grounded in networks, assemblages, and circulatory systems, as well as forms of legal ordering that resist cartographic capture altogether: Indigenous jurisdictionalities,[20] oceanic cosmologies,[21] algorithmically mediated normativities.[22] Only by cultivating such renewed spatial imagination can International Law remain meaningfully *on the map* – not as a legacy discipline recycling a Eurocentric vision of the globe but as a mode

[17] See Grégoire Chamayou, *A Theory of the Drone*, trans. Janet Lloyd (New York: The New Press, 2015); and Annelise Riles, *Collateral Knowledge: Legal Reasoning in the Global Financial Markets* (Chicago: University of Chicago Press, 2011), 9–20.

[18] Shoshana Zuboff, *The Age of Surveillance Capitalism* (New York: Public Affairs, 2019), 312–16; and Dan Jerker B. Svantesson, *Solving the Internet Jurisdiction Puzzle* (Oxford: Oxford University Press, 2017), 52–55.

[19] Approaches include Gilles Deleuze and Félix Guattari, *A Thousand Plateaus: Capitalism and Schizophrenia*, trans. Brian Massumi (Minneapolis: University of Minnesota Press, 1987), 16–20; Jane Bennett, *Vibrant Matter: A Political Ecology of Things* (Durham, NC: Duke University Press, 2010), 45–49; and Benjamin H. Bratton, *The Stack: On Software and Sovereignty* (Cambridge, MA: MIT Press, 2016), 98–102.

[20] See John Borrows, *Canada's Indigenous Constitution* (Toronto: University of Toronto Press, 2010).

[21] Upolu Lumā Vaai, "Philosophical Vectors of Oceanic Diplomacy and Development: The Samoan Wisdom of Restraint Meets the Australian Indigenous Relationalist Ethos," *Australian Journal of International Affairs* 77 (2023): 677–81.

[22] Denise Garcia, "Algorithms and Decision-Making in Military Artificial Intelligence," *Global Society* 38, no. 1 (2024): 24–33; Joshua A. Kroll et al., "Accountable Algorithms," *University of Pennsylvania Law Review* 165, no. 3 (2017): 633–705; and Karen Yeung, "Algorithmic Regulation: A Critical Interrogation," *Regulation & Governance* 12, no. 4 (2018): 505–23.

of legal thought responsive to the dynamic spatial architectures that now configure global power.

Politically, recent appeals for national reassertion and geopolitical restoration reflect a nostalgic desire to recover the ontological security once promised by the cartographic World Map of states.[23] These calls express a broader anxiety provoked by the erosion of spatial certainties – when identity, authority, and geography no longer align neatly within the territorial grid. Yet this perceived unravelling obscures the imperial and racialized foundations of the modern legal map, which was built through logics of enclosure, domination, and exclusion.[24] Efforts to preserve or restore this mapped order frequently conceal its historically contingent and hierarchical origins. To confront this inheritance critically is not to reject cartographic ordering itself but to interrogate how emergent spatial logics – such as digital sovereignty,[25] planetary risk governance,[26] and climate-induced displacement[27] – are being grafted onto the legal architectures of cartographic modernity. These new geographies do not displace classical legal categories such as territory, sovereignty, or jurisdiction; rather, they hybridize them, generating layered, sometimes contradictory, formations of governance that international lawyers must learn to navigate and theorize.[28]

23 John Agnew, "The Territorial Trap: The Geographical Assumptions of International Relations Theory," *Review of International Political Economy* 1, no. 1 (1994): 77–80; see also Chris Rumford, "Theorizing Borders," *European Journal of Social Theory* 9, no. 2 (2006): 155–69.

24 Antony Anghie, *Imperialism, Sovereignty and the Making of International Law* (Cambridge: Cambridge University Press, 2005), 32–40; Lauren Benton, "Anomalies of Empire," in *A Search for Sovereignty: Law and Geography in European Empires, 1400–1900* (Cambridge: Cambridge University Press, 2010), 1–39.

25 See Chenchen Zhang and Carwyn Morris, "Borders, Bordering and Sovereignty in Digital Space," *Territory, Politics, Governance* 11 (2023): 1051–58.

26 See Duncan McLaren and Olaf Corry, "Clash of Geofutures and the Remaking of Planetary Order: Faultlines Underlying Conflicts over Geoengineering Governance," *Global Policy* 12, no. S1 (2021): 20–33.

27 Cristiano d'Orsi and Gino J. Naldi, "Climate-Induced Displacement in the Sahel: A Question of Classification," *International Review of the Red Cross* 103 (2021): 1029–65.

28 See Mariana Valverde, "Theorizing the Space and Time of Law," in *Chronotopes of Law: Jurisdiction, Scale and Governance* (New York: Routledge, 2015), 30–53.

This is not a moment of disciplinary decline but one of generative dislocation – a rupture that opens space for reimagining the spatial imaginaries at the heart of international legal thought.[29] The cartographic inheritance of the discipline may endure, but it can no longer serve as the sole compass for navigating the plural, dynamic, and contested terrains of global legality. To remain epistemically responsive, disciplinary International Law must reimagine its mapping of the legal globe – not to recover a lost coherence but to render visible the emergent legal forms[30] – assemblages, infrastructures, atmospheres – that now constitute global ordering. Only by recalibrating its conceptual repertoire can the discipline enhance its relevance – both within the coordinates of a familiar map and within a legal world whose spatial grammars are still being written. The task, then, is not to discard the incumbent World Map but to expose it as a constructed and unfolding text. Through critical and imaginative engagement with the spatial assumptions being reworked by overlapping legal, technological, and environmental forces, International Law may avoid the temptations of *Retromania* and reorient itself within trans-territorial landscapes that increasingly define the legal globe.

Mapping the Innumerable

Reimagining International Law in an era of spatial rupture requires confronting not only the cartographic logic of conventional legal thought but also its epistemic mediums. If maps have historically shaped the way modern law perceives space, so too has *the book* shaped how it thinks. The ensuing challenge, then, is not merely one of spatial remapping but of intellectual mediumship: how International Law conceptualizes, constructs, and circulates its core ideas. In this context, the future of the book is not a question of form alone but also of disciplinary capacity.

[29] Some examples include: David Delaney, *The Spatial, the Legal and the Pragmatics of World-Making: Nomospheric Investigations* (New York: Routledge, 2010); and Andreas Philippopoulos-Mihalopoulos, *Spatial Justice: Body, Lawscape, Atmosphere* (London: Routledge, 2015).

[30] For example, consider how the perception of territory may be re-examined relative to property: Nicholas Blomley, "Precarious Territory: Property Law, Housing, and the Socio-Spatial Order," *Antipode* 52, no. 1 (2020): 36–57.

The medium of the book has long served as a vehicle for theoretical synthesis and conceptual innovation in International Law. It is the format through which landmark arguments have been staged and scholarly lineages established – from Lauterpacht and Chimni to Koskenniemi, and from Kennedy, Knop, and Orford to Anghie – to name but a few. These texts have done more than inform; they shape the contours of disciplinary memory, anchoring debates across generations. Yet the monograph today finds itself increasingly *off the map* of institutional value. The reasons are both structural and philosophical: The generative temporality required for the book – slow thinking, recursive development, speculative inquiry – is at odds with the accelerative demands of the metrified university.[31]

Recent decades have witnessed an escalating emphasis on research metrics, performance benchmarking, and knowledge valorization.[32] These managerial frameworks increasingly determine what kind of scholarship counts, how it circulates, and where it sits within hierarchies of institutional prestige.[33] Under such governance, the book is often framed as a costly and an imposing albatross, where the return on intellectual investment is difficult to quantify,[34] and its temporal horizon often exceeds the reporting cycles of research output audits.[35] Accordingly, this preface offers an apt moment to reflect on the changing place of the book in international legal thought amid the rise of digital media, research assessment regimes, and accelerated publication cultures.[36]

31 Maarten Hillebrandt and Michael Huber, "Quantifying Higher Education: Governing Universities and Academics by Numbers," *Politics and Governance* 8, no. 2 (2020): 1–5; see also Benjamin Ginsberg, *The Fall of the Faculty: The Rise of the All-Administrative University and Why It Matters* (New York: Oxford University Press, 2011).

32 See Ingo Venzke, "Against Impact," *Leiden Journal of International Law* 37, no. 4 (2024): 757–62.

33 See Deborah Lupton, *The Quantified Self* (Cambridge: Polity, 2016).

34 Wendy Laura Belcher, *Writing Your Journal Article in Twelve Weeks: A Guide to Academic Publishing Success* (Chicago: University of Chicago Press, 2019), 5–7.

35 See Stefano Collini, *What Are Universities For?* (London: Penguin, 2012), 168–77; see also William Germano, *Getting It Published: A Guide for Scholars and Anyone Else Serious about Serious Books*, 3rd ed. (Chicago: University of Chicago Press, 2016).

36 Sally Engle Merry, *The Seductions of Quantification: Measuring Human Rights, Gender Violence, and Sex Trafficking* (Chicago: University of Chicago Press, 2016), 9–21.

It asks how the book might be relocated – not nostalgically defended but critically repositioned – in a scholarly landscape increasingly structured by speed, visibility metrics, and compressed formats. Under such managerialism, knowledge becomes legible primarily through quantifiable outputs: citation indexes, impact scores, h-index rankings, and grant income.[37] These instruments have transformed scholarly value from a question of intellectual contribution to one of statistical visibility.[38] As Maggie Berg and Barbara Seeber observe, the "supermarket model" of research tends to prioritize output over insight and performance over patience.[39] Monographs, by their nature, resist such economization. As a result, they are frequently cast as indulgences: viable perhaps for the senior – or delinquent – scholar with institutional security but risky for those navigating academic precarity. To write my book in such a time has often felt like an act of resistance, rather than an essential journey needed for disciplinary reflection and, possibly, regeneration.

This epistemic marginalization has implications beyond institutional career pathways. As the book is marginalized as a contribution of academic value, the forms of thought it sustains – genealogical excavation, conceptual synthesis, historical contextualization – are rendered more difficult to maintain. In a discipline that must now grapple with algorithmic governance, climate collapse, and noncontiguous territorialization, this is no minor loss. The book supports a long arc of inference, allowing ideas to traverse temporal, disciplinary, and methodological registers in ways shorter formats cannot.

The proliferation of legal blogs and digital platforms has only intensified this shift. Websites such as *EJIL: Talk!*, *Opinio Juris*, and *Just Security* have become critical spaces for real-time engagement with international legal events. They facilitate dialogue and

[37] Sarah de Rijcke et al., "Evaluation Practices and Effects of Indicator Use: A Literature Review," *Research Evaluation* 25, no. 2 (2016): 161–69.

[38] David Barton and Sharon McCulloch, "Negotiating Tensions around New Forms of Academic Writing," *Discourse, Context & Media* 24 (2018): 8–15.

[39] Maggie Berg and Barbara K. Seeber, *The Slow Professor: Challenging the Culture of Speed in the Academy* (Toronto: University of Toronto Press, 2016), 57–58: "Slowing down is about asserting the importance of contemplation, connectedness, fruition, and complexity. It gives meaning to letting research take the time it needs to ripen.… It gives meaning to periods of rest, an understanding that research does not run like a mechanism; there are rhythms, which include pauses and periods that may seem unproductive."

incubation and broaden the field's public reach.[40] In doing so, they have altered the public face of international legal scholarship. However, these platforms also privilege particular epistemic aesthetics, which demands clarity, speed, and topicality. Legal commentary flirts with a genre of "performance"[41] – the timely insight, the authoritative voice, the conclusive tone. These constraints are not merely formal. As Marshall McLuhan famously argued, the medium of communication structures the very thought it conveys.[42] Digital platforms prioritize brevity, linearity, and summary. They resist recursion, contradiction, and slow synthesis. They are optimized for shareability rather than difficulty. The consequence is an epistemic contraction, wherein thought is increasingly flattened to match the logics of the platforms that host it. As Richard Lanham noted, "the economics of attention" now shape not only what is written but also how and why it is written.[43]

In such an ecology, the book assumes renewed critical importance. It offers a different scale of argument as well as a different mode of engagement. It supports temporality rather than urgency, reflection rather than reaction, structure rather than succession. It allows law to think genealogically, historically, and speculatively. In the face of planetary disruptions and normative uncertainty, these are essential capacities. To advocate for the book, then, is not to reject the blogosphere or digital scholarship. It is to insist on a broader epistemic ecology – one that values the complementary affordances of different media. Legal blogs are vital for immediate response; books, for reflection. Blogs facilitate entry into the debate; books can transform its grammar. What is at stake is not preference but possibility: the kind of knowledge International Law can generate and the kind of futures it can envision. If legal blogs provide the first word, books

[40] See Panagiotis A. Kyriakou, "International Law Shaping and Digital Ecosystems: Between Sensationalism and Empowerment," *Asian Journal of International Law* 15, no. 1 (2025): 232–51, https://doi.org/10.1017/S2044251324000328

[41] See Jeffrey C. Alexander, *Performance and Power* (Cambridge: Polity, 2011).

[42] Marshall McLuhan, *Understanding Media: The Extensions of Man* (Cambridge, MA: MIT Press, 1994), 7–21.

[43] Richard A. Lanham, *The Economics of Attention: Style and Substance in the Age of Information* (Chicago: University of Chicago Press, 2006); see also Kathleen Fitzpatrick, *Planned Obsolescence: Publishing, Technology, and the Future of the Academy* (New York: NYU Press, 2011).

are often essential for the second thought: the reflective, speculative, and recursive thinking that underpins serious legal theory. And if International Law is to remain intellectually responsive to planetary conditions, infrastructural entanglements, and plural legal orders, it must preserve the scholarly ecologies that make such thinking possible.

To relocate the book within the epistemic map of International Law is to reposition thought itself. It is to affirm that form shapes content, that intellectual labor requires time, and that theory needs room to unfold. Being *off the map*, in this sense, is not a loss but an opening. It is an opportunity to rethink what International Law sees, as well as how it sees – to imagine anew the media through which law thinks. To remain *on the map* in a world of shifting legal geographies, International Law must also reflect critically on the spatial and institutional coordinates of its own knowledge production. This reflection includes revaluing the temporal, epistemic, and conceptual affordances of the book – not as a nostalgic artefact but as a vital medium through which International Law might yet think otherwise.

As with any project that unfolds across shifting conceptual and disciplinary terrains, the arguments assembled here did not emerge all at once but rather through earlier avenues of inquiry. Portions of the arguments developed in this book first appeared along various itineraries of thought. Several chapters draw upon, revise, and considerably expand fragments of my previous writings, including "On Fragments and Geometry: The International Legal Order as Metaphor and How it Matters" (2013), "The Visual Conquest of International Law: Brute Boundaries, the Map and the Legacy of *Cartogenesis*" (2018), "International Law and the Ides of March: A Response to David Kennedy" (2018), "The European Union and Critical Legal Cartography: Old Geopolitics, Worn Geopoetry, and the Return of Geopower" (2022), and "What Is the Global? Reassembling How International Lawyers See Space and Time" (2025). These earlier texts served less as blueprints than as provisional coordinates – conceptual waypoints that helped orient the broader cartographic and theoretical journey undertaken here. While this book recasts those materials through new vantage points and expanded argumentation, I acknowledge their presence as part of the evolving cartography of ideas that ultimately gave shape to *Off the Map*.

Mapping the Incontiguous: Acknowledgments

Every book is a journey, and book writing rarely follows a straight line. This book, like many others, was written along discontinuous paths – through detours, hesitations, and moments of both clarity and doubt. My intellectual trajectory cannot be fully mapped by institutional affiliations or disciplinary coordinates alone. Rather, it is indebted to a more intricate and incontiguous geography of support: one formed across time, space, and people.

Acknowledgments, like maps, are selective and inevitably incomplete. They cannot capture the full terrain of gratitude or trace every influence with precision. They nonetheless gesture toward the broader ecology within which scholarship emerges: a field composed not only of citations and conferences, but also of shared meals, read drafts, enjoyed drinks, and encouragement offered at just the right moment. In what follows, I offer thanks to those whose presence – near and far, continuous and intermittent – shaped this book's becoming. These connections form their own kind of cartography: layered, shifting, and *off the map*, but no less real for it.

How one enters a field of inquiry profoundly shapes how its horizons are perceived and navigated. Before turning to academic International Law, I was a litigation lawyer practicing in domains where the legal and extra-legal were deeply entangled. Whether working on matters involving medical malpractice, commercial transactions, corporate governance or labor grievances, the cases I encountered were never merely legal disputes. They were complex assemblages of juridical form, social context, institutional dynamics, and affective undercurrents.

Success in litigation often depended as much on doctrinal mastery as on an interpretive sensibility attuned to adjacent fields – medicine, finance, business, organizational culture, and human psychology. To lead a case effectively required grasping how legal and nonlegal elements co-constituted its stakes and form.

Yet as I transitioned from legal practice into academic scholarship, I was struck by a curious inversion in the ethos. Where practice demanded a capacity to traverse boundaries, to draw pragmatically and creatively across knowledge domains, disciplinary International Law seemed consumed by a logic of boundary maintenance. Disciplinary rigor was measured not by capacious synthesis or interpretive dexterity, but by fidelity to methodologically enclosed terrains – doctrinal, historical, or theoretical. Interdisciplinary gestures were sometimes tolerated and often suspicious, and thus rarely integral. The governing imaginary was one of jurisdictional demarcation and preservation, rather than of intellectual bridging and innovation.

This shift was more than merely stylistic; it revealed deeper assumptions about what constitutes relevant knowledge – and who may be recognized as an "international" lawyer. In practice, knowledge is often situated, contingent, and improvisational. It emerges through embodied encounters, interpretive leaps, and an attunement to the entangled legal and extra-legal dimensions of complex problems. In this sense, the move from practice to theorizing was not merely a change in vocation – it was a crossing into a different epistemic geography, one that often conceals its borders even as it polices them. Entering this space, I often felt intellectually *off the map*: familiar with the terrain, but unsure of my coordinates within it.

It is for these reasons that I begin my acknowledgments with David Kennedy. His founding of the Institute for Global Law and Policy at Harvard Law School (IGLP) has been profoundly transformative, shaping both my own trajectory and that of a generation of international legal scholars seeking to navigate the field otherwise. For many of us, the IGLP offered a refuge from rigid disciplinary cartographies: a space where the boundaries of legal scholarship could be stretched, challenged, and redrawn. It has served as a rare intellectual commons – a site for those whose inquiries routinely traverse doctrinal, historical, political, and economic dimensions. The IGLP became a space where being *off the map* was not a liability, but a virtue. David could have used his intellectual capital to further entrench the discipline's dominant maps. Instead, he chose to redraw them – investing outward, not inward; opening space rather than enclosing it. It reflects a vision of the field as dynamic and revisable, and of scholarship as something capacious enough to accommodate voices and horizons not yet *on the map*.

Within the IGLP, I encountered some of the most generative and intellectual relationships of my academic life – colleagues, sparring partners, and friends who accompanied me along unmarked paths and unexpected turns. I am deeply grateful to Antony Anghie, Diamond Ashiagbor, Maddy Chiam, Dan Danielsen, Dennis Davis, Aziza Ahmed, Arnulf Becker Lorca, Cyra Choudhury, Richard Clements, Seamus Darby, Karen Engle, Günter Frankenberg, Chris Gevers, John Haskell, Jason Jackson, Vidya Kumar, Lucas Lixinski, Vasuki Nesiah,

Daniel Pinheiro Astone, Hani Sayed, Poul Kjaer, Michelle Le Roux, Martti Koskenniemi, Zina Miller, Vasuki Nesiah, Scott Newton, Zoran Oklopčić, Akbar Rasulov, Kerry Rittich, Leo Specht, Chantal Thomas, Kristen Verdeaux, Dina Waked, Robert Wei, and Lucie White. This book is indebted to that vision, and to the people and many places that have made it possible to find my bearings without always needing to stay on the charted path.

The erratic topography of a scholarly life is rarely traversed alone. It requires perseverance and imagination alongside the presence of devoted mentors, colleagues, and friends – intellectual sherpas who, for reasons that remain both humbling and cosmic, saw value in my questions and potential in my voice. I have been extraordinarily fortunate to journey alongside some of the most courageous, generous, and unwavering companions one could hope for. From the very inception of the project, they believed not only in the viability of this book, but in the possibility that it might matter – that it could chart something worth reading on the intellectual terrain of International Law.

I am especially grateful to Friedrich Kratochwil, who took a chance on a litigator-turned-PhD-candidate and opened the door to a new academic world. To Nicholas Onuf (and his wife, Sandy), who has been a steadfast presence throughout this journey – a wise interlocutor, a generous mentor, and one of the earliest champions of this book. His belief in the project gave me confidence long before the arguments had coalesced. Hans Lindahl has offered not only deep and sincere friendship but has also been an institutional and intellectual anchor – mentoring me with care, supporting this project with conviction, and investing in its promise from its earliest, most speculative phase. Geert Vervaeke, my former Dean at Tilburg Law School, grasped the arc of this research with a clarity that surprised and moved me. His expressions of confidence, and the concrete steps he took to carve out the institutional space and time for this work to take shape, were pivotal. I am grateful to John Haslam and Carrie Parkinson at Cambridge University Press for providing their sound guidance during my drafting process.

There is also a broader network of allies and friends whose support – extended at key moments – proved indispensable. One pivotal supporter was the European University Institute (EUI). Joanne Scott, then Head of the EUI Law Department, granted me a Ferdinand Braudel Fellowship that enabled the earliest chapters to be drafted. Together with Erik Jones of the Robert Schuman Centre, she also co-sponsored a collaborative research workshop at the EUI, which provided a space for exchange and reflection that deeply influenced my thinking. Later, Nicolas Petit, Joanne's successor as Department Head, generously extended my Visiting Fellow status over several years, ensuring that I could access the remarkable resources of the EUI Library. Equally formative was the engagement of the International Law Working Group at the EUI, which hosted two seminars on my early draft chapters.

Yet the network of allies behind this project extended far beyond Tilburg or Florence, tracing a variegated and generous geography of guest lectures, workshops, and scholarly encounters that enabled me to road-test, refine, and rethink the arguments that unfold in these pages. Each stop along the way added a topographic layer – new vantage points from which the contours of the project came into sharper focus. John Haskell arranged what proved to be a breakthrough moment: my first invited lecture on the book's central claims, delivered at Mississippi College of Law in Jackson. In Tokyo, Takao Suami of Waseda University generously hosted me for two days of sustained scholarly exchange. During that time, a remarkable group of scholars from across Japan convened to engage each chapter of the manuscript. In South Africa, Juanita Pienaar and Nicola Smit supported and organized a collaborative workshop at Stellenbosch University, which opened up new conceptual pathways, particularly around questions of scalar geometries, jurisdictional layering, and trans-territorial rule.

Further north, Pål Wrange arranged a seminar at Stockholm University, where I benefited from conversations with Jens Bartelson and Anne Orford. Their insights, each from distinct but intersecting critical traditions, helped me rethink the book's theoretical framing. Soon after, Carl Lewis welcomed me to the Asser Institute in The Hague, where I had the opportunity to present the work to a multidisciplinary audience of scholars and practitioners. Each of these encounters – across vastly different institutional and geographic settings – contributed to the reshaping of the manuscript in crucial ways. They reminded me that scholarly thinking is always embedded in place, even when it aspires to move beyond inherited maps.

The project also developed considerably through an annual mini-course I co-taught at the IGLP Global Scholars Academy, held in Bangkok (with Günter Frankenberg), Budapest (with Hani Sayed), and later in Stellenbosch (with Scott Newton and Marius Pieterse), titled "Mapping the World: Law in the Global Geography." These teaching encounters became conceptual laboratories where ideas were sharpened through dialogue with emerging scholars and policy leaders from across the world. Each of these moments, though geographically dispersed and temporally staggered, helped to reorient the project at key junctures.

Writing any manuscript is a marathon – marked as much by moments of fatigue as by flashes of insight and clarity. What sustains that journey, beyond scholarly community, are friendships that remind one of life's richness beyond the page. Throughout this long process, I have been fortunate to share time with a remarkable group of friends whose presence brought levity, perspective, and joy to even the most demanding phases of writing. These companions – diverse in background, temperament, and geography – offered a kind of companionship that is difficult to name, let alone footnote, but remains indelibly etched in memory. My heartfelt thanks go to: Tanja Aalberts, Guillaume Boutry and Marie-Hélène Pineau; Michele Capecchi and Elia Nichols; Jin-Young Chung; Elai and Iveta Davicioni; Caterina de'Medici and Alberto Statti; Jeffrey Dunoff, Thomas Gammeltoft-Hansen; Vivek Hajarnavis; Juho Harkonen; Madeleine Hallward and Alex Purkiss; Konrad and Katarzyna Jagodzinski; Alex Killoch and Heather Fraser; Gail Lythgoe; Iassen "Punky" Lazarov; Rob and Kim Murgatroyd; Noora Arajärvi; Hannes Peltonen; Sergio Puig and Negi Katirai; Sofia Ranchordas and Gianluca Rossi; Vikas Saraf and Joli Divon; Gavin Sullivan; Martin and Sonia Simich; Bill Tompson and Gabriella Meloni; Neil Walker. Each of you, in your own way, made this long road lighter – and far more interesting.

Last but not least, no journey of this scale unfolds without the enduring shoulders of family – those who, often without fanfare or formal recognition, absorb the temporal, emotional, and practical dislocations that academic writing entails. Writing a book involves a preoccupation that often feels opaque to those not living inside its pages. That my family understood – even when they could not always see – why I needed to disappear into thought is a generosity. More than that, they helped create the conditions for this work to happen: making room for solitude, protecting time for writing, and offering support that was as logistical as it was emotional. Foremost I am grateful to our children, Aleksander and Viktoria, for their presence, and invigorating me with their energy, curiosity, and fun. To my supportive wife, Anna Sobczak, for her care, compassion, and sacrifices, and for reminding me of the importance of finishing the book. Special thanks to my dearest and caring mother, Dragica Rajković, my kind in-laws, Jerzy and Natalia Sobczak, and generous Aunt Lida for providing many important weeks and months of support at home. My appreciation to Daniel Rajković (brother), Ljubiša Ristić, Slavica and Bojan Stamenković, Ivana and Milan Nikolić, Nedeljko and Ružica Vukomanović, Marko and Marija Jovanović, Čedo Stepanović, and Anna-Maria and Kristina Kaneff for their sincere interest in this project. My gratitude to my nieces, Mina Milovanović and Natalija Rajković, for their assistance at home during my final phase of drafting. While my father, Božidar Rajković†, is no longer with us, I can imagine his anima is smiling somewhere *off the map*. To the many more who shared their care and interest, but have gone unnamed through my oversight: Thanks to you all!

1 The Enigma
International Law's Forgotten Geography

Geography occupies an enigmatic place within the discipline of International Law. It is at once ubiquitous and unspoken – present in the everyday assumptions and categories through which legal reasoning unfolds, yet largely absent as an object of sustained theoretical reflection. International lawyers routinely engage with geographic terms and logics – territory, territoriality, jurisdiction, borders, extraterritoriality – without necessarily interrogating the conceptual histories or spatial imaginaries that underpin them.[1] Geography, in this respect, functions more as an implicit background condition than as a critical interlocutor.

Despite this apparent marginality, International Law has long been entangled with geographic thought. Indeed, during the formative centuries of European and colonial expansion,[2] the emergence of International Law relied heavily upon spatial ontologies constructed by Eurocentric geographers. The state system, juridical territoriality, and the cartographic ordering of the planet emerged through overlapping cartographic and legal rationalities. Geography, in this context, did not merely describe space; it produced it, giving form and authority to legal concepts that underwrite the statist international order.

And yet, few legal scholars today recognize the extent and influence of this historical and ontological association. This is in part because statist cartography – so central to both the emergence of disciplinary International Law and the political imaginary of modern Europe – achieved such dominance that its geographic foundations became

[1] Sir Daniel Bethlehem, "The End of Geography: The Changing Nature of the International System and the Challenge for International Law," *European Journal of International Law* 25, no. 1 (2014): 9–24.

[2] Jordan Branch, "Mapping the Territorial State," in *The Cartographic State: Maps, Territory, and the Origins of Sovereignty* (Cambridge: Cambridge University Press, 2014), 68–71; see also Denis Wood, *The Power of Maps* (New York: Guilford Press, 1992).

naturalized.[3] By the founding of the United Nations, cartographic conventions had rendered the spatial logic of International Law seemingly self-evident: sovereign states enclosed within bounded territories, arranged across a flat, gridded map of the Earth.

But the story of geography does not end with the institutional triumph of statist mapping. Contemporary Geography, as a discipline, has undergone significant internal transformations, distancing itself from its earlier affiliations with imperial mapping, determinism, and spatial fixity. Today, many geographers – particularly those working in critical, historical, and human geography – strenuously reject the legacy of cartographic essentialism and instead advance plural, relational, and dynamic accounts of space.[4] They inquire into the politics of scale,[5] the infrastructures of mobility,[6] and the atmospheric,[7]

[3] Bruno Latour, "*Onus Orbis Terrarum*: About a Possible Shift in the Definition of Sovereignty," *Millennium: Journal of International Studies* 44, no. 3 (2016): 305–20, at 308–9.

[4] Rob Kitchin et al., "Unfolding Mapping Practices: A New Epistemology for Cartography," *Transactions of the Institute of British Geographers* 38, no. 3 (2013): 480–96; Rob Kitchin and Martin Dodge, "Rethinking Maps," *Progress in Human Geography* 31, no. 3 (2007): 331–44; Rob Kitchin and Oliver Dawkins, "Digital Twins and Deep Maps," *Transactions of the Institute of British Geographers* 50, no. 1 (2025), e12699, https://doi.org/10.1111/tran.12699; Matthew H. Edney, "Cartography and Its Discontents," *Cartographica* 50, no. 1 (2015): 9–13; Matthew H. Edney, "Historical Geography and the Cartographic Illusion of Exceptionalism," *Journal of Historical Geography* 88 (2025): 27–38; Anne Kelly Knowles, "Why We Must Make Maps: Historical Geography as a Visual Craft," *Historical Geography* 42 (2014): 3–26; and Matthew David Unangst, "(De)Colonial Historical Geography and Historical GIS," *Journal of Historical Geography* 79 (2023): 76–86.

[5] Simone Tulumello and Roberto Falanga, "Homeland as a Multi-Scalar Community: (Dis)continuities in the U.S. Security/Safety Discourse and Practice," *Environment and Planning C: Politics and Space* 40 (2021): 143–64; Danny MacKinnon, "Reconstructing Scale: Towards a New Scalar Politics," *Progress in Human Geography* 35 (2010): 21–36; and Rowan Rush-Morgan, "Geographies of Queer Economies," *Geography Compass* 17, no. 8 (2023): e12719, https://doi.org/10.1111/gec3.12719

[6] Rob Kitchin et al., "Data Mobilities: Rethinking the Movement and Circulation of Digital Data," *Mobilities* (2025): 1–19, https://doi.org/10.1080/17450101.2025.2481309; Mei-Po Kwan and Tim Schwanen, "Geographies of Mobility," *Annals of the American Association of Geographers* 106, no. 2 (2016): 243–56, https://doi.org/10.1080/24694452.2015.1123067

[7] Michael Cassidy et al., "The Ethics of Volcano Geoengineering," *Earth's Future* 11, no. 10 (2023), 1–17, https://doi.org/10.1029/2023EF003714; Andy Parker et al., "Stopping Solar Geoengineering through Technical Means: A Preliminary Assessment of Counter-Geoengineering," *Earth's Future* 6, no. 8 (2018): 1058–65, https://doi.org/10.1029/2018EF000864

algorithmic,[8] and affective dimensions of spatial governance. In doing so, they challenge the very coordinates that continue to underpin much of international legal reasoning.

What emerges from this disciplinary disjunction is a provocative question: What might it mean for International Law to revisit its own forgotten geography? To move beyond tacit reliance on inherited spatial assumptions and instead engage critically with contemporary geographic thought? This introductory chapter begins that inquiry by unpacking the historical intimacy between cartographic and legal projects, tracing how the conceptual architecture of International Law has been shaped – often invisibly – by geographic imaginaries. It also invites international lawyers to consider how those imaginaries might be rethought in light of the critical spatial theories that have emerged over recent decades.

Far from a peripheral concern, geography remains central to how International Law imagines its jurisdictional reach, organizes authority globally, and encodes legal responsibility. To ignore shifts in geographic thinking is thus to risk intellectual detachment. To engage them, however, is to open new conceptual terrain – one that promises to recast foundational legal categories and expand the horizons of international legal thought itself.

Yet one need not rely solely on the claims of contemporary geographers to perceive this shift. International lawyers, after all, were not absent when disciplinary Geography itself voiced a decisive departure from the ontological foundations of Eurocentric cartography. A particularly illuminating episode in this regard is the rise and fall of the International Map of the World (IMW) – a century-long cartographic endeavor that, although once administered by the League of Nations and later the United Nations, remains virtually unknown within legal

[8] Mei-Po Kwan, "Algorithmic Geographies: Big Data, Algorithmic Uncertainty, and the Production of Geographic Knowledge," *Annals of the American Association of Geographers* 106, no. 2 (2016): 274–82, https://doi.org/10.1080/00045608.2015.1117937; Thomas Skou Grindsted, "Algorithmic Finance: Algorithmic Trading across Speculative Time-Spaces," *Annals of the American Association of Geographers* 112, no. 5 (2022): 1390–402, https://doi.org/10.1080/24694452.2021.1963658; Louise Amoore, "Cloud Geographies: Computing, Data, and Sovereignty," *Progress in Human Geography* 42, no. 1 (2018): 4–24, https://doi.org/10.1177/0309132516662147; and Louise Amoore, "Algorithmic War: Everyday Geographies of the War on Terror," *Antipode* 41, no. 1 (2009): 49–69.

scholarship. Its cancellation in 1986 is especially revealing, not because it failed on technical grounds but because it collapsed under conceptual pressure – specifically, doubts voiced from within the geographic and cartographic community about whether a singular "World Map" could ever faithfully represent a geographic state of nature.

First proposed by geographer Albrecht Penck in 1891 and formally launched in 1913,[9] the IMW was among the most ambitious cartographic undertakings of the twentieth century (see Figure 1.1). Envisioned as a universal, standardized, and objective representation of the Earth's physical geography, the project aimed to consolidate global geographic knowledge into a coherent visual framework.[10] It would do so through a series of national contributions to a standardized "base map" at a scale of 1:1,000,000 – approximately sixteen miles to the inch – intended to serve as an authoritative reference for both scientific and geopolitical use.[11] Rooted in the positivist aspirations of its age, the IMW reflected the belief that cartography could produce a single, universal image of terrestrial reality, free from interpretive contingency.[12]

And yet, after decades of meticulous labor, numerous international symposia, and over 800 map sheets submitted by contributing states,[13] the United Nations officially dissolved the project just shy of its completion – missing only Greenland, Antarctica, and parts of southern Africa.[14] On the face of it, the decision may

9 See Albrecht Penck, "The Construction of a Map of the World on a Scale of 1:1,000,000," *The Geographical Journal* 1, no. 3 (1893): 253–61.

10 Alastair W. Pearson and Michael Heffernan, "Globalizing Cartography? The International Map of the World, the International Geographical Union, and the United Nations," *Imago Mundi* 67, no. 1 (2015): 58–80, at 59.

11 A. R. Hinks, "The International One-in-a-Million Map of the World," *Royal Engineers Journal* 17 (1913): 77–86, at 78.

12 Hinks, "The International One-in-a-Million Map of the World," 77–78; William Rankin, "Zombie Projects, Negative Networks, and Multigenerational Science: The Temporality of the International Map of the World," *Social Studies of Science* 47, no. 3 (2017): 353–75, at 356–57.

13 United Nations Economic and Social Council, *Report of the Meeting of the United Nations Ad Hoc Group of Experts on the International Map of the World on the Millionth Scale (IMW), 9–11 December 1986: Papers Submitted by the United Nations Secretariat at the Fourth United Nations Regional Cartographic Conference for the Americas, 23–27 January 1989, Item 5(f) of the Provisional Agenda* (New York: United Nations, 1989).

14 United Nations, *Status of Publication of IMW Sheets as at 31 December 1986*, U.N. Doc. ST/ESA/SER.D/17, Supp. 3 (New York: United Nations, 1987).

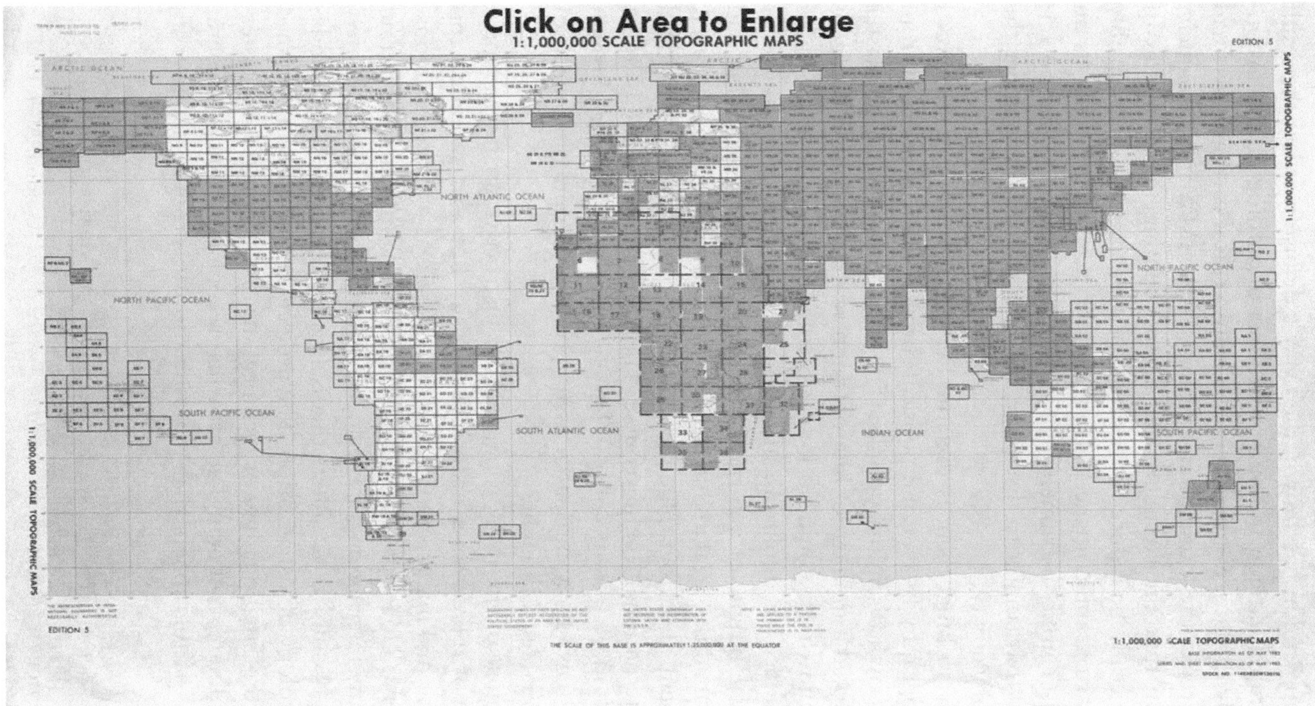

Figure 1.1 IMW, 1:1,000,000 sheet index (global grid). The IMW scheme divides the globe into 2,160 sheets. Public domain image courtesy of the Perry-Castañeca Library Map Collection, University of Texas Libraries, accessed November 24, 2025, https://maps.lib.utexas.edu/maps/imw/index_world.html

appear perplexing: Why abandon a project so close to fruition? But as William Rankin has shown, the IMW's demise was less the result of institutional fatigue and more a product of ontological disillusionment.[15] By the late twentieth century, many critical cartographers had begun to reject the foundational premise of the IMW itself – namely, the notion that the complex, plural, and contingent spatialities of the Earth could be reduced to a single, homogeneous, and ostensibly neutral cartographic image.[16] They came to see the IMW not as an innocent scientific instrument but as an enactment of spatial power: a strategy that sought to discipline and universalize space under the guise of objectivity.

What is striking, then, is that the IMW's collapse was not forced upon Geography by external political forces; rather, it emerged from within its own disciplinary ranks. The abandonment of the "master map" marked a moment of internal rupture – a recognition that geographic knowledge could no longer pretend to speak from nowhere or to produce an apolitical, all-encompassing view from above. It signaled the fatigue of a particular spatial imaginary – one that had also informed the legal architecture of international order. However, this moment of cartographic reckoning has passed almost unnoticed within international legal discourse. The IMW project – and its quiet demise – offers a profound, if largely forgotten, episode through which to reexamine the spatial assumptions still animating much of international legal thought.

The demise of the IMW is particularly instructive for international lawyers, not merely as a historical curiosity but as a revealing episode in the making of spatial ontology. Here was a United Nations-administered global project – rooted in the same institutional terrain where many international legal doctrines take shape – that ultimately collapsed because geographers themselves had reassessed its foundational ontology of visualization. The project's abandonment stemmed not from diplomatic failure or technical incapacity but from an internal disciplinary reckoning: a growing recognition among geographers and cartographers that the aspiration to produce a universal,

[15] Rankin, "Zombie Projects, Negative Networks, and Multigenerational Science," 357.

[16] Jerry Brotton, *A History of the World in Twelve Maps* (London: Allen Lane, 2012), 443–45.

objective map of the world was neither ontologically neutral nor politically innocent.[17]

For disciplinary International Law, this episode raises profound, if largely unacknowledged, questions. The IMW's collapse highlights how a discipline equally invested in representing and ordering planetary space came to critically question its own practices.[18] One might expect a comparable reflexivity within International Law,[19] particularly given the extent to which legal doctrines of territory, jurisdiction, and statehood have drawn from earlier geographic and cartographic logics.[20] Yet, despite the IMW unfolding within the very institutional architecture of the United Nations, its ontological significance has gone almost entirely unremarked in legal discourse.[21]

The disciplinary boundaries have proven remarkably resilient. International legal thought remains tethered to what might be called a "Westphalian base map" – a visual and conceptual schema in which global authority is imagined as a mosaic of discrete, bordered sovereignties plotted across a stable terrestrial grid.[22] This image continues to structure how legal claims are visualized, how jurisdictional reach is conceptualized, and how international space is ordered. But unlike disciplinary Geography, which has largely moved beyond this static imaginary, International Law has yet to confront the ontological implications of its own spatial assumptions.[23]

This enduring reliance on a cartographic imaginary questioned by its original disciplinary source invites serious reflection. It suggests that International Law's conceptual and visual architecture may be

[17] William Rankin, *After the Map: Cartography, Navigation, and the Transformation of Territory in the Twentieth Century* (Chicago: University of Chicago Press, 2016), 65–69.

[18] Rankin, *After the Map*, 65–69.

[19] See Cedric Ryngaert, "Representations of the (Extra)Territorial: Theoretical and Visual Perspectives," *Utrecht Law Review* 13, no. 2 (2017): 1–6.

[20] Stuart Elden, *The Birth of Territory* (Chicago: University of Chicago Press, 2013), 322–27.

[21] United Nations, *Report of the Secretary-General: Termination of the International Map of the World Project*, E/CONF.82/9 (1986), ¶ 11; Rankin, *After the Map*, 69.

[22] See Nikolas M. Rajkovic, "The Visual Conquest of International Law: Brute Boundaries, the Map, and the Legacy of Cartogenesis," *Leiden Journal of International Law* 31, no. 2 (2018): 267–88.

[23] Martti Koskenniemi, "The Politics of International Law: 20 Years Later," *European Journal of International Law* 20, no. 1 (2009): 24–26.

increasingly out of step with the spatial realities it purports to govern. If legal doctrine continues to rely on inherited cartographic abstractions, it risks reproducing forms of reasoning that obscure rather than illuminate the shifting conditions of global legal ordering.[24] The death of the IMW, in this sense, is not a marginal cartographic event – it is a diagnostic moment, revealing the need for international legal scholarship to reengage critically with the spatial foundations of its own normative world-making.

1.1 International Law and Geographic Forgetting

What, then, explains International Law's apparent indifference to the spatial critiques that have reshaped disciplinary Geography over the past half century? Enigmatic problems, by their nature, resist simple explanation. They emerge not from a single cause but from the convergence of multiple, interwoven dynamics – disciplinary habits, conceptual inheritances, institutional inertia. The chapters that follow will examine several of these dynamics in detail. But part of what makes such enigmas especially persistent is their apparent simplicity. Foundational presumptions, long internalized and rarely questioned, can create the illusion of clarity even as they obscure deeper complexities. What appears canonical or intuitive may in fact be the residue of older ontologies – ones that go unchallenged until disciplinary reflexivity demands their excavation.

That reflexivity, when it does occur, is rarely smooth.[25] As with other disciplinary reckonings, it often arises only through a kind of intellectual disruption – an intradisciplinary food fight, as it were. A useful parallel can be drawn here with the pathbreaking critique offered by Martti Koskenniemi several decades ago, when he called attention to the way International Law had largely ignored its entanglement with liberal political and social theory. As he wrote:

24 See John Pickles, "What Do Maps Represent?" in *A History of Spaces: Cartographic Reason, Mapping and the Geo-Coded World* (London: Routledge, 2004), 27–59.

25 For example, in relation to the history "turn" in International Law, see: Anne Orford, "History and the Turn to the International," in *International Law and the Politics of History* (Cambridge: Cambridge University Press, 2021), 70–104.

> [T]he whole of international legal "talk" is an extended effort to solve problems created by a particular way of understanding the relationship between descriptions and prescription, facts and norms in international life. My argument is that the persisting disputes within the realms of theory and doctrine result from the fact that these disputes bear a close relationship to controversial topics encountered beyond specifically "legal" discourses. The ideas of statehood, authority, legitimacy, obligation, consent, and so on which stand at the heart of international law are also hotly debated issues of social and political theory. In each of these realms the problems turn on the justifiability of assumptions about what the character of the present social world is and how it should be changed. It would be futile to assume that the assumptions which characterize modern social and political discourse are different, or separable from those which control legal discourse on these same matters.[26]

Koskenniemi's intervention marked a turning point in international legal scholarship – compelling many to acknowledge that the doctrinal core of the discipline was structured, in part, by unstated political and philosophical commitments. The argument advanced here builds on that reflexive move, extending it into another domain of conceptual silence: the spatial and geographic. Why is it that a discipline whose very name – International Law – signals a constitutive relationship to space, geography, and the spherical Earth remains so curiously disengaged from contemporary geographic thought? Why has there been so little sustained reflection on the spatial assumptions embedded within international legal thought?

The absence is not merely incidental. It reveals a deeper ontological and normative void, one that is arguably as significant as the neglect of political and social theory that Koskenniemi identified. And as with that earlier silence, interrogating it opens the door to interdisciplinary engagement. One of the virtues of cross-disciplinary inquiry is that fundamental questions in one field often have analogues in another. They may not be direct counterparts, but they often circle shared concerns – concerns that, when translated with care, can illuminate disciplinary blind spots.

The earlier story of the IMW was offered to illustrate precisely this point: that neighboring disciplines – particularly Geography and

[26] Martti Koskenniemi, *From Apology to Utopia: The Structure of International Legal Argument* (Cambridge: Cambridge University Press, 2006), 4–5.

International Relations – may contain insights of direct relevance to international legal thought. Consider, for instance, J. B. Harley's influential 1989 critique of statist cartography. Writing from within the discipline of Geography, Harley warned of the degree to which the iconic World Map had come to imprison that field's own ways of seeing – limiting the capacity to imagine alternative spatial orderings.[27] His intervention helped catalyze the emergence of Critical Geography and Critical Cartography, both of which have since become central to spatial theory.[28] These movements did not merely offer new methods; they challenged the very ontological and political foundations of how space had been visualized and governed.

The provocation for international lawyers is clear. If disciplinary Geography has confronted the limits of its visual regimes and reoriented its conceptual architecture accordingly, what prevents disciplinary International Law from undertaking a comparable reckoning? If inherited cartographic imaginaries have been revealed as instruments of spatial power in one discipline, might they not operate similarly in another – particularly one so invested in the governance of global space?

Yet to detour into the full literature of Critical Geography at this point would be premature. A more pointed entry can be made by stating directly what is at stake: Critical Geography challenges the canonical spatial imaginary that continues to underpin much of international legal thought. Put bluntly, International Law's visual and doctrinal privileging of the approximately 280,000 kilometers of state borders has long obscured the material and juridical significance of other,[29] equally consequential, global infrastructures – such as the 64 million kilometers of highways,[30] 2 million kilometers of oil and gas

[27] J. B. Harley, "Deconstructing the Map," *Cartographica* 26, no. 2 (1989): 1–20, esp. 2–5.

[28] See Reuben Rose-Redwood, "Introduction: The Limits to Deconstructing the Map," in "Deconstructing the Map: 25 Years On," special issue, *Cartographica* 50, no. 1 (2015): 1–8; Martin Dodge and Chris Perkins, "Reflecting on J. B. Harley's Influence and What He Missed in 'Deconstructing the Map'," *Cartographica* 50, no. 1 (2015): 37–50.

[29] Central Intelligence Agency, "Land Boundaries," *The World Factbook*, accessed August 10, 2025, www.cia.gov/the-world-factbook/about/archives/2022/field/land-boundaries

[30] Central Intelligence Agency, "Roadways: World (2023)," *The World Factbook*, accessed August 10, 2025, www.cia.gov/the-world-factbook/about/archives/2023/field/roadways/

pipelines,[31] 1.1 million kilometers of railways,[32] and over 1.4 million kilometers of undersea internet cables.[33] These are not merely technical systems; they are lines of trans-territorial authority, legal rule, and spatial (re)ordering.

In this light, the discipline's continued emphasis on state-centric cartographies appears curiously limited and even anachronistic. International legal scholars, like many social scientists, have inherited an ahistorical and overly static image of spatial order – one that struggles to grasp how contemporary global authority is continually materialized through the interplay of algorithmic governance, biometric identification tools, ISO standards, EU directives, World Bank performance metrics, satellite data, port security procedures, customs regulations,[34] and even the data analytics of private corporations such as Google, Meta, OpenAI, and Palantir.[35] These developments signal a shift in the spatial logic of power – from territorial sovereignty to infrastructural and informational control – yet legal doctrine continues to depict global space through the inherited optic of statist cartography.

31 GlobalData, "Oil and Gas Pipelines Length and Capital Expenditure (CapEx): Market Analysis," product page, April 17, 2023, accessed August 10, 2025, www.globaldata.com/store/report/oil-and-gas-pipelines-length-and-capital-expenditure-market-analysis/

32 World Bank, "Rail Lines (Total Route-km)," *World Development Indicators* (indicator IS.RRS.TOTL.KM; source: UIC Railisa), accessed August 10, 2025, https://data.worldbank.org/indicator/IS.RRS.TOTL.KM; see also United Nations, *LLDCs Global Report* (2017), table "Rail lines, total route (km)" (listing "World: 1,051,839"), accessed August 10, 2025, https://sdgs.un.org/sites/default/files/2021-10/LLDCs-Globl-Report_11_25_2017_SPREAD_LowVersion.pdf

33 TeleGeography, "Frequently Asked Questions about Undersea Submarine Cables," *TeleGeography Blog*, accessed August 10, 2025, https://blog.telegeography.com/frequently-asked-questions-about-undersea-submarine-cables; see also Parag Khanna, *Connectography: Mapping the Global Network Revolution* (New York: Random House, 2016), 11; Douglas Guilfoyle, "Reading *The City and the City* as an International Lawyer: Reflections on Territoriality, Jurisdiction and Transnationality," *London Review of International Law* 4, no. 1 (2016): 195–207; and Deborah Cowen, *The Deadly Life of Logistics: Mapping Violence in Global Trade* (Minneapolis: University of Minnesota Press, 2014).

34 Mark B. Salter, "Introduction: Making Assemblages International," in *Making Things International 2: Catalysts and Reactions*, ed. Mark B. Salter (Minneapolis: University of Minnesota Press, 2016), xvi.

35 See Keller Easterling, *Extrastatecraft: The Power of Infrastructure Space* (London: Verso, 2014), 16–19; Benjamin H. Bratton, *The Stack: On Software and Sovereignty* (Cambridge: MIT Press, 2016).

This raises urgent questions for the discipline: How are boundaries of authority to be visualized when geopolitical and geoeconomic practices increasingly transcend the lines drawn on traditional maps? Has international authority evolved beyond the spatial coordinates that modern cartography once offered as the base map of legal reality? Has the visual grammar inherited from modern cartography outlived its capacity to render global legal space intelligible? These are not abstract inquiries. They are the real, material conditions under which international legal authority is now constituted and contested. This book addresses them through an interdisciplinary lens, illustrating the scope of what has been overlooked and inviting international lawyers to pursue similar inquiries at the intersection of International Law and contemporary geographic thought.

To do so is to confront an uncomfortable truth: While International Law has long relied on cartographic assumptions and spatial forms of reasoning, it has rarely acknowledged them as such. Trained to prioritize doctrinal coherence and internal consistency, International Law has long eschewed questions about its own spatial premises.[36] Yet for how much longer can traditional textbooks, methodologies, and terminologies sustain this silence? As global authority diffuses across public and private actors, the inherited maps and taxonomies of the discipline appear increasingly strained. When companies such as X or Meta exercise jurisdiction-like powers across national boundaries – through content moderation, data governance, or algorithmic sorting – the cartography of authority on which International Law has historically relied demands critical reexamination.

For some time, however, the discipline has sought to address these pressures obliquely. The rise of Transnational Law and Global Administrative Law (GAL) has often been treated as a way of filling ontological cracks in the doctrinal edifice without disturbing its cartographic foundations. By layering new accounts of functional governance, administrative coordination, and norm diffusion on top of the classical doctrines, these approaches have enriched the field empirically but left intact the underlying ontology of a world imagined as a mosaic of contiguous, sovereign polygons. In effect, they have offered a functionalist supplement rather than a conceptual rupture: introducing new layers of practice without interrogating the cartographic

[36] Martti Koskenniemi, "What Is International Law For?" in *International Law*, ed. Malcolm D. Evans (Oxford: Oxford University Press, 2024), 41–43.

imaginaries that continue to structure the doctrinal core. As such, their contributions – valuable though they are – have rarely been mobilized to challenge International Law's reliance on inherited spatial assumptions or to reflect on its curious lack of engagement with spatial theorizing.

What is needed is a renewed and explicit engagement with geographic and spatial theory – an inquiry into the premises and visual infrastructures that have long conditioned how International Law imagines authority, space, and boundary.[37] Spatial categories such as "international," "transnational," "global," and "regional" are not neutral descriptors. They are socially constructed "frames,"[38] encoded and materially reinforced by rules, norms, metrics, and institutionalized practices that harden what begins as conceptual into seemingly naturalized fact.[39] They are further embodied through legitimating visual devices – above all, the iconic World Map of states, which has functioned simultaneously as a symbol and an infrastructure of legal cognition. That this optic has become so deeply naturalized underscores its productive and structuring power (see Chapter 3): Statist cartography has shaped not merely how we see "the world" but also how International Law has learned to govern it.[40]

This both confirms and critiques the salience of social constructivism for international legal theorizing. Constructivist approaches rightly reveal the contingency of categories such as sovereignty, territory, and jurisdiction, but they often stop short of asking how such

37 Nikolas M. Rajkovic, "On Fragments and Geometry: The International Legal Order as Metaphor and How It Matters," *Erasmus Law Review* 6, no. 1 (2013): 6–16; Philip Liste, "Colliding Geographies: Space at Work in Global Governance," *Journal of International Relations and Development* 19, no. 2 (2016): 199–221, at 200–201; and David Koller, "and New York and the Hague and Tokyo and Geneva and Nuremberg and … The Geographies of International Law," *European Journal of International Law* 23, no. 1 (2012): 97–119.

38 On the significance of "framing" for "fixing the limits of possible knowledge for modern minds and the conditions of rule in the modern world," see: Nicholas Greenwood Onuf, *The Mightie Frame: Epochal Change and the Modern World* (Oxford: Oxford University Press, 2018), 1–11, at 9.

39 Branch, "Mapping the Territorial State," 68–71; J. B. Harley, "Historical Geography and the Cartographic Illusion," *Journal of Historical Geography* 15, no. 1 (1989): 80–91, at 85; Boaventura de Sousa Santos, "Law: A Map of Misreading. Toward a Postmodern Conception of Law," *Journal of Law and Society* 14, no. 3 (1987): 279–302, at 282.

40 Latour, "*Onus Orbis Terrarum*," 309.

categories are materially sedimented. Once institutionalized, these imaginaries are cognitively sustained and reinforced through, for example, treaties, procedural norms, bureaucratic routines, and statistical practices that give them tangible durability. In other words, the very "constructedness" of International Law's spatial categories is precisely what makes them so hard to dislodge: They are not merely ideas but infrastructures of practice.

Nevertheless, even deeply embedded imaginaries – however foundational – must eventually respond to changing material and normative practices. The cartographic logic that has long structured international legal reasoning is increasingly out of step with the cellular, incontiguous, and pointillistic geographies of authority and power that now shape global governance (see Chapter 5). While state borders and territorial controls persist, they are increasingly supplemented – and in many cases eclipsed – by material infrastructures such as data centers, logistics corridors, biometric databases, and satellite constellations, as well as by normative practices of algorithmic regulation, corporate rule-setting, and standards-based coordination across borders. Legal anthropologists describe these as forms of "spatial discipline" and "static violence,"[41] highlighting how new modalities of exclusion and control are encoded both in territorial lines and in infrastructures of digital surveillance,[42] algorithmic governance,[43] and remote-sensing technologies.[44]

[41] Andrea M. Brighenti, "Lines, Barred Lines: Movement, Territory and the Law," *International Journal of Law in Context* 6, no. 3 (2010): 217–27, at 221; see also Michel Foucault, *Security, Territory, Population: Lectures at the Collège de France, 1977–78*, ed. Michel Senellart, trans. Graham Burchell (Basingstoke: Palgrave Macmillan, 2007).

[42] Stephen L. Roberts and Stefan Elbe, "Catching the Flu: Syndromic Surveillance, Algorithmic Governmentality and Global Health Security," *Security Dialogue* 48, no. 1 (2017): 46–62; Samuel N. Chambers and Gabriella Soto, "The Geography of Intent: The Bodily Implications of Border Surveillance Technologies," *Political Geography* 120 (2025): 103332, https://doi.org/10.1016/j.polgeo.2025.103332

[43] Carola Westermeier, "From Flows towards Updates: Security Regimes and Changing Technologies for Financial Surveillance," *Review of International Studies* 49, no. 4 (2023): 615–36; Rocco Bellanova and Marieke de Goede, "The Algorithmic Regulation of Security: An Infrastructural Perspective," *Regulation & Governance* 16, no. 1 (2022): 102–18, https://doi.org/10.1111/rego.12338; and Fleur Johns, "Global Governance through the Pairing of List and Algorithm," *Environment and Planning D: Society and Space* 34, no. 1 (2016): 126–49.

[44] Katharine Hall Kindervater, "The Emergence of Lethal Surveillance: Watching and Killing in the History of Drone Technology," *Security Dialogue* 47, no. 3 (2016): 223–38, at 224.

Faced with these shifts, core categories of International Law – sovereignty, jurisdiction, territorial integrity – are compelled to stretch, mutate, or double back on themselves, straining to accommodate phenomena that no longer conform to the planar geometries of statist cartography. Consider jurisdiction: Traditionally tethered to territory, it is now reconfigured through data localization laws that tie authority to server locations, or through corporate content moderation systems that regulate expression across millions of users irrespective of state borders. Sovereignty, too, is recast when Arctic seabed claims hinge on geological continuities beneath melting ice, or when satellite-based monitoring allows states to assert control over airspace and maritime zones at scales far beyond their territorial borders. In such cases, the core categories of International Law function less as stable foundations than as unstable placeholders – invoked to preserve doctrinal coherence even as the practices they are meant to capture increasingly bypass, perforate, or recast boundaries.

These developments do not merely augment the contiguous border; they transform the very meaning of boundary-making on the legal globe.[45] Yet international legal scholarship has only lightly engaged with what such transformations imply for its inherited frameworks. Doctrinal assumptions remain tethered to a visual grammar defined by statist cartography, even as operative sites of legal and political authority increasingly exceed or perforate territorial boundaries.[46] This is not simply a matter of updating doctrine to accommodate new actors or regulatory instruments. The deeper issue is conceptual:

45 Vijay Varadharajan, and Neeraj Suri, "Security Challenges When Space Merges with Cyberspace," *Space Policy* 67 (2024): 101600, https://doi.org/10.1016/j.spacepol.2023.101600; Benjamin Johnson, "Sensing the Arctic: Situational Awareness and the Future of Northern Security," *International Journal* 76, no. 3 (2021): 404–26; Huub Dijstelbloem et al., "Surveillance at Sea: The Transactional Politics of Border Control in the Aegean," *Security Dialogue* 48, no. 3 (2017): 224–40; Lars Gjesvik, and Johann Ole Willers, "Beyond Control? The Political Economy of Private Interception, Intrusion, and Surveillance Markets," *Review of International Political Economy* 31, no. 6 (2024): 1840–64; Didier Bigo, "Security, Borders, and the State," in *Borders and Border Politics in a Globalizing World*, ed. Paul Ganster and David E. Lorey (Lanham, MD: Rowman & Littlefield, 2005), 109–21; and Foucault, *Security, Territory, Population*, 11–13.

46 See Quinn Slobodian, *Cracked-Up Capitalism: Market Radicals and the Dream of a World without Democracy* (London: Penguin Random House, 2023).

a persistent set of spatial assumptions continues to structure how international legal thought visualizes "the World."[47]

This spatial imaginary – reproduced through maps, textbooks, and jurisdictional schemas – has not kept pace with the transscalar, non-contiguous, and often intangible architectures through which authority is now exercised. Reliance on the state-centric map constrains the legal imagination, narrowing the capacity to apprehend governance mechanisms that operate through data infrastructures, logistics networks, borderless enforcement regimes, and corporate platforms. The result is a growing disjuncture between the inherited image of international legal space and the dispersed, infrastructural, and often opaque practices that now organize global authority.

What is at stake is not simply a call for interdisciplinarity, but a more fundamental rethinking of how disciplinary International Law imagines and represents space. The tools for such reflection already exist – for example in the critiques advanced by Critical Geographers, in the reconceptualizations of space emerging from Science and Technology Studies, and even within the legal field's own peripheral discourses.[48] But drawing those tools into the disciplinary mainstream requires recognizing that International Law's conceptual and visual infrastructures are not neutral.[49] They are historically contingent artefacts – forms of legal seeing – that must be reevaluated if the discipline is to remain responsive to the spatial dynamics of the unfolding present. To recognize this is to accept that if the discipline is to remain responsive to the spatial dynamics of the present, it must subject its own cartographic foundations to sustained critique and reimagination.

[47] Karin Mickelson, "The Maps of International Law: Perceptions of Nature in the Classification of Territory," *Leiden Journal of International Law* 27, no. 3 (2014): 621–39, at 639; see also Branch, "Mapping the Territorial State."

[48] See Daniel Neep, "State-Space beyond Territory: Wormholes, Gravitational Fields, and Entanglement," *Journal of Historical Sociology* 30, no. 3 (2017): 466–95, at 467; Rankin, *After the Map*, 357; Floor M. Fleurke et al., "Constitutionalizing in the Anthropocene," *Journal of Human Rights and the Environment* 15, no. 1 (2024): 4–22; Itamar Mann, "Law and Politics from the Sea," *International Theory* 16, no. 1 (2024): 78–101.

[49] See Marshall McLuhan, *Understanding Media: The Extensions of Man* (1964; repr., Berkeley, CA: Gingko Press, 2013), 8–9.

1.2 The Reign of Statist Cartography

The visual legacy of statist cartography has not only shaped how international lawyers imagine space; it has also insulated the discipline from confronting the ontological significance of novel material and normative developments. In recent decades, the rise of Transnational Law, GAL, and Informal International Law-Making (IN-LAW) has illuminated transborder practices that diverge sharply from the orthodox World Map. These literatures have highlighted new modalities of authority – decentered, informal, privately enacted, or digitally encoded – yet their implications for International Law's underlying spatial assumptions remain largely unexplored. Despite their empirical richness, they have not dislodged the conceptual and visual hegemony of the World Map of states.

Indeed, one reason for this persistence is that these fields often operate as functional supplements rather than conceptual ruptures. By documenting emergent practices of regulation and coordination, they add empirical density to the picture of global governance, but they do so without disturbing the cartographic ontology that underwrites International Law's doctrinal core. The World Map remains the silent backdrop against which transnational, administrative, and informal practices are narrated, leaving untouched the deeper question of how spatial imaginaries organize the discipline's categories and claims to authority.

In this way, statist cartography is not simply left intact – it is subtly reinforced. By treating the state map as a naturalized canvas upon which new legal practices unfold, these literatures reproduce its authority even as they describe its limits. The effect is paradoxical: The more International Law expands its descriptive range to include, for example, transnational and informal practices, the more it recenters the statist map as the unquestioned framework of intelligibility. What emerges is less a displacement of statist cartography than its quiet revalidation, ensuring its continued reign as the conceptual and visual infrastructure of international legal thought.

Against this backdrop arises a critical challenge: How might International Law renew its dormant dialogue with spatial theory to better theorize legal authority as it is actually constituted, practiced, and spatialized in the present? This is a deliberately large question – one that signals the need for sustained interdisciplinary engagement.

It rests on a simple proposition: international legal authority cannot be fully understood in abstraction from the spatial theories and visual infrastructures that define what counts as "international" in the first place. The visual construction of legal space is not a peripheral concern; it is central to how authority is recognized, enacted, and contested.

The chapters that follow therefore issue a broader scholarly invitation: to reconsider the conceptual and empirical terrain of the discipline by recovering the analytical significance of spatial thought, theory, and visualization. Such a reorientation opens new pathways for understanding the legal, geopolitical, and socio-technical practices that now shape global boundary-making. It also asks a pressing follow-up to a long-standing concession: While it is now widely acknowledged that state, substate, and non-state actors participate in global boundary practices, the more difficult – and necessary – task is to leverage that recognition to interrogate the enduring hold of statist cartography over the discipline's spatial imagination.

At the heart of this problem lies the naturalization of core disciplinary concepts such as territoriality and jurisdiction. These categories are often treated as self-evident features of legal space – as if they were stable, objective, or geologically given.[50] This reflects what historical sociologists have described as the naturalization or *reification illusion*: the transformation of contingent legal and political arrangements into seemingly immutable features of global order (see Chapter 4).[51] In the case of International Law, this has allowed the cartographic "base map" of states to harden into a default ontological frame[52] – one that resists scrutiny precisely because of its apparent familiarity and simplicity.[53]

[50] See Robert David Sack, *Human Territoriality: Its Theory and History* (Cambridge: Cambridge University Press, 1986); Jean Gottmann, "The Evolution of the Concept of Territory," *Social Science Information* 14, no. 3 (1975): 29–47.

[51] John M. Hobson, "What's at Stake in 'Bringing Historical Sociology Back into International Relations'? Transcending 'Chronofetishism' and 'Tempocentrism' in International Relations," in *Historical Sociology of International Relations*, ed. Stephen Hobden and John M. Hobson (Cambridge: Cambridge University Press, 2002), 6.

[52] Onuf, *The Mightie Frame*, 9–11.

[53] See Richard T. Ford, "Law's Territory (A History of Jurisdiction)," *Michigan Law Review* 97, no. 4 (1999): 843–930, at 843–45.

Dislodging this framework requires more than critique at the level of doctrine or discourse.[54] While linguistic and doctrinal analysis can expose the rhetorical dominance of territorial language, the deeper challenge is to destabilize the ontological and visual infrastructure that continues to shape international legal reasoning. On this front, disciplinary Geography and International Relations (IR) have proven more reflexive. Both fields have developed extensive bodies of empirical and theoretical work that interrogate the spatial grammar of global rule.[55] International Law, by contrast, has often engaged these insights only tangentially – treating spatial transformations as factual developments rather than as conceptual or epistemological challenges to its foundational cartographies.

This distinction is critical. It marks the difference between accommodating new facts within an old map versus reimagining the map itself. As the next section will illustrate, even when empirically rich alternatives to the statist imaginary are developed – whether within International Law or International Relations (IR) – the World Map of states has shown remarkable resilience. Its visual and conceptual authority persists, often undisturbed by the very evidence that ought to challenge it.

1.2.1 *Territoriality and Jurisdiction as a State of (Geographic) Nature*

A major development in recent international legal scholarship has been the emergence of what is broadly characterized as postnational legal thought. Key strands of this work – Transnational Law,[56]

[54] Katja Freistein and Philip Liste, "Introduction: Fragmented Territoriality," *Journal of International Relations and Development* 19, no. 2 (2016): 193–98, at 194–95; see also Philip Liste, "Geographical Knowledge at Work: Human Rights Litigation and Transnational Territoriality," *European Journal of International Relations* 22, no. 1 (2016): 217–39.

[55] Some notable exemplars are: John Agnew, "Sovereignty Regimes: Territoriality and State Authority in Contemporary World Politics," *Annals of the Association of American Geographers* 95, no. 2 (2005): 437–61; Elden, *The Birth of Territory*; Gearóid Ó Tuathail (Gerard Toal), *Critical Geopolitics: The Politics of Writing Global Space* (Minneapolis: University of Minnesota Press, 1996).

[56] See Peer Zumbansen, "Transnational Legal Pluralism," *Transnational Legal Theory* 1, no. 2 (2010): 141–89; Peer Zumbansen, "Transnational Law: Theories and Applications," in *The Oxford Handbook of Transnational Law*, ed. Peer Zumbansen (Oxford: Oxford University Press, 2021), 3–30.

GAL,[57] and IN-LAW[58] – have generated compelling empirical accounts of authority that transcend state borders and conventional jurisdictional frameworks. These bodies of research have significantly expanded the field's descriptive and analytical scope, particularly by documenting how authority and power are exercised across institutions, scales, and actors that do not conform to the familiar architecture of inter-state relations.

Yet this empirical richness has not unsettled the conceptual terrain upon which disciplinary International Law continues to rest. Instead of revising the field's spatial foundations, postnational innovations are often treated as exceptions to, or functional extensions of, an underlying normative order still presumed to be defined by state-centric legality. Trans-territorial practices may be acknowledged, but they are positioned at the doctrinal periphery, while the state-based imaginary remains entrenched at the conceptual core.

This tendency is clearly visible in the early framing of GAL. In their widely cited formulation, Krisch and Kingsbury described the emergence of GAL in terms that acknowledged profound change, while simultaneously maintaining a metaphorical distinction between doctrinal stability and empirical flux:

> Globalization and the rise of global governance are transforming the structure of international law, though much of this transformation takes place beneath the surface of the international legal order and often goes unnoticed. Global administrative law … starts from the observation that much of global governance can be understood as regulation and administration, and that we are witnessing the emergence of a "global administrative space": a space in which the strict dichotomy between domestic and international has largely broken down, in which administrative functions are performed in often complex interplays between officials and institutions on different levels, and in which regulation may be highly effective despite its predominantly

[57] Nico Krisch, and Benedict Kingsbury, "Introduction: Global Governance and Global Administrative Law in the International Legal Order," *European Journal of International Law* 17, no. 1 (2006): 1–13; See also Nico Krisch, *Beyond Constitutionalism: The Pluralist Structure of Postnational Law* (Oxford: Oxford University Press, 2010).

[58] Joost Pauwelyn et al., eds., *Informal International Lawmaking* (Oxford: Oxford University Press, 2012), 13–15; Joost Pauwelyn et al., "When Structures become Shackles: Stagnation and Dynamics in International Lawmaking," *European Journal of International Law* 25, no. 3 (2014): 733–63.

non-binding forms. In practice, the increasing exercise of public power in these structures has given rise to serious concerns about legitimacy and accountability, prompting patterns of responses to those concerns in many areas of global governance.[59]

The significance of this passage lies not only in its descriptive acuity but also in what it inadvertently reveals about the spatial architecture of international legal thought. The metaphor of transformation "beneath the surface" presupposes a hierarchical geography of legal space: informal or trans-territorial practices are situated in a subordinate stratum beneath the canonical plane of state-based authority. Even as GAL seeks to capture the regulatory complexity of global governance, its imagery subtly reasserts the primacy of the state by relegating novel practices to a metaphorical subsurface. In doing so, it reinforces the very spatial assumptions that its empirical content seems poised to contest.

This tension raises a deeper question: What determines whether a legal practice is conceptualized as foundational or peripheral, visible or submerged, within the field's cognitive map? The answer is not found in empirical visibility or functional importance but in the theoretical categories that define what counts as legally intelligible. There is no natural "surface" of International Law, no geological divide separating the doctrinal from the marginal. These distinctions are historically contingent, reproduced through the spatial grammars the discipline has long employed to render authority legible.

Comparable problems are visible beyond International Law. In IR, John Agnew's critique of the "territorial trap" challenged the assumption that state territory constitutes a natural, fixed unit of political space. His intervention catalyzed a broader rethinking of how spatial categories organize global analysis. Yet even there, insufficient attention has been paid to the material and visual infrastructures – maps, diagrams, territorial schemas – that silently reproduce state-centric assumptions and confer upon them cognitive durability.

Agnew's key insight – that territoriality is not given but produced – has clear implications for legal thought. It demands that we interrogate not only the formal categories of jurisdiction and territory but

[59] Benedict Kingsbury et al., "The Emergence of Global Administrative Law," *Law and Contemporary Problems* 68, nos. 3–4 (Summer–Autumn 2005): 15–62, at 15.

also the visual and material techniques through which they are constructed and stabilized. In International Law, territoriality and jurisdiction continue to draw their normative weight from entrenched cartographic conventions – conventions that depict the world as a mosaic of bounded, statist units. This appearance of naturalness is the effect of a visual ontology – a legacy of how international lawyers have been trained to see, map, and order legal space.

Chapter 2 takes up Agnew's critique in greater depth, drawing out its implications for international legal thought. In particular, it explores how Agnew's deconstruction of territorial assumptions has resonated within IR while remaining largely unexamined in our neighboring legal discipline. For now, it is sufficient to register both the critical force of his intervention and the notable silences it leaves intact – silences that reveal how spatial perception is as much a product of visual habits and institutional aesthetics as of conceptual insight.

Confronting this legacy does not require abandoning territorial categories altogether. What it does demand is a critical engagement with their historical contingency, their spatial mediations, and their visual scaffolding. The task is not to replace one binary with another – doctrinal versus nondoctrinal, formal versus informal – but to move beyond such oppositions toward more flexible and adaptive theoretical vocabularies. As in horticulture, transformation rarely advances through rupture; it proceeds through accretion and recomposition, with new growth altering inherited structures even as it emerges from them. By the same token, international legal thought must learn to treat its maps less as static containers than as grafted landscapes – layered, provisional, and open to reconfiguration. Only then can the discipline begin to rethink the visual and conceptual premises through which it maps, understands, and legitimates the legal globe.

1.2.2 The World Map and Its Visual Infrastructure

Agnew's "Territorial Trap" spurred a wave of critical scholarship across the social sciences, emphasizing that geographic space is not absolute but historically contingent.[60] This ontological shift paralleled earlier theoretical developments influenced by Derrida, Foucault,

[60] John Agnew, *Geopolitics: Re-Visioning World Politics*, 2nd ed. (London: Routledge, 2003), 76–80.

and others, in which critique focused on the discursive architectures underpinning dominant social and political meanings. The effort was to deconstruct not only what was said, but also how meaning was spatially arranged and institutionally sedimented.[61]

Yet this fertile critique ultimately encountered a spatial impasse – akin to the limitations observed earlier in GAL's disciplinary reception within International Law. On the one hand, the "Territorial Trap" catalyzed rich discursive analyses that challenged the fixity of territorial categories. On the other, it left largely unexamined the bounding practices that visually and institutionally stabilized the very cartographies of statism it questioned. As Neil Brenner and Stuart Elden have noted, the turn to discourse often encouraged a pivot toward new semantic categories – such as place, scale, or networks – without a corresponding interrogation of the visual and material infrastructures that sustained the illusion of perfected and permanent territorial order.[62] Consequently, the problem of "clear spatial demarcation" – which Agnew had originally identified as central – remained undertheorized.[63] The critique faltered when it came to analyzing how state authority is authenticated visually, through repeated exposure to maps that naturalize the world as a discrete collection of sovereign units.

What this reveals is a disjunction: a rejection of territorial fixity at the level of theory coexisting with the uncritical retention of the very cartographic forms that instantiate it. Visual infrastructures – especially the repeated depiction of the globe as a World Map of states – play a central role in legitimating legal order. As Mark Salter has argued in the context of sovereignty, critical discourse must attend

[61] Peter Andreas, "Redrawing the Line: Borders and Security in the Twenty-first Century," *International Security* 28, no. 2 (2003): 78–111; Arjun Appadurai, *Modernity at Large: Cultural Dimensions of Globalization* (Minneapolis: University of Minnesota Press, 1996); Deborah D. Avant et al., eds., *Who Governs the Globe?* (Cambridge: Cambridge University Press, 2010); Darin Barney, *The Network Society* (Cambridge: Polity, 2004); Ulrich Beck, *Cosmopolitan Vision* (Cambridge: Polity, 2006); Manuel Castells, *The Rise of the Network Society* (Oxford: Blackwell, 1996); Yale H. Ferguson and Richard W. Mansbach, *Remapping Global Politics: History's Revenge and Future Shock* (Cambridge: Cambridge University Press, 2004); Andreas Osiander, "Sovereignty, International Relations, and the Westphalian Myth," *International Organization* 55, no. 2 (2001): 251–87; Ó Tuathail, *Critical Geopolitics*.

[62] Neil Brenner and Stuart Elden, "Henri Lefebvre on State, Space, Territory," *International Political Sociology* 3, no. 4 (2009): 353–77, at 356.

[63] Agnew, "Territorial Trap," 53–54.

not only to meaning but also to the material media through which meaning is stabilized and circulated:

When we look at the architecture of particular discourses, practices, institutions, or installations, there can be a tendency to focus on the deconstruction of meanings rather than on the physical circulation of documents or the medium of communication. The best kinds of these analyses acknowledge that these discourses are not abstract and immaterial, but rather come in very material packages. Ideas are expressed in language, which is printed, posted, broadcast, and read. Culture is written, performed, and received. Ideas are discussed, debated, written down, transmitted, translated into forms, evaluated. While we connect ideas and signifiers together to create *post hoc ante* a coherent or messy discourse about sovereignty from treaties, UN declarations, diplomatic talk, and day-to-day life, these ideas and words circulate in very material ways: as diplomatic cables, as interdepartmental memos, as briefing notes, as newspaper stories, as memes on the Internet, as buildings, as posters, as practices. If we look at the material expressions of discourse, rather than a disembodied discourse, then we reveal other kinds of power at work.[64]

Salter's insistence here is crucial. Legal practices, like all social practices, are never immaterial. They come to life through documents drafted and archived, speeches delivered and recorded, rituals performed in courtrooms and conference halls, and, not least, through the visual technologies that orient actors toward a particular conception of "the World." What Salter describes with respect to sovereignty applies even more forcefully to territorialization. Territorial rule is not merely represented but actively enacted. Boundaries acquire durability because they are repeatedly drawn and redrawn, written into treaties, marked on maps, taught in classrooms, invoked in judicial reasoning, circulated in government communiqués, enforced through police orders, materialized through customs forms, and made visible through fences, checkpoints, and boundary markers. Territorialization is thus inseparable from the material practices through which it is continually reproduced.

The challenge, then, is not only discursive but irreducibly material. International Law has long been shaped by a cartographic regime that spans centuries of map-making – an enduring visual infrastructure that compresses legal, political, and social life into the bounded frame

[64] Salter, "Introduction," xvi.

of the state. As Anssi Paasi has argued, such maps constitute a process of "spatial socialization," rendering "the World" legible through a singular visual schema.[65] Yet this schema privileges a narrow set of forms – maps, atlases, globes, GIS projections – even though territorialization in practice depends on a much wider range of artefacts, performances, and infrastructures.

Historically, globes, atlases, and classroom wall maps trained the eye to see "the World" as a mosaic of bordered states. Today, authority and power are increasingly projected through pointillism and pixels: Satellite imagery, digital mapping platforms, and algorithmically generated borders render territory as constellations of data-points, layers, and coordinates (see Chapter 5). These technologies potentially open up new ways to trace how territory is enacted – for example, by visualizing flows, networks, or shifting boundaries that conventional cartography cannot capture. Yet within international legal practices, these expanded possibilities remain largely peripheral. The International Court of Justice annexes sketch maps to its judgments in boundary and maritime delimitation cases, where they do more than illustrate – they structure the Court's reasoning in drawing lines across seas and landmasses. International Law textbooks likewise reproduce political maps that present the state-based world as natural and given, shaping generations of students' spatial imagination. In these sites, a cartographic ontology keeps the material register narrow, privileging a handful of familiar visual infrastructures over the broader repertoire that emerging technologies and other social practices could make visible.

Broadening the spectrum of material practices that International Law acknowledges is therefore essential if the discipline is to grasp how territorialization actually works today. To decompress this visual legacy does not mean rejecting it wholesale. Rather, it requires a more supple conceptual metaphor and methodological posture – one capable of recognizing both continuity and transformation. As noted earlier, the metaphor of horticulture is instructive: New forms of thought do not displace what came before, but reshape it. In that spirit, this book calls for an accretive critique – one that challenges the narrowing cartographic ontology of International Law while remaining attentive to

65 Anssi Paasi, "Bounded Spaces in a 'Borderless World': Border Studies, Power, and the Anatomy of Territory," *Journal of Power* 2, no. 2 (2009): 213–34, at 226.

the wider spectrum of material practices, old and new, through which legal space is made and remade. Decompression, in other words, is the necessary precondition for grafting: loosening the grip of inherited cartographic forms so that conceptual innovations can take root in more fertile ground.

1.2.3 Returning the G-word and Spatial Theorizing to International Law

To move beyond the conceptual constraints that continue to shape how International Law imagines space, the discipline must cultivate a form of development that is neither reformist nor ruptural, but grafted. The metaphor of grafting suggests that conceptual innovation proceeds not by abandoning inherited forms, but by recombining them into new configurations responsive to unfolding conditions. This approach captures the disciplinary challenge ahead: developing theoretical tools that remain attuned to the shifting spatial logics of legal authority while critically reworking the conceptual materials inherited from earlier thought.

Despite increasing awareness of legal pluralism and regulatory complexity, the conceptual architecture of International Law remains tethered to a spatial imaginary structured by assumptions of territorial contiguity and exclusivity. That foundational image – reinforced by the cartographic infrastructures discussed earlier – continues to visualize the world as neatly organized into bounded statist units. It has shaped not only how legal space is imagined, but also how emerging juridical formations are interpreted. Overlapping, diffuse, and reticulated forms of authority are too often treated as marginal or exceptional rather than as integral features of global legal ordering. The result is a persistent disjuncture between the categories through which legal authority is conceptualized and the spatial configurations through which it is increasingly exercised.

Acknowledging these shifts – however frequent in scholarly discourse – has too often remained descriptive. References to "multi-level" or "polycentric" governance proliferate,[66] yet rarely precipitate

[66] Rakhyun E. Kim, "Is Global Governance Fragmented, Polycentric, or Complex? The State of the Art of the Network Approach," *International Studies Review* 22, no. 4 (2020): 903–31; Maria Koinova, "Polycentric

a sustained rethinking of the spatial assumptions that underpin international legal thought. The more urgent task is to ask: how can International Law more fully engage the diverse and dynamic spatial formations through which global authority is now constituted? What conceptual resources might enable us to move beyond inherited models of boundary-making? And how might such resources be cultivated within international legal theory in ways that are both critical and generative?

Answering the spatial challenges facing international legal thought requires more than doctrinal supplementation. It demands engagement with adjacent intellectual traditions – particularly in Geography, Constructivist International Relations, and spatial theory – that have long examined the production of space as a legal, political, and ontological project. For international legal scholars, this entails revisiting a largely occluded disciplinary relationship: the formative entanglement between legal, spatial and geographic thought. Restoring this connection is not merely an exercise in interdisciplinarity, but a means of recovering conceptual tools that have long existed at the field's margins sidelined by efforts to consolidate doctrinal coherence.

This book takes up that challenge. Organized as a series of interlinked inquiries, each chapter interrogates a different dimension of the spatial logics that continue to structure international legal reasoning, while proposing alternative frameworks grounded in critical geography, spatial theory, and socio-legal analysis.

Chapter 2, *Don't Look [Down]!*, begins by examining the conspicuous absence of spatial theorizing within International Law, particularly in comparison to the trajectory of IR. While IR underwent a spatial turn during its "Third Great Debate" – most notably through John Agnew's critique of the "Territorial Trap" – International Law has not pursued a comparable reckoning. The chapter situates this divergence in a set of historical and conceptual conditions, including postwar sensitivities around geopolitical language and a disciplinary

Governance of Transit Migration: A Relational Perspective from the Balkans and the Middle East," *Review of International Studies* 48, no. 3 (2022): 461–83; Ernst-Ulrich Petersmann, "Strengthening Multilevel Governance of Public Goods through Democratic and Republican Constitutionalism," *Cambridge International Law Journal* 11, no. 2 (2022): 180–201; and Tanja A. Börzel, "Multilevel Governance or Multilevel Government?" *The British Journal of Politics and International Relations* 22, no. 4 (2020): 776–83.

preference for the triad of territory, sovereignty, and jurisdiction. Drawing on the work of Carl Schmitt and the cultural geography of "geopoetics," it shows how International Law's spatial perception has remained shaped by pastoral and statist imaginaries – limiting its capacity to engage emerging spatial forms of global legal authority.

Chapter 3, *Potere Incognito*, turns to the historical and ontological entanglement between legal authority and cartographic practice. It elaborates the concept of *cartographization* to describe the process through which maps have not only represented but structured legal space. Far from neutral instruments, cartographic forms have functioned as world-making devices that embed spatial assumptions into the ontological foundations of international legal thought. Drawing from critical geography, media theory, and constructivist IR theory, the chapter critiques the liberal-legalist tendency to bracket power, demonstrating how visual conventions have shaped what becomes legible within legal discourse and what remains occluded.

Chapter 4, From Jurisdictions to *Juriscapes*, shifts from critique to conceptual reconstruction. It proposes *juriscapes* as a complementary analytic to the conventional framework of jurisdiction. While jurisdiction remains central to organizing legal authority through bounded territorial logics, it tends to prioritize system maintenance and formal hierarchies. *Juriscapes*, by contrast, highlight the morphogenetic processes through which authority is constituted and distributed across noncontiguous, infrastructurally mediated, and trans-territorial spaces. The chapter draws on legal anthropology, infrastructure studies, and critical geography to foreground how authority and power are enacted through for example ports, data flows, supply chains, and algorithmic systems that often exceed the ontological register of a conventional jurisdictional map.

Chapter 5, *Vidi et Vici*, further develops this line of inquiry by tracing how the formation of mapped legal space was historically tied to imperial practices of extraction, enclosure, and spatial abstraction. Cartography, it argues, was not simply a descriptive device but a juridical means that enabled a vision of global order premised on segmentation and calculability. In contrast, the contemporary spatial logic of legal authority is increasingly defined by *pointillistic geographies*: fragmented but strategically connected sites – such as logistics hubs, data centers, and free trade zones – through which authority and power are exercised across territorial discontinuities. Business Logistics plays a key role in sustaining these arrangements, facilitating the projection of authority across infrastructural nodes. The chapter calls for a reorientation of spatial analysis in International Law, one that is historically grounded and sensitive to the material and transscalar conditions of contemporary rule.

The concluding chapter, Chapter 6, The Crisis of *Kartenpolitik*, synthesizes the book's core themes by examining the limits of the cartographic imaginary that has long anchored international legal thought. It argues that the spatial ontology of bordered statehood – visually stabilized by the iconic World Map of states – can no longer account for the distributed, overlapping, and often cellular spatial arrangements through which global authority and power are now extended. Developments such as climate governance, digital infrastructure, and global value chains increasingly challenge the coherence of state-centric territorial frameworks.

Rather than abandoning mapping, the chapter calls for its critical reconstitution. Revisiting the etymological meaning of *cartography* – to "write the earth" – it proposes that international lawyers develop new visual grammars and spatial vocabularies capable of engaging the diverse geographies of legal ordering. Legal authority today operates through formations such as extraterritorial sanctions, carbon accounting systems, drone corridors, and undersea cables – networks that defy inherited cartographic assumptions and demand more flexible analytic tools.

These developments do not displace conventional jurisdictional frameworks, but they do require their reconceptualization. The concept of *juriscapes*, introduced in the book, offers one such tool for analyzing how legal authority is enacted across spatially discontinuous, relational, and infrastructural domains. As the final chapter argues, meeting the challenges of contemporary global ordering demands a more responsive spatial imagination – one that neither fetishizes the coherence of the past nor ignores the complex spatialities of the present. The task is not to discard the map, but to rethink how we draw, read, interpret and use it.

2 Don't Look [Down]!

International Law and Its Worn Geopoetry

International Law is not only a product of formal legal sources but also of spatial narratives – geographic imaginaries that frame how legal authority is envisioned, bounded, and enacted. This foundational interplay between law and geography has largely escaped systematic scrutiny within the discipline, even though its traces are omnipresent. The discipline's operative metaphors – jurisdictional "reach," "territorial" scope, legal "landscapes," and "boundaries" of authority – bear the imprint of a deep-seated cartographic rationality. Terms such as "extraterritoriality," "European" Law, "Global" Administrative Law, or "Mediterranean" migration encode spatial designations that are both legal and geographic, structured by an implicit reliance on mapped representations of the Earth's surface.

As Chapter 1 argued, this conjunction is neither incidental nor merely semantic. Rather, disciplinary International Law's enduring attachment to a spatial order defined by statist units reflects the conceptual sedimentation of modern cartographic reason. The "World Map" of states – gridded, bordered, and color-coded – continues to shape how international legal claims are visualized, how authority is understood, and how rule is enacted. A map-mindedness visibly shades the workings of International Law, perhaps similar to how disciplinary geology casts its profile over geography.[1] Yet, unlike this latter profile, international lawyers scarcely ponder the surface they toil upon and, consequently, the need to examine modern geography's legacy in

[1] See Boaventura de Sousa Santos, "Law: A Map of Misreading. Toward a Postmodern Conception of Law," *Journal of Law and Society* 14 (1987): 279; Cedric Ryngaert, "Representations of the (Extra)Territorial: Theoretical and Visual Perspectives," *Utrecht Law Review* 13 (2017): 1; Nikolas M. Rajkovic, "The Visual Conquest of International Law: Brute Boundaries, the Map and the Legacy of Cartogenesis," *Leiden Journal of International Law* 31, no. 2 (2018): 267–88.

conditioning the disciplines' worldview. The World Map remains an object of reference rather than of reflection.

This absence of spatial self-awareness stands in contrast to the disciplinary evolution of Geography, which has long grappled with its imperial and scientific legacies. While geographers have deconstructed the ontological and ideological regimes embedded in mapmaking, international legal scholars have largely left untouched the spatial foundations that structure their own field. Geography is typically treated as external to legal inquiry, surfacing episodically in the context of war, revolution, or state succession, but seldom as a constitutive dimension of legal thought. This marginalization is symptomatic of a deeper epistemic condition: Spatial categories such as territoriality and jurisdiction have become so entrenched in the discipline's conceptual grammar that they appear as natural, self-evident features of international legal reasoning.[2]

This chapter builds on the argument advanced in Chapter 1: that International Law's dominant spatial ontology is both historically contingent and conceptually fragile. It has been maintained through what might be termed a cartographic unconscious – a deep reliance on ontological, ideological and visual conventions inherited from statist geography and Enlightenment cartographic science.[3] Figures like Alexander von Humboldt and Karl Ritter helped formalize a global spatial imaginary based on territorial coherence and geometrical segmentation, one that continues to inform how legal authority is mapped, even in the face of contemporary spatial complexities.[4] The enduring influence of this mapped imaginary has narrowed the discipline's conceptual aperture, constraining its ability to theorize emerging spatial formations – including investor–state arbitration and hybrid tribunals; GDPR-style extraterritorial data protection and supply-chain due-diligence regimes; sanctions and export-control architectures; the legal ordering of the high seas and orbital space; and the infrastructural geographies of cloud regions and submarine cables – that exceed traditional statist containers.

2 Jordan Branch, "Mapping the Territorial State," in *The Cartographic State: Maps, Territory, and the Origins of Sovereignty* (Cambridge: Cambridge University Press, 2014), 68–71.

3 J. B. Harley, "Historical Geography and the Cartographic Illusion," *Journal of Historical Geography* 15 (1989): 80, 85.

4 Karl Schlögel, *In Space We Read Time: On the History of Civilization and Geopolitics* (New York: Bard Graduate Center, 2016), 6.

It is in this context that the metaphor and provocation of this chapter – *Don't Look Down!* – takes on significance. For more than a century, international legal thought has moved forward atop spatial assumptions it has rarely examined. The triadic ontology of territory, sovereignty, and jurisdiction has served as the conceptual infrastructure upon which the field has elaborated its rules, institutions, and claims to authority. Yet this architecture conceals as much as it reveals. The question now, as posed in debates over spatial ontology, is not simply "what is space?" but rather "what forms of space are assumed to exist – and to what effect?" Translated into disciplinary terms: What kind of legal space does disciplinary International Law presuppose in its foundational concepts – and what forms of spatial ordering are rendered invisible or unintelligible as a result?

To be clear, the spatial silence in International Law is not wholly unique. Across the wider field of international studies, geographic assumptions have long shaped disciplinary worldviews.[5] But the timing, depth, and outcome of critical interventions have varied. A striking contrast emerges in relation to IR, which faced a decisive ontological reckoning during its so-called Third Great Debate (3GD) in the late 1980s and early 1990s.[6] Sparked by challenges to positivist and state-centric paradigms, the 3GD brought renewed attention to the spatial foundations of IR, including John Agnew's influential critique of the "territorial trap" – the assumption that

[5] See Latour, "Onus Orbis Terrarum"; John Gerard Ruggie, "Territoriality and Beyond: Problematizing Modernity in International Relations," *International Organization* 47, no. 1 (1993): 139–74; Neil Brenner, "Beyond State-Centrism? Space, Territoriality, and Geographical Scale in Globalization Studies," *Theory and Society* 28, no. 1 (1999): 39–78; Andreas Osiander, "Sovereignty, International Relations, and the Westphalian Myth," *International Organization* 55, no. 2 (2003): 251–87; Gearóid Ó Tuathail, *Critical Geopolitics: The Politics of Writing Global Space* (London: Routledge, 1996); Saskia Sassen, *Territory, Authority, Rights: From Medieval to Global Assemblages* (Princeton, NJ: Princeton University Press, 2006).

[6] Yosef Lapid, "The Third Debate: On the Prospects of International Theory in a Post-Positivist Era," *International Studies Quarterly* 33, no. 3 (1989): 235–54; Friedrich Kratochwil and John Gerard Ruggie, "International Organization: A State of the Art on an Art of the State," *International Organization* 40, no. 4 (1986): 753–75; Richard Ashley and R. B. J. Walker, "Speaking the Language of Exile: Dissident Thought in International Relations," *International Studies Quarterly* 34, no. 3 (1990): 259–68; and Jim George, "International Relations and the Search for Thinking Space: Another View of the Third Debate," *International Studies Quarterly* 33, no. 3 (1989): 269–79.

state power, identity, and political legitimacy are all bound to fixed territorial units.[7]

Although IR's internal debates were far from unified in outcome, they reflected a willingness to revisit foundational spatial assumptions and develop alternative conceptual frameworks for global politics. That willingness is instructive. International Law, by contrast, has remained largely sheltered from such introspection. The World Map of states continues to serve not only as a representational tool but as a normative framework – structuring the distribution of rights, obligations, and responsibilities across legal space. The discipline has yet to undertake a comparable spatial turn or to acknowledge the historical contingencies and visual regimes that structure its spatial worldview.

This chapter does not offer a comprehensive history of that omission. Nor does it seek to mimic IR's trajectory. Rather, it argues for the necessity of cultivating a spatial self-awareness within disciplinary International Law – one that can illuminate the conceptual blind spots, inherited cartographies, and visual assumptions that continue to shape its legal imaginary. This is not a call to abandon territorial concepts wholesale, but to historicize and recontextualize them – to see their conceptual architecture not as fixed, but as mutable and contested. By doing so, international lawyers may begin to develop the critical tools needed to engage with the increasingly fragmented, networked, and noncontiguous forms of legal authority that define the contemporary global condition. *Looking down*, in this sense, is not a gesture of disciplinary retreat – but a conceptual necessity.

2.1 The Third Great Debate and a Broader Paradox

As this chapter will explore, International Law followed a markedly different trajectory from that of IR: a discipline that, whether by

7 Friedrich Kratochwil, *Rules, Norms, and Decisions: On the Conditions of Practical and Legal Reasoning in International Relations and Domestic Affairs* (Cambridge: Cambridge University Press, 1989); Nicholas Onuf, *World of Our Making: Rules and Rule in Social Theory and International Relations* (Columbia: University of South Carolina Press, 1989); Emanuel Adler, "Seizing the Middle Ground: Constructivism in World Politics," *European Journal of International Relations* 3, no. 3 (1997): 319–63; Richard Ashley, "The Poverty of Neorealism," *International Organization* 38, no. 2 (1984): 225–86; and R. B. J. Walker, *Inside/Outside: International Relations as Political Theory* (Cambridge: Cambridge University Press, 1993).

disposition or design, largely avoided confronting the ontological foundations of its statist mapping. The point here is not simply to rehearse a familiar cross-disciplinary contrast or to reignite interdisciplinary rivalries. While it is true that Hans Morgenthau – a founding figure of IR – was trained as an international lawyer and famously turned away from the field in frustration,[8] such biographical footnotes risk obscuring a more significant divergence: how two closely related "international" disciplines arrived at such different levels of reflexivity regarding the spatial assumptions at the core of their respective analytical frameworks.

In IR, the late Cold War period witnessed a major epistemological and ontological reckoning. The so-called 3GD, which unfolded from the mid 1980s through the 1990s, was catalyzed in part by IR's inability to anticipate or account for the relatively peaceful collapse of the Soviet bloc.[9] This geopolitical blind spot prompted internal critiques of the dominant Realist paradigm, which had long treated the international system as a fixed and competitive arrangement of sovereign states. Scholars working within Constructivist, Liberal, Political Economy, and Poststructuralist traditions questioned the taken-for-granted status of the state as the natural unit of international analysis.[10] They challenged both the descriptive adequacy and the normative desirability of state-centrism as the field's defining axiom.

This disciplinary rupture gave rise to a wave of scholarship that interrogated not just state behavior, but the very spatial ontology that sustained the Realist worldview. John Agnew's influential critique of

[8] Martti Koskenniemi, "Out of Europe: Carl Schmitt, Hans Morgenthau, and the Turn to 'International Relations'," in *The Gentle Civilizer of Nations: The Rise and Fall of International Law, 1870–1960* (Cambridge: Cambridge University Press, 2001), 471.

[9] See Onuf, *World of Our Making*; Kratochwil, *Rules, Norms, and Decisions*; see also R. Koslowski and Friedrich Kratochwil, "Understanding Change in International Politics: The Soviet Empire's Demise and the International System," *International Organization* 48 (1994): 215.

[10] Susan Strange, *States and Markets* (London: Pinter Publishers, 1987); Alexander Wendt, "Anarchy Is What the States Make of It: The Social Construction of Power Politics," *International Organization*, 46 (1992): 391; Alexander Wendt, "The Agent–Structure Problem in International Relations" *International Organization* 41, no. 3 (1987): 335–70; Jim George, *Discourses of Global Politics: A Critical (Re)Introduction to International Relations* (Boulder, CO: Lynne Rienner Publishers, 1994).

the "Territorial Trap" – the assumption that state power, identity, and policy are all territorially contained – became emblematic of this broader rethinking. IR began to explore how global politics might be theorized through more dynamic spatial configurations: networks, regions, and empires that transcend the geometrical grid of cartographic statehood.

The paradox, then, is not simply that IR problematized state space while International Law did not. It is that IR, a discipline with no formal role in regulating legal authority or governing territory, proved more willing to question the spatial frameworks inherited from statist cartography. International Law, by contrast, has continued to work within those inherited coordinates – even as it engages with practices that increasingly exceed them. The statist ontology that IR scholars came to view as a conceptual limitation remains a normative foundation in much of international legal thought. This chapter argues that this divergence deserves closer attention – not to valorize one field over the other, but to understand how disciplinary habits of thought have shaped what kinds of spatial problems are seen, named, and rendered intelligible in international legal discourse.

Notably, that statist axiom met one of its most significant challenges with the publication of John Agnew's seminal article, the "Territorial Trap."[11] Appearing during the height of IR's 3GD, Agnew's intervention represented not only a critique of Realism's spatial assumptions but also a broader ontological provocation. He argued that IR scholars – and by extension, much of the social sciences – had become ensnared in a view of the world that reified territory as a fixed and natural container of political life. What had become normalized as the "geographical division of the world into mutually exclusive territorial states,"[12] he contended, was in fact a historically specific configuration – one whose role and meaning had evolved over time but had been rendered static by a dominant disciplinary paradigm. Few appreciated, he argued, that the World Map of states was "spatio-temporal framing," which did not represent a "body of fixed facts … essentially the same today as 200 years ago."[13]

11 John Agnew, "The Territorial Trap: The Geographical Assumptions of International Relations Theory," *Review of International Political Economy* 1, no. 1 (1994): 53–80.

12 Agnew, "Territorial Trap," 53.

13 Agnew, "Territorial Trap," 56.

As Agnew wrote:

> [W]hat are the geographical assumptions that have led to the privileging of a territorial conception of the state in the first place? First, state territories have been reified as set or fixed units of sovereign space. This has served to dehistoricize and decontextualize processes of state formation and disintegration ... Second, the use of domestic/foreign and national/international polarities has served to obscure the international between processes operating at different scales: for example, the link between the contemporary globalization of certain manufacturing industries and the localization of economic development policies ... Third, the territorial state has been viewed as existing prior to and as a container of society.[14]

What made the "Territorial Trap" particularly significant, however, was not only its challenge to IR orthodoxy but also its method of critique. Agnew's was a fundamentally interdisciplinary intervention, drawing on critical geography and geopolitics to expose the substrate assumptions that had long underpinned IR's state-centric worldview. In doing so, he revealed how these assumptions were not exclusive to IR, but in fact permeated the social sciences more broadly – often without sufficient recognition of their intellectual origins or conceptual fragility. The article illuminated how a naturalized view of territorial sovereignty had been sustained by inherited visual grammars and unexamined geopolitical metaphors.

Moreover, Agnew's argument resonated far beyond IR. It contributed to a wider disciplinary conversation – particularly within Critical Geography,[15] Political Science,[16] and Sociology[17] – about the adequacy of territorial models in explaining contemporary global transformations. Emerging at a moment when scholars were debating the implications of globalization, transnational governance, and economic integration, the "Territorial Trap" helped crystallize a broader challenge to the state-centric paradigm. The article became a touchstone in debates about "deterritorialization" and respatialization,[18] prompting

14 Agnew, "Territorial Trap," 59. 15 Brenner, "Beyond State-Centrism?," 39.
16 Branch, "Mapping the Territorial State."
17 Saskia Sassen, "When Territory Deborders Territoriality," *Territory, Politics, Governance* 1, no. 1 (2013): 21–45.
18 Stuart Elden, "Missing the Point: Globalization, Deterritorialization and the Space of the World," *Transactions of the Institute of British Geographers* 30, no. 1 (2005): 8–19; Gearóid Ó Tuathail, "Borderless Worlds? Problematizing Discourses of Deterritorialization," *Geopolitics* 4, no. 2 (1999): 139–54.

scholars to shift their analytical focus from static conceptions of sovereignty to the historical and material processes that produced – and continue to reconfigure – territorial authority.[19]

In this sense, Agnew's intervention was not merely corrective; it was generative. It reoriented IR toward the spatial foundations of its disciplinary worldview and reconnected it to critical currents in geography and spatial theory. In doing so, it foregrounded a crucial insight: that spatial arrangements are not simply reflective of geopolitical "facts" but are themselves products of historically situated knowledge practices.[20] The World Map of states – long treated as a mirror of political reality – was thus revealed to be an ontological and normative regime, one that organized global space through specific territorial imaginaries and representational conventions.[21]

Put plainly, the "Territorial Trap" demonstrated how the dominance of state-centrism in global thought rested not on empirical inevitability, but on theoretical premises and visual codes that had come to define what counts as "international" or "global."[22] It called attention to the visual economy of mapped authority – a spatial ontology so familiar that it appeared natural, yet whose political and ontological stakes are far from neutral. For international lawyers, the import of this critique lies not only in its challenge to spatial complacency but also in its reminder that the ontological and visual scaffolding of legal thought is itself spatially structured. Understanding law's globality requires, in part, understanding the spatial formations – mapped, imagined, and enacted – that sustain it.

2.2 Carl Schmitt and the Eluded Debate in International Law

At this point, some international lawyers may detect a sense of *déjà vu*. The spatial concerns articulated in Agnew's "Territorial Trap" – and

[19] Nisha Shah, "The Territorial Trap of the Territorial Trap: Global Transformation and the Problem of the State's Two Territories," *International Political Sociology* 6, no. 1 (2012): 57–76.

[20] Rajkovic, "The Visual Conquest of International Law," 267–88.

[21] Jens Bartelson, "The Social Construction of Globality," *International Political Sociology* 4, no. 3 (2010): 219–35.

[22] Neil Brenner and Stuart Elden, "Henri Lefebvre on State, Space, Territory," *International Political Sociology* 3, no. 4 (2009): 353–77, at 353, 356.

the broader disciplinary reorientation it precipitated in IR – resonate in ways that are not entirely foreign to disciplinary International Law.[23] Indeed, the entanglement of law, geography, and spatial ordering is not wholly absent from the legal field. It has, at times, surfaced as a latent current, murmuring beneath doctrinal argumentation and occasionally crystallizing in conceptual reflection.[24] Yet, unlike in IR, this current never coalesced into a sustained disciplinary reckoning with the spatial ontology underpinning international legal thought.

There are historical and intellectual reasons for this. Among them is the contested legacy of one of the few figures in International Law to grapple explicitly with questions of space and order: Carl Schmitt.[25] His *The Nomos of the Earth*, published in 1950, remains a pivotal – if polarizing – text in the field's sporadic engagement with spatial theory.[26] Schmitt's appeal here is not only his direct engagement with the spatial foundations of international order but also his reliance on metaphors of global landscaping – treating the division and cultivation of the earth's surface as a conceptual entry point into law's ordering logics. His intervention parallels Agnew's in some important respects: both foreground the normative and conceptual centrality of spatial

[23] For example: Richard T. Ford, "Law's Territory (A History of Jurisdiction)," *Michigan Law Review* 97, no. 4 (1999): 843–930.

[24] See Martti Koskenniemi, "Carl Schmitt and International Law," in *The Oxford Handbook of Carl Schmitt*, ed. Jens Meierhenrich and Oliver Simons (Oxford: Oxford University Press, 2017), 593:

> The booming Schmitt commentary of the past two decades has not spread into international law as much as one might have expected. Even as his international law texts have been reflected on by political theorists and international relations experts; international lawyers have not immersed themselves in Schmitt exegesis. This may result from their instinctive avoidance of conflictual items, inextricable from their self-image as representatives of a cosmopolitan peace project and their activist role in precisely the international institutions that Schmitt would have indicted as parts of Anglo-American global hegemony. In part, no doubt, this may be explained by the predominantly technical and positivist orientation of the field. International lawyers do not see themselves as representatives of an intellectual discipline. Their humanitarian sensibilities are not based on any well-articulated theory but have been imbibed practically unconsciously with the profession's technical routines.

[25] Bardo Fassbender, "Stories of War and Peace: On Writing the History of International Law in the 'Third Reich' and After," *European Journal of International Law* 13, no. 2 (2002): 479–512, at 498.

[26] Carl Schmitt, *The Nomos of the Earth in the International Law of the Jus Publicum Europaeum*, trans. G. L. Ulmen (New York: Telos Press Publishing, 2003).

ordering in structuring political authority; both challenge the assumption that existing spatial arrangements are timeless; and both critique the abstraction of universalist discourses that obscure the historically contingent production of global space.

Yet there are also critical divergences. Schmitt's project is deeply inflected by his broader entanglement with the German conservative revolution. His audience was primarily jurists and legal historians, not social scientists. His conceptual tools – *nomos*, *Großraum*, *Katechon*[27] – were steeped in theological and philosophical registers far removed from Agnew's social scientific idiom.[28] And most crucially, Schmitt's intellectual legacy has been shadowed by his associations with the Nazi regime, raising enduring ethical and methodological questions about the uses and limits of his thought within legal scholarship.

Notwithstanding these differences, *The Nomos of the Earth* introduced into international legal discourse a serious inquiry into the spatial foundations of legal order – an inquiry that has not been taken up with comparable intensity or breadth. While Schmitt has garnered both admiration[29] and criticism,[30] his core claim – that the spatial distribution of authority is a constitutive rather than derivative feature of international legal order[31] – has received curiously little sustained debate.[32] Unlike Agnew's intervention in IR, which helped catalyze a wave of interdisciplinary scholarship and conceptual innovation,[33] Schmitt's spatial theorizing remains more often cited than engaged, acknowledged but less interrogated on its own terms. This disciplinary

[27] Julia Hell, "Katechon: Carl Schmitt's Imperial Theology and the Ruins of the Future," *The Germanic Review: Literature, Culture, Theory* 84, no. 4 (2009): 283–326.

[28] For example: Carl Schmitt, *The Concept of the Political*, trans. George Schwab (Chicago: University of Chicago Press, 1996); Carl Schmitt, *Roman Catholicism and Political Form*, trans. G. L. Ulmen (Westport, CT: Greenwood Press, 1996).

[29] Friedrich Hayek, *Law, Legislation and Liberty* (London: Routledge, 1990), 485.

[30] Benno Teschke, "Fatal Attraction: A Critique of Carl Schmitt's International Political and Legal Theory," *International Theory* 3, no. 2 (2011): 179–227.

[31] William Hooker, *Carl Schmitt's International Thought: Order and Orientation* (Cambridge: Cambridge University Press, 2009), 69.

[32] Koskenniemi, "Carl Schmitt and International Law," 593.

[33] Stephen Legg, ed., *Spatiality, Sovereignty and Carl Schmitt: Geographies of the Nomos* (London: Routledge, 2011).

silence is significant.[34] For it raises two questions that are more than historical curiosities: Why did the spatial turn that Schmitt gestured toward fail to ignite a broader ontological debate within International Law? And why should that missed opportunity matter for how the field conceptualizes legal authority in the present?

These questions are not merely retrospective; they touch on the deeper architecture of international legal cognition. If, as this chapter contends, disciplinary International Law has continued to operate within a spatial ontology defined by statist cartography – one that is treated more as a background given than as a site of inquiry – then understanding why the field failed to develop a robust internal critique of its spatial foundations becomes a matter of disciplinary self-reflection. The absence of such debate is not simply an intellectual lacuna; it is a symptom of a broader reluctance to engage with the conceptual and visual infrastructures that shape how international legal space is imagined, represented, and governed.

The subsections that follow take up these questions in turn. First, by revisiting the reception of Schmitt's work within International Law, situating it within its postwar context, and considering the institutional and ideological factors that shaped its limited uptake. Second, by exploring what a more thorough engagement with spatial theory – drawing from geography, spatial humanities, and critical legal thought – might yield for the discipline. In doing so, the chapter aims to show that the absence of a spatial debate is not incidental, but constitutive: It reveals something fundamental about how international legal knowledge has been structured, and what it has systematically deferred.

2.2.1 [Schmitt's] Inferno: International Law's Untouchable Space

Any scholarly intervention occurs within a particular historical, institutional, and intellectual ecology – one that shapes the reception, uptake, or dismissal of its arguments. John Agnew's "Territorial Trap," as discussed earlier, emerged in the context of IR's 3GD, a moment when the discipline was unusually open to epistemological, ontological, and methodological reflection. The climate of critique that characterized this period provided fertile ground for a challenge to foundational

[34] Koskenniemi, "Carl Schmitt and International Law," 593.

spatial assumptions. By contrast, Carl Schmitt's interventions into spatial thought, especially his *The Nomos of the Earth*, confronted an entirely different milieu – one defined by postwar reconstruction, ideological purification, and the reassertion of liberal universalisms within the field of International Law.[35] These conditions deeply affected the trajectory – and ultimately the containment – of spatial inquiry within the discipline.

To understand this dynamic, it is instructive to recall that Schmitt's engagement with spatial concepts long preceded *The Nomos of the Earth*. As early as 1928, he developed the notion of *Großraum* – a concept of "greater spaces" that sought to capture the de facto expansion of legal and political authority beyond state borders.[36] Schmitt argued that emerging forms of spatial order, such as the Monroe Doctrine, revealed a new principle of international legality based not on formal equality among states, but on spatial hierarchies and spheres of influence structured around dominant powers. *Großraum*, in this view, marked a departure from classical International Law's insistence on mutual recognition among formally sovereign states. It pointed instead to an unfolding spatial logic in which authority was exercised over integrated geography through security guarantees, economic dependency, and industrial organization.[37]

Yet *Großraum* was conceptually distinct from the *Nomos*.[38] Where the former described a geopolitical formation anchored in asymmetrical power relations, the latter aimed to articulate the foundational principle through which global space was historically partitioned and normatively ordered. In *The Nomos of the Earth*, Schmitt located the origins of modern International Law in the "spatial revolution" of the Age of Discovery – a moment in which European powers, through

[35] Jan-Werner Müller, *A Dangerous Mind: Carl Schmitt in Post-War European Thought* (New Haven, CT: Yale University Press, 2003), 245.

[36] Anne Orford, "Regional Orders, Geopolitics, and the Future of International Law," *Current Legal Problems* 74 (2021): 162; Rüdiger Voigt, ed., *Großraum-Denken: Carl Schmitts Kategorie der Großraumordnung* (Stuttgart: Franz Steiner Verlag, 2008).

[37] Carl Schmitt, "The Großraum Order of International Law with a Ban on Intervention for Spatially Foreign Powers: A Contribution to the Concept of Reich in International Law (1939–41)," in *Writings on War*, ed. Timothy Nunan (Cambridge: Polity, 2011), 75, 87–88.

[38] G. L. Ulmen, "Translator's Introduction," in Schmitt, *The Nomos of the Earth*, 19.

acts of appropriation, partitioned the globe into discrete zones of legal authority. This *nomos*, or concrete spatial order, gave rise to a juridical logic that conflated land with authority, territory with sovereignty, and mapping with lawmaking.

It is precisely here, however, that historical context and semantic proximity became decisive. While Schmitt's spatial concepts were generative in analytic terms, they became ideologically and morally entangled with the catastrophic politics of their time. The conceptual vocabulary of *Großraum* and *Nomos* did not exist in isolation; it belonged to a wider semantic field of spatial thought that, by the 1930s and 1940s, had been co-opted and weaponized by the Nazi regime.[39] Terms such as *Lebensraum* (living space), *Ostraum* (eastern space), and *Volk ohne Raum* (a people without space) were not only linguistic constructs – they were instruments of imperial ambition and racialized violence, used to justify territorial expansion and the genocidal reordering of Europe.[40]

In this sense, Schmitt's spatial theorizing – however distinct in purpose or argument – became tainted by association.[41] His personal affiliations with the Nazi regime, including his juridical justifications for its early measures, rendered his later work suspect, even where its theoretical insights might have warranted closer engagement. The shadow of complicity hung over *The Nomos of the Earth*, making its spatial argumentation politically precarious and professionally untouchable for many international lawyers in the postwar period. What might otherwise have spurred a deeper inquiry into the spatial ontology of legal order was instead bracketed, archived, or cautiously referenced with caveats.

This legacy has had lasting effects. While *The Nomos of the Earth* has enjoyed periodic revivals – particularly within critical legal studies, political theology, and European constitutional theory – its core spatial claims have not generated the kind of sustained disciplinary debate that Agnew's "Territorial Trap" catalyzed within IR. In disciplinary International Law, the very notion of spatial critique has remained underdeveloped, often treated as historically contaminated

[39] See Joseph W. Bendersky, "Carl Schmitt at Nuremberg," *Telos* 72 (Summer 1987): 91–96; Joseph W. Bendersky, *Carl Schmitt: Theorist for the Reich* (Princeton, NJ: Princeton University Press, 1983), 270.

[40] Bendersky, *Carl Schmitt: Theorist for the Reich*, 270.

[41] Schlögel, *In Space We Read Time*, 33–34.

or theoretically extraneous. The result is a double silence: one imposed by the political burden of Schmitt's biography, and another sustained by the field's own reluctance to interrogate its visual and spatial foundations.

Yet this silence is revealing in itself. It exposes how certain forms of theoretical inquiry – especially those touching on space, territory, and order – remain cordoned off from the discipline's core self-understanding. It suggests that International Law's aversion to spatial theorizing is not merely a matter of intellectual oversight, but a symptom of deeper anxieties about the normative and historical conditions under which legal space has been constituted. In the subsections that follow, this chapter explores how this occlusion came to be institutionalized and what might be gained by recovering a more reflexive approach to the spatial architecture of international legal thought.

This conflation between spatial theory and its wartime instrumentalization became a powerful inhibitor to the development of international legal theory. The semantic proximity of concepts like *Großraum* or *Nomos* to the terminologies of National Socialism produced a kind of conceptual quarantine – rendering geography, and spatial reflection more broadly, into untouchable terrain.[42] Even as international legal scholars began, in the post-Cold War decades, to register growing discrepancies between traditional spatial templates and the emergent geographies of legal practice, those realizations rarely translated into a systematic reckoning with the field's spatial foundations.

One important, and widely cited, exception is Sir Daniel Bethlehem's 2014 inaugural lecture for the Sir Eli Lauterpacht series, provocatively titled "The End of Geography," and published with canonical weight by the *European Journal of International Law*. There, Bethlehem acknowledged the mounting inadequacy of International Law's prevailing geographic assumptions – especially the enduring grip of territorial jurisdiction as the default mode of legal spatiality. As he observed:

> [O]ur current conception of jurisdiction is overwhelmingly territorial in character, even in its non-obviously territorial dimensions. It is rooted in analyses of the 1930s that have developed little since then. While the challenges of the future may continue to be squeezed into this framework,

[42] Benno Teschke, "Decisions and Indecisions: Political and Intellectual Receptions of Carl Schmitt," *New Left Review* 67 (2011): 61–95, at 79.

with greater or lesser adequacy and effectiveness, this is not ideal. Issues of cyber, of the global environment, and of other transboundary matters could do with some creative thinking about how we approach questions of jurisdiction. [...]

Geographers have a good fortune that lawyers are denied. The law is not about eternal things. It is about the here and now. It is about how humankind organizes and manages its society. We hope that the law is of consequence, and it is our calling to work to this end. But the law can become old-fashioned. Mountains may only rarely change their position, and oceans only very rarely empty themselves of water. But the law is both more vulnerable and more adaptable. The place of geography in the international system is changing. It presents challenges to international law. These are challenges to which we must all rise.[43]

"The End of Geography," according to Bethlehem, meant recognizing that International Law had over-relied on *a particular* geography, overlooking the ahistorical nature of that geographic template and its spatial poverty over time.[44] With current legal practices being, in fact, vastly broader and more transversal – spatially – than the state-centric map assigned by the United Nations system. Yet, there was a bigger problem that Bethlehem touched upon: the substantive and, even, nominal absence of geographic or spatial theorizing within the discipline's repertoire.[45] This atrophy flowing from how select premises falsely naturalized statist cartography as the inherent map of geo-institutional ordering. As Bethlehem noted, such premises struggled versus novel global practices and boundaries, which had already begun reshaping geo-institutional and geo-legal ordering. To such an extent, there was a rethink needed on geographic assumptions that had long dominated the doctrinal field.

However, while Bethlehem's emphasis on dated geography did break ground, the substance of that recognition fell short of something groundbreaking for the discipline. It only touched the surface of a deeper conceptual void: International Law rarely acknowledged, or reflected on, the grand theory of space, that is state-centrism, that lurked in its normative basement. That lack of acknowledgement visible even in

[43] Daniel Bethlehem, "The End of Geography: The Changing Nature of the International System and the Challenge for International Law," *European Journal of International Law* 25, no. 1 (2014): 9–24, at 22–24.

[44] Bethlehem, "The End of Geography," 23.

[45] Bethlehem, "The End of Geography," 20

Bethlehem's own critical wording cited earlier: He framed disciplinary Geography as unitary and homogeneous, and seminal notions such as theory and space became obscured via geological metaphors, a plea for "creative thinking," and the vague assertion of a "framework."[46] The image of "mountains" and "oceans" gestured toward permanence, while law was framed as temporally contingent. What remained absent was an acknowledgement that the legal ordering of space – no less than the space of law – is itself a theoretical project.

This elision is telling. It suggests that International Law's discomfort with spatial theorizing is not merely a vestige of Schmitt's ideological shadow, but a deeper disciplinary condition. Few international lawyers conceive of their field as intellectually proximate to disciplinary Geography, let alone as indebted to its theoretical legacies.[47] This estrangement has reinforced the longstanding binary whereby International Law is understood as doctrinal rather than theoretical, practical rather than philosophical, technical rather than conceptual.[48] As a result, even when international lawyers sense the inadequacy of their inherited spatial models – as Bethlehem clearly did – they often lack the conceptual grammar to articulate alternative frameworks.

This disciplinary estrangement becomes especially apparent when Bethlehem's intervention is contrasted with Agnew's. Where Agnew drew directly on Critical Geography and spatial theory to expose the epistemological and ontological premises of IR's statist worldview, Bethlehem's critique remained limited to the level of doctrinal recalibration. Agnew exposed the "Territorial Trap" as a conceptual artifact that structured geopolitical perception; Bethlehem, by contrast, called for new ways to "approach" jurisdiction without scrutinizing the theoretical architecture of jurisdiction itself. The contrast underscores the consequences of International Law's self-imposed distance from the traditions of spatial thought.

Reengaging those traditions is not merely an academic exercise – it is essential for any serious reconsideration of legal space in an era marked by spatial transformation. To rethink geography beyond the statist model, as Bethlehem proposes, requires more than "creativity."

46 Bethlehem, "The End of Geography," 22.
47 Rajkovic, "The Visual Conquest of International Law," 267–68.
48 See Fuad Zarbiyev, "Of Theory and Reality, and Airplanes and Helicopters," *European Journal of International Law* 36, no. 1 (2025): 147–64.

It demands recognition of spatial theory as foundational to International Law's conceptual infrastructure. This is a difficult move for the discipline, precisely because spatial thought has long been occluded – its presence distorted by its misappropriation during the 1930s and 1940s, and its broader lineage either forgotten or dismissed.

Yet this historical framing is misleading. The theoretical tradition of Geography is far older, richer, and more diverse than its fascist distortions. It includes figures such as Immanuel Kant, Alexander von Humboldt, Karl Ritter, Albrecht Penck, and Walter Benjamin – none of whom were complicit in, or reducible to, the political semantics of the Third Reich. Their work contributed to a longstanding conversation about the relationship between space, order, and representation – conversations that remain of enduring relevance to international legal thought. To reduce Geography to the semantic residue of *Lebensraum* is to overlook its deeper genealogies and theoretical resources.

What is at stake, then, is not merely the rehabilitation of geography within legal scholarship, but the recovery of a spatial imagination that has long been marginalized. Disciplinary International Law has operated for too long with a flattened spatial ontology – one in which space is assumed rather than theorized, mapped rather than made sense of. To move beyond this condition requires returning to neglected traditions of spatial thought, not as a nostalgic exercise but as a generative framework for reimagining legal authority in an age of spatial reconfiguration. In the next subsection, this chapter turns back to *The Nomos of the Earth* – not to revisit the specter of Schmitt's geopolitics, but to draw attention to the underexplored conceptual insight that animated his project: a spatial *gaze* and *geopoetics* that, while compromised, still offers provocation for how we might begin to see the legal ordering of space differently.

2.2.2 Schmitt's Gaze: The Nomos and Its Circumferential Logic

To suggest that International Law operates through a "gaze" may seem unusual – perhaps even unsettling – for many within the discipline.[49]

[49] A notable exception from Constitutionalism Theory is Zoran Oklopčić, "The Nomos and the Gaze: Beyond Self-Determination (II)," in *Beyond the People: Social Imaginary and Constituent Imagination* (Oxford: Oxford University Press, 2018), 193–230.

The term connotes a way of looking that is not neutral but shaped by position, intent, and power.[50] It implies that how one *sees* the "international" is never disinterested, and that vision itself structures legal perception. Yet, this notion of the gaze remains alien to International Law's doctrinal vocabulary, professional self-understanding, and methodological conventions. It cuts against the grain of the formalist ethos that has long defined the discipline's labor – an ethos concerned with rules, texts, institutions, and practice, rather than the spatial or visual mediation of legal meaning.

Still, the question remains: Is the "gaze" so foreign to the actual work of international lawyers? Is it not the case that legal interpretation – whether of territory, jurisdiction, or the international community itself – is always conditioned by ways of seeing? Returning to this chapter's title, "Don't Look [Down]," we are reminded that the issue is not whether lawyers look, but where and how they are trained to direct their sight.[51] The gaze, in this context, refers to the habitual visual orientation of the discipline – an orientation structured by inherited spatial categories such as territory, sovereignty, and jurisdiction.

This insight pushes us to recognize that looking is never neutral. It is shaped by techniques, traditions, and positionalities. The gaze is thus not simply about what is visible, but about the terms through which visibility is structured. As such, it informs what is perceived as legally relevant or intelligible. Kenneth Burke helps frame this idea through his concept of "circumferential logic" – a logic that expands or contracts the radius of meaning depending on one's interpretive orientation:

> In time[s] of adversity one can readily note the workings of "circumferential" logic, in that [persons] choose to define their acts in terms of much wider orbits than the orbit of the adversity itself. The "solace of religion", for instance, may have its roots not in a mere self-deception, whereby one can buoy [themselves] up with false promises or persuade [themselves] that the situation is not bad when it is so palpably bad; but it may stem from an accurate awareness that one can define human nature and human actions

[50] Definition of "gaze" in the *Oxford English Dictionary*: www.oed.com/viewdictionaryentry/Entry/77224

[51] Nikolas M. Rajkovic, "International Law and the Ides of March: A Response to David Kennedy," *Tilburg Law Review* 23, no. 1 (2018): 121–24, at 122; see also David Shim, "Remote Sensing Place: Satellite Images as Visual Spatial Imaginaries," *Geoforum* 51 (2014): 152–60, at 153.

> in much wider terms than the particularities of his immediate circumstances would permit; and this option is not an "illusion", but a fact, and as true as a fact as any fact in his immediate circumstances.[52]

Burke's insight suggests that interpretive acts – including those undertaken by international lawyers – are bounded by the orbit of their gaze. That gaze defines what counts as a legal problem, what is considered relevant context, and what spatial arrangements are rendered legible.

Derek Gregory deepens this insight through his analysis of "scopic regimes," which he describes as historically specific ways of seeing the "world-as-exhibition".[53] According to Gregory, such regimes are not merely visual in the sensory sense, but also discursive and disciplinary. They are "culturally constructed and prescriptive, socially structured and shared."[54] Within this framework, the gaze is not merely a function of ocular intensity or position – in a sheer biological sense. It is also about the "productive power"[55] of visual "observation" and – returning to Burke – how disciplinary, cultural, and technological mediation influences a contraction or expansion of circumferential vision and logic.

From this perspective, one might argue that disciplinary International Law has long operated within a specific (and notably European) scopic regime – a visual and conceptual orientation that imagines the planet as a gridded surface of states. This is precisely the gaze that Carl Schmitt sought to both analyze and embed in *The Nomos of the Earth*. Despite (or perhaps because of) the ideological burden attached to Schmitt's name, his account of the spatial foundations of international legal order offers a powerful, if unsettling, example of circumferential legal vision.

That gaze – wide, elevated, and imperial in posture – proceeds through a *world-as-exhibition* narrative. Schmitt did not merely theorize the emergence of international legal space; he visualized it, casting the globe itself as the object of geopolitical division and legal inscription. His narrative opens with an epic and sublime moment of spatial

52 Kenneth Burke, *A Grammar of Motives* (Berkeley and Los Angeles: University of California Press, 1969), 84.

53 Derek Gregory, *Geographical Imaginations* (Oxford: Blackwell, 1998), 14.

54 Derek Gregory, "From a View to a Kill: Drones and Late Modern War," *Theory, Culture & Society* 28, nos. 7–8 (2011): 188–215, at 190.

55 Michael Barnett and Raymond Duvall, "Power in International Politics," *International Organization* 59, no. 1 (2005): 39–75, at 55.

awakening,[56] in which the Earth becomes a measurable object, calling forth legal partition:

> No sooner had the contours of the earth emerged as a real globe – not just sensed as myth, but apprehensible as fact and measurable as space – than there arose a wholly new and hitherto unimaginable problem: the spatial ordering of the earth in terms of international law …
>
> The first attempts in international law to divide the earth as a whole according to the new global concept of geography began immediately after 1492 … [T]he struggle among European powers for land-appropriations made necessary certain divisions and distributions. These sprang from what I call *global linear thinking*, which represents a chapter in the historical development of spatial consciousness. It began with the discovery of a "new world" and the start of the "modern age," and kept pace with the development of geographical maps and of the globe itself …
>
> The question was political from the start; it could not be dismissed as "purely geographical." As scientific, mathematical, or technical disciplines, geography and cartography certainly are neutral … Despite the neutrality of geography as a science, purely geographical concepts can generate a political struggle.[57]

This passage reveals how Schmitt identified the visual and spatial foundations of International Law not as byproducts of legal reasoning, but as its enabling condition. The modern *nomos* emerged, in his view, from the conjuncture of cartographic representation and imperial conquest. It was through this gaze – from above, across oceans and continents – that the global spatial order was imagined, divided, and legalized. His notion of *global linear thinking* captured the practice of inscribing power onto space via lines: lines of demarcation, sovereignty, jurisdiction, and colonial appropriation.

Yet Schmitt also hints at a deeper point: that legal geography is never simply technical or neutral. Even "purely geographical" concepts can serve as vehicles for normative and political claims. The fact that geography appears neutral only underscores its structural power (see Chapter 3). In this regard, Schmitt's gaze exposes the fiction of spatial neutrality in International Law – a fiction that continues to underpin the discipline's prevailing cartographic imaginary.

[56] William Hooker, *Carl Schmitt's International Thought: Order and Orientation* (Cambridge: Cambridge University Press, 2009), 72.

[57] Schmitt, *The Nomos of the Earth*, 86–88.

The challenge for international lawyers, then, is to reflect on the gaze that has oriented the discipline's thinking. What circumferences define the spatial imagination of legal reasoning? What visual conventions determine what is seen and what is obscured in the mapping of legal authority? And how might that "gaze" be expanded, redirected, or contested to apprehend the new spatial formations shaping global legal order?

2.2.3 Schmitt's Geopoetry and Law's Pastoral Circumference

This is where the notion of *geopoetry* becomes particularly significant when reading Schmitt's passages on the global ordering of legal space. At first glance, *The Nomos of the Earth* appears grounded in descriptive realism – a cartographic rendering of global partitioning based on geopolitical facts and juridical consequences.[58] Its tone evokes an almost elemental inevitability, as though Schmitt were recounting a natural history of legal space, anchored in the certitudes of geology and geography. Yet closer scrutiny reveals a more literary construction at work: a teleological narrative woven through evocative imagery and aesthetic cadence. What cultural geographers have termed *geopoetry* is at play in Schmitt's narration of the "new global concept of geography."[59] Modern cartography has always leveraged geopoetics to sustain its social purchase and reigning imaginary,[60] and Schmitt's *Nomos* provides a rare window into how geopoetry gently affixed International Law's gaze to a (European) pastoral circumference.

To appreciate this dimension, it is necessary to understand what geographers mean by *geopoetics*. As a term, geopoetry came to prominence in disciplinary geography over thirty years ago.[61] It was advanced – as already noted – by cultural geographers, who questioned and criticized

[58] See Oliver Simons, "Carl Schmitt's Spatial Rhetoric," in *The Oxford Handbook of Carl Schmitt*, ed. Jens Meierhenrich and Oliver Simons (Oxford: Oxford University Press, 2017), 776–802.

[59] See Angela Last, "We Are the World? Anthropocene Cultural Production between Geopoetics and Geopolitics," *Theory, Culture & Society* 34, nos. 2–3 (2017): 147–68.

[60] Last, "We Are the World?," 151.

[61] Federico Ferretti, "From the Drought to the Mud: Rediscovering Geopoetics and Cultural Hybridity from the Global South," *Cultural Geographies* 27, no. 4 (2020): 597–613, at 598.

the traditional nature/culture divide of modern mapping.[62] The noun serves to highlight two underexamined dimensions of geographic knowing: its conceptual politics and the salience of a social imaginary. As such, core notions – notably "geography" or "geopolitics" – were revisited as bundled concepts, fusing geophysical features with varying social, cultural, and ideological narratives.[63] What is more, geopoetics became grasped as essential to the making of a ruling imaginary, and thus a perceived "geographic reality."[64] As Angela Last explains:

> [G]eopoetics "make us see ... perceive ... feel" – not reality itself but "the ideology from which it is born, in which it bathes, from which it detaches itself as art, and to which it alludes." Through making ideology and cultural engagements with geography (rather than earth forces) tangible, geopoetics render tangible the shuttling back and forth between geography and its representation. To paraphrase Judith Butler, poetic practices engage in a struggle over "the regulation of the sphere of appearance ... to establish what will count as reality and what will not".[65]

In this sense, Schmitt's *Nomos* is not simply a work of spatial theorization – it is also a work of geopoetic composition. It seeks to *make visible* a particular worldview, and to imbue that view with historical inevitability and normative weight.[66] The appeal to sacred origins, primal appropriations, and pastoral imagery is not accidental; it is the vehicle through which legal geography is rendered legible as destiny. Nowhere is this more explicit than in Schmitt's account of the constitutive act of land-appropriation:

> [T]he constitutive process of a land-appropriation is found at the beginning of the history of every settled people, every commonwealth, every empire. This is true as well for the beginning of every historical epoch. Not only logically, but also historically, land-appropriation precedes the order that follows from it. It constitutes the original spatial order, the source of all further concrete order and all further law. It is the reproductive root in the normative order of history ... The traditional history of international law also is a history of land-appropriations.[67]

62 Angela Last, "Fruit of the Cyclone: Undoing Geopolitics through Geopoetics," *Geoforum* 64 (2015): 56–64, at 57.
63 Last, "We Are the World?" 149.
64 Ferretti, "From the Drought to the Mud," 600.
65 Last, "Fruit of the Cyclone," 59–60.
66 Hooker, *Carl Schmitt's International Thought*, 73.
67 Schmitt, *Nomos of the Earth*, 48.

This passage exemplifies Schmitt's pastoral geopoetics. By portraying land appropriation as both the ontological origin and historical predicate of law, he assigns (Eurocentric) legal ordering a mythic attachment to the Earth.[68] The legal becomes natural; law's geography is framed not as contingent, but as foundational – rooted in soil, sacralized by time, and inherited by tradition. This pastoral framing is no mere rhetorical flourish. It functions as a disciplinary horizon, delimiting the spatial imagination of International Law. It suggests that the terrestrial map of sovereign states is not only historically grounded, but normatively unassailable.[69] Such teleology becomes most vivid in Schmitt's etymology of *nomos*:

> The Greek word for the first measure of all subsequent measures, for the first land-appropriation understood as the first partition and classification of space, for the primeval division and distribution, is *nomos*. ... [I] want to restore to the word *nomos* its energy and majesty. [...] *Nomos* comes from *nemein* – a [Greek] word that means both "to divide" and "to pasture." Thus, *nomos* is the immediate form in which the political and social order of a people becomes spatially visible ... In Kant's words, it is the "distributive law of mine and thine," or, to use an English term that expresses it so well, it is the "radical title." *Nomos* is the measure by which the land in a particular order is divided and situated ... In particular, *Nomos* can be described as a wall, because, like a wall, it, too, is based on sacred orientations.[70]

Here, *nomos* becomes both legal measure and sacred metaphor – a pastoral and juridical architecture rolled into one. Its function is not merely to describe how land was divided, but to *sacralize* that division as an enduring form of order. It is this very blending of sublime, spatial, and legal registers that gives Schmitt's text its geopoetic power. The reader is not simply being told how International Law arose spatially; they are being invited to feel its archaic weight, to see legal geography as an inheritance rather than a construct.

But that same geopoetic move also serves to demarcate the epistemic authority of International Law from the broader field of Geography.[71]

[68] Hooker, *Carl Schmitt's International Thought*, 78.
[69] Hooker, *Carl Schmitt's International Thought*, 83.
[70] Schmitt, *Nomos of the Earth*, 67–70.
[71] Wendy Brown, *Walled States, Waning Sovereignty* (New York: Zone Books, 2010), 57.

Schmitt's invocation of sacred space, radical title, and pastoral division constructs an exceptionalist frame: a vision of legal geography that stands apart from – and hierarchically above – the empirical and pluralistic inquiries of disciplinary Geography. To refer back to the words of Angela Last, *nomos* framed how to "see ... perceive ... [and] feel" the sacrosanct reality of international legal geography. In this case, *nomos* does not just describe the Earth – it defines who gets to engender it, and on what terms. This exceptionalism is consequential. It helped sustain the illusion that International Law's spatial concepts – sovereignty, territory, jurisdiction – were self-evident and universal, rather than geopoetically produced and historically contingent.[72] It reinforced the treatment of statist geography as a given spatial framework, limiting critical reflection within International Law on the visual and conceptual infrastructures that have shaped how legal space is imagined and governed.

Yet vulnerabilities were always latent in this pastoral frame. Chief among them: a tendency toward ahistoricism and spatial reification. By rooting law's spatial order in sacralized origins, *The Nomos of the Earth* effaced the social and political agency that has shaped geographic perception over time. For example, Schmitt's notion of *global linear thinking* – though evocative – obscures the complex cartographic histories and geopolitical contests that shaped nineteenth-century Europe's legal imagination. That period marked not just the rise of formalized sovereignty, but the expansion of imperial infrastructures and racialized borders – all inscribed through cartographic practices that were anything but neutral.

This history of cartographization – the process through which the Earth's complex materiality was rendered legible and governable via mapped, institutionalized spatial forms – is notably absent from Schmitt's geopoetic account. His pastoral framing of *nomos* occludes the representational and imperial techniques by which legal space was historically produced. Yet, understanding this process is essential for grasping how disciplinary International Law became entangled with projects of cartographic rationalization and spatial conquest. By revisiting the cartographic techniques that transformed the Earth into a gridded legal tableau, international lawyers can begin to interrogate not only the pastoral circumference of *nomos*, but also the deeper

[72] Schmitt, *Nomos of the Earth*, 88.

assumptions that have allowed a single cartographic imaginary – the Earth as a grid of bordered states – to dominate the legal field.

What is at stake, then, is not merely a critique of Schmitt's narrative, but a recovery of the contingent and constructed nature of legal spatiality that his work implicitly conceals. To move beyond the geopoetic coherence offered by the *nomos* is to open disciplinary International Law to alternative spatial imaginaries – ones attentive not to inherited geometric rationalities, but to emergent and contested geographies of legal meaning, authority, and global power. Such a shift invites a reorientation of the field's spatial grammar away from cartographic closure and toward spatial plurality.

2.3 Worn Geopoetry and Regimes of Geographic Perception

It now seems fitting to return to Agnew's deconstruction of state-centrism in IR and the chapter's opening query: Why did International Law not undergo a comparable "Third Great Debate"? Schmitt's *The Nomos of the Earth* provided a useful historical counterpart to Agnew's "Territorial Trap," particularly in how each addressed the origins and production of international geography. Schmitt broke ground by linking modern geography's globe-making to the spatial construction of international legal order. But when read through the lenses of inferno, gaze, and geopoetry, his contribution also reveals a deeper epistemic void and striking contrast with Agnew's more systematic critique.

The theme of inferno helped illustrate how spatial theorizing became tainted – if not taboo – within International Law after the Second World War, as fascist and Nazi misappropriations cast suspicion over spatial semantics. The gaze revealed how a circumferential logic, filtered through territoriality and jurisdiction, shaped what international lawyers saw – and failed to see – in legal space. Geopoetry, finally, disclosed the subtle aesthetic and ideological narrative through which statist cartography was naturalized in legal thought: a pastoral vision that masked the contingent nature of global spatial ordering.

In sum, *The Nomos of the Earth* exposed a geopoetic scaffolding that continues to buttress statist cartography within disciplinary International Law. In contrast to Agnew's dissection of the territorial state as a historically contingent construct, Schmitt projected a teleology that presented it as legal destiny. His gaze did not just reflect a personal worldview but gave voice to a larger disciplinary inheritance: the deep attachment of International Law to a cartographic imagination grounded in contiguous enclosures. The triad of inferno, gaze, and geopoetry reveals how this imaginary functions not only as doctrinal assumption but as a regime of geographic perception, structuring the visual and conceptual coordinates of international legal reasoning. This brings us to pivotal questions: What are the implications of such geopoetic entrenchment for the discipline? And how might international lawyers begin to reengage spatial theorizing in ways that challenge, rather than reproduce, the inherited geometries of power?

These questions animate Chapters 3 and 4. Chapter 3, "*Potere Incognito*: Seeing, Power, and the Cartographic World Order," turns to the ontological and visual infrastructures that have long conditioned what international lawyers recognize as legal space. It traces how Renaissance perspectivalism, Cartesian geometry, and imperial mapping practices converged to render the Earth governable as a gridded tableau of bordered states. This visual order, the chapter argues, did not merely represent legal space – it actively produced it. Cartographic projection became an epistemic device through which power was made legible and spatial order materialized. Through this process of cartographization, International Law internalized a flattened, geometric imaginary that disguised its co-constitution with imperial visual regimes. What emerges is a critique of the discipline's occluded *potere incognito* – its failure to see how its own authority was built on an inherited and unexamined visual grammar.

Chapter 4, "From Jurisdictions to *Juriscapes*: Toward a Transformative Theory of Territorialization," shifts from critique to conceptual reconstruction. If Chapter 3 interrogates how a singular legal map came to dominate international legal thought, Chapter 4 asks how we might theorize legal spatiality beyond that map. The chapter introduces *juriscapes* as a heuristic for understanding the morphogenetic processes through which legal authority today is reconstituted, redistributed, and reenacted. Rejecting the static containers of traditional jurisdiction, it emphasizes the infrastructural, trans-scalar, and networked configurations through which legal norms travel and take effect – across ports, data cables, sanctions regimes, and supply chains. Drawing on legal pluralism, critical geography, and anthropology, the *juriscapes* framework reorients international lawyers toward the material and spatial heterogeneity of contemporary global rule.

Together, these chapters excavate the foundations of international legal spatiality and offer tools to reimagine its contours. They reveal how visual infrastructures and inherited geometries have constrained legal thought while opening pathways to theorize law's emergent geographies more precisely and critically. If Chapter 2 diagnosed International Law's entrapment in a worn geopoetic imaginary, Chapters 3 and 4 offer a way forward – toward a more reflexive, spatially attuned international legal scholarship.

Looking outward, Agnew's critique also gestures to a broader shift that now spans the social sciences and beyond. In recent years, a geovisual revolution has emerged, propelled by the democratization of mapping technologies and the proliferation of spatial data. This revolution has challenged the visual monopoly long held by the state, giving rise to what geographers call "people's cartography."[73] Whether in climate visualization, satellite mapping of migration flows, or digital platforms tracking carbon emissions and transnational political alignments, new spatial grammars are becoming central to how global space is interpreted and contested.[74]

Contrary to Sir Daniel Bethlehem's suggestion that geography is a stable external given, disciplinary Geography today is a site of vibrant theoretical debate and methodological experimentation. Across multiple domains, scholars are confronting the epistemic limits of statist cartography and illuminating how all geographic representations are historically situated, politically charged, and ontologically contestable. For international lawyers, this suggests a productive path forward: to recognize that legal geography is never self-evident, but always constructed through visual, conceptual, and institutional choices.[75] It is a product of what might be called geo-institutional bargains – historically specific settlements about how the Earth should be seen, divided,

[73] Jeremy Crampton and John Krygier, "An Introduction to Critical Cartography," *ACME: An International Journal for Critical Geographies* 4, no. 1 (2006): 12.

[74] Christine Leunenberger and Izhak Schnell, *The Politics of Maps: Cartographic Constructions of Israel/Palestine* (Oxford: Oxford University Press, 2020), 2.

[75] Jeremy Crampton, "Cartography: Maps 2.0," *Progress in Human Geography* 33, no. 1 (2009): 91.

and governed. The World Map of states, long taken as legal fact, is better understood as one such grand bargain – powerful in its reach, but no longer uncontested in its logic.

The juxtaposition of Agnew and Schmitt thus speaks to a broader epistemic tension in this moment of geographic vertigo. Where Agnew emphasizes the historical contingency of state-centrism and invites critical unbuilding, Schmitt dramatizes the pastoral and sacral investments that continue to sustain it. Together, they chart the divergence between IR and IL in how each discipline has responded to the spatial crisis of the present. In disciplinary International Law, the territorial grid still holds sway – not merely as a doctrinal convenience, but as a governing ontology. Despite the growing mismatch between legal practices and mapped space, the discipline remains tethered to an iconic cartography: the World Map of states. In Chapter 3, we examine how this iconic order was produced, naturalized, and juridically encoded. In so doing, we begin to unearth how the geopoetic, epistemic and ontological infrastructure of *cartographization* gave statist geography its compelling graphic reality.

3 Potere Incognito

Seeing, Power, and the Cartographic World Order

What is the relationship between international law and politics? This is a perennial question. The usual responses emerge from distinct disciplinary silos, each narrating a separate "International" – one legal, the other political. Beneath this bifurcation lies a deeper inheritance: the liberal tradition's presumption that law stands in contrast to power.[1] Traditionally, within International Law, this has long enabled a strategic bracketing of power – assigning it as another discipline's proper noun and conceptual terrain. Hans Morgenthau's foundational schism made this division explicit.[2] Yet, that bracketing maneuver has always come with a shelf-life, due to its conceptual shallowness and lethargy.[3] Power and law have never been universal or one-size-fits-all concepts, with each differentiated by many types and nuances. More critically, certain forms of power are not external to law but constitutive of it.[4] This chapter opens a window onto that entanglement. It argues that productive and structural forms of power are not merely conditions for law's application but fundamental to International Law's visual, spatial, and conceptual architecture.

[1] See Nikolas M. Rajkovic, "Global Law and Governmentality: Reconceptualizing 'Rule of Law' as Rule 'Through' Law," *European Journal of International Relations* 18, no. 1 (2012): 29–52.

[2] See Hans J. Morgenthau, *Politics among Nations: The Struggle for Power and Peace*, 6th ed. (New York: Alfred A. Knopf, 1978), 31–32: "[N]ot every action that a nation performs with respect to another nation is of a political nature. Many activities are normally undertaken without any consideration of power, nor do they normally affect the power of the nation undertaking them. Many legal, economic, humanitarian, and cultural activities are of this kind." See also Koskenniemi, *The Gentle Civilizer of Nations*, 465–73.

[3] This relates to Giovanni Sartori's seminal intervention on conceptual stretching and its key pitfall. See Giovanni Sartori, "Concept Misformation in Comparative Politics," *American Political Science Review* 64, no. 4 (1970): 1033–53, at 1035: "It appears that we can cover more – in travelling terms – only by saying less, and by saying less in a far less precise manner."

[4] See Friedrich Kratochwil, *The Status of Law in World Society: Meditations on the Role and Rule of Law* (Cambridge: Cambridge University Press, 2014), 7.

Perspective, after all, is an artefact. It flows from where one stands in place and time – and, crucially, how one is trained to see. So, how do international lawyers see? Pedantic question, you might say. Put that intuition on hold for a moment, because we will explore it. What conditions shape the perceptual orientation of international legal reasoning?

One answer lies in the visual forms through which space has been rendered familiar and manageable. Cartographic images, in particular, have long offered a sense of orientation by compressing the world into a coherent surface, inviting trust in their lines and proportions. Precisely because this visual ordering appears stable and reassuring, it has been easy to relegate images to the background of legal reasoning – treating them as secondary, illustrative aids rather than as formative conditions of how space, authority, and power come into view. Academic discourse has formalized this tendency through the axiom of "image-as-illustration,"[5] according to which legal seeing is mediated primarily by specific texts – treaties, casebooks, *travaux préparatoires* – while images serve, at most, as supplemental aids. In this ontological hierarchy, certain texts are substance and images are accessories.

This chapter challenges that ordering. The hierarchy of text over image obscures how visuality – not merely textuality – has shaped the very ways international lawyers apprehend space, authority, and legality. To some, the title of this chapter may suggest a familiar critique: an excavation of how statist cartography has shaped the geographic, geopolitical, and geo-legal imagination of the Earth. That reading aligns with Jordan Branch's seminal account of how modern territorial maps structured the inter-state imaginary and institutionalized a visual grammar of international order.[6] But such an interpretation may end this chapter before it even begins. It would allow the bracketing maneuver to slip out the back door once again – failing to confront how International Law's perception has always been cartographically governed, and perhaps even iconographically captured. To unbracket

[5] See Michael Crutcher and Matthew Zook, "Placemarks and Waterlines: Racialized Cyberspaces in Post-Katrina Google Earth," *Geoforum* 40, no. 4 (2009): 523–34; Philip Kingsbury and John Paul Jones, "Walter Benjamin's Dionysian Adventures on Google Earth," *Geoforum* 40, no. 4 (2009): 502–13.

[6] See Jordan Branch, *The Cartographic State: Maps, Territory, and the Origins of Sovereignty* (Cambridge: Cambridge University Press, 2014).

"power" requires *seeing* law's cartographization as parcel of a far deeper and wider history of what Nicholas Onuf called *world-making*:

> the metaphor *world* is exceptionally evocative and usefully ambiguous. We speak of worlds – *any world* – in the usual way of observers in every world. We also speak of *the world* more concretely as the Western world – a geographically bounded world of societies related by culture and history. Finally we speak of this world as having taken on planetary proportions. For the most salient properties of this world, we often use the adjective *global.*
>
> We take this last world to be geographically inclusive, not to mention culturally invasive, thanks to the success that Western societies have had in spreading certain of their practices and institutions. None are more important than the practices and institutions that we put together and call international relations. The globalization of the Western world is recent, rapid, laden with ramifications for so many other worlds.[7]

Cartographization produced a geographic imaginary of a geometrically divisible planet, which became the visual prehistory for the inter-state system and, later, the institutionalization of International Law. This imaginary became the visual basis for engaging the planet: an essential part of *seeing* "the World" *as it is* versus what it *may otherwise be*.[8] However, the construction of such a reigning imaginary involved more than just disseminating and popularizing cartographic maps to form a graphic regime. Above all, cartographization was a complex process that involved multiple and intersecting types of power, which together manifested demarcations, borders, territories, and states as proclaimed mimetic reflections of planetary reality. The historical outcome being a dense landscape of transgenerational mappings, which have given certain geometric frames, categories or units

[7] Nicholas G. Onuf, "Worlds of Our Making," in *Making Sense, Making Worlds: Constructivism in Social Theory and International Relations* (London: Routledge, 2013), 21–22; see also Nicholas G. Onuf, *World of Our Making: Rules and Rule in Social Theory and International Relations* (Columbia: University of South Carolina Press, 1989).

[8] See Christian Jacob, *The Sovereign Map: Theoretical Approaches in Cartography throughout History* (Chicago: University of Chicago Press, 2006), 2:

> The map is mechanism that shows what no eye could ever see, even when the map represents the most familiar territory – the space marked out by daily experience ... Maps suggest ways of thinking as well as seeing. They materialize a view of the mind more than of external reality. They project an order of reason onto the world and force it to conform to a graphic rationale, a cultural grid, a conceptual geometry.

of "the World" (e.g., state territory) the appearance of cosmological perfection.[9] In sum, historical progress bequeathed ostensibly a cartographic grid that made nature and society *finally* knowable, calculable and thus controllable.[10]

Accordingly, the impact of cartographization represents more than just a story about how statist cartography came to shape the *seeing* of law's rule on a global scale. Cartographization also illustrates the deeply typological nature of power, and how the interplay of productive and structural types of power are inherent in the making of how the international legal orders are perceived spatially and temporally. It helps challenge a fundamental presumption: International lawyers stand at a measured distance from both the political and the arch-antonym of power. In this manner, a way to unbracket power is by *seeing* the "image-as-illustration" axiom in reverse: to consider how (legal) text likely served and elaborated a reigning cartographic medium, and not simply vice versa. It is a disruptive proposition no doubt, because it cuts against the textual grain of much international legal theorizing and doctrinal canon. No less, challenging established canon remains an abiding cause, since critical reflection is sometimes the only path toward disciplinary renewal and continued social purchase.

To understand cartographization's deep influence on International Law thus requires a heightened sensitivity to power's visual and spatial operations. By outsourcing the analysis of power to disciplines like IR, international lawyers have provincialized their own understandings of how power works upon and through vision. Reversing the text–image hierarchy allows us to see how particular cartographic

9 On the significance of cosmological elements for the (re)making of international orders, see Bentley B. Allan, *Scientific Cosmology and International Orders* (Cambridge: Cambridge University Press, 2018), 11–12:

> Cosmological elements are central to understanding change ... Political purposes ... are infused with meanings drawn from the broader cosmological ideas. Cosmological elements define purposes by providing a narrative of humanity's place in the universe that suggests what ends political agents should pursue ... So, cosmological elements are powerful because they infuse the beliefs and institutions that order collective life with meaning and motivate actors by placing them in narratives that structure time and space.

10 This follows from the Weberian ideal of control through scientific rationalization and control. See Max Weber, *The Vocation Lectures*, ed. David Owen and Tracy B. Strong (Indianapolis: Hackett, 2004), 22–23.

media – underwritten by specific modes of power – became foundational to the discipline's worldview. This is not merely a matter of optics; it is a matter of ontology.

This conjunction of power and perception will guide the chapter in two steps. Section 3.1 develops a typology of power that departs from the conventional Weberian lens, in which power is narrowly defined as the use of material resources to coerce or influence others. Instead, it foregrounds a deeper register of power: the shaping of sight itself – what is seen, unseen, and rendered imaginable. Viewed through this frame, International Law appears as a field historically imbued with multiple dimensions of power that have shaped its authority from the outset. Section 3.2 turns to the disciplinary effects of cartographic reason. It examines how legal and political seeing has been discursively – and arguably colonially – shaped by visual regimes derived from Enlightenment mapping practices. Yet this visual imperium now frays, as geo-economic and geopolitical practices (and crises) increasingly operate through trans-territorial scales of authority and emergent proto-domains.

3.1 *Seeing* Cartographic Power

How have notions of space and place – those foundational coordinates of human meaning – been constructed? How have ideas about the legal "World" been generated and stabilized? Or, more pointedly still, how have international lawyers – among many others – been made to *see* that world? These questions mark the turn this chapter now takes. They invite a shift in focus: from cartographic representations as passive illustrations, to the ways visuality itself has served as a vehicle of incipient power. Across recent centuries, the practice of Earth mapping has shaped how territory, nature, society, and politics are apprehended. Cartographic images – produced for diverse purposes across geographic, geological, political, military, economic, and climatic domains – have become so commonplace as to appear benign. Yet their history tells a different story. Through multiple traditions, cartographic practices have not simply reflected preexisting realities; they have constituted scientific knowledge, produced geographic "facts," and trained the eye to privilege certain spatial logics over others. They have cultivated a cartographic mindset – a way of seeing the Earth through the grid of the geometric map. In the words of Leuenberger and Snell: "Maps are ubiquitous. Climate maps inform us of weather patterns. Political maps designate nations, boundaries, and state capitals. Economic maps reveal a region's natural resources and economic activities ... Maps – whether they depict weather patterns, national boundaries, or election results – help us understand and navigate the world around us ... Maps helped create nations, boundaries, spatial imaginations, and national identities."[11]

It would be a steep and implausible claim to suggest that International Law has somehow stood outside or above this mapped ubiquity. Indeed, as Chapter 2 demonstrated, the discipline has long operated within a "cartographic unconscious" – a deep and largely unexamined reliance on the visual grammars inherited from Enlightenment geography and statist mapping practices. Yet few within the field have interrogated the implications of *cartographization* – understood not merely as a technical process but as a broader epistemic condition – on the shaping of international legal thought itself. This absence is striking. After all, the visual construction of the cartographic globe predated – and arguably helped to facilitate – the emergence of the modern inter-state system, alongside the conceptualization of international legal order.[12] Cartography's geometrical aesthetics and its hegemonic imaginary enabled, and later naturalized, the concept of territory as the basic spatial unit of international law. As J. B. Harley famously put it: "the map maker has always played a rhetorical role in defining the configurations of power ... in the visible landscape."[13] Harley's insight reminds us that maps are not neutral reflections but political artefacts – devices of persuasion, world-making, and power projection. The rhetorical function of mapping has long shaped the spatial imagination of modernity. That this dynamic would have bypassed international legal thought is not only unlikely, but conceptually unsustainable.

And yet, a puzzling lacuna persists. On the one hand, elements of legal scholarship and case law have, explicitly or implicitly,

11 Christine Leuenberger and Izhak Schnell, *The Politics of Maps: Cartographic Constructions of Israel/Palestine* (Oxford: Oxford University Press, 2020), 1.

12 See Jens Bartelson, "The Social Construction of Globality," *International Political Sociology* 4, no. 3 (2010): 219–35, at 220.

13 J. B. Harley, "Maps, Knowledge, and Power," in *The New Nature of Maps: Essays in the History of Cartography*, ed. Paul Laxton (Baltimore: Johns Hopkins University Press, 2001), 51–81, at 81.

acknowledged the role of the map in structuring territorial claims, border disputes, and jurisdictional authority. On the other hand, these acknowledgements have rarely extended to a deeper interrogation of the *dominance* of cartographic reason – its role not merely in representing, but in *governing*, legal visualizations of space, place, and life on Earth. This contradiction – between the sporadic recognition of maps as evidence or instruments, and the widespread neglect of cartographical mapping as an ontological regime – deserves more scrutiny. To begin addressing this void, it is useful to turn to several exemplars that reveal how cartographic power operates not through overt prescription, but through an elusive normalization across both legal scholarship and international legal practice.

3.1.1 Legal Space and Its Immaculate Sovereign

Among those who have drawn illuminating parallels between law and cartography, Boaventura de Sousa Santos stands out. His use of the map metaphor has been influential in linking legal cognition to spatial perception. "The relations law entertains with social reality," he observed, "are much similar to those between maps and spatial reality. Indeed, laws are maps; written laws are cartographic maps; customary, informal laws are mental maps."[14] However, de Sousa Santos also applied a critical voice by emphasizing how cartography "inevitably distorts reality,"[15] because its purpose is to generalize, edit and manipulate how the landscape is depicted. He further noted an inherent tension and "unstable compromise"[16] that existed within mapping, a constant dialectic between (a) convenient orientation for the user versus (b) accurate representation of spatial surroundings. To Illustrate that tension and how it may be approached, de Sousa Santos made reference to a now-famous allegory drawn from Jorge Luis Borges:

> the emperor ... ordered the production of an exact map of this empire. He insisted that the map should be exact to the most minute detail. The best cartographers of the time were engaged in this important project. Eventually, they produced the map and, indeed, it could not possibly be more exact ...

[14] de Sousa Santos, "Law: A Map of Misreading," 282.
[15] de Sousa Santos, "Law: A Map of Misreading," 282.
[16] de Sousa Santos, "Law: A Map of Misreading," 283.

However, to their frustration it was not a very practical map, since it was of the same size as the empire. [...] To be practical a map cannot coincide point by point with reality ... [T]he distortion of reality thus produced will not automatically involve the distortion of truth, if the mechanisms by which the distortion of reality is accomplished are known and can be controlled.[17]

This parable, for de Sousa Santos, exemplified the inescapable trade-off between fidelity and functionality in legal and cartographic representation alike. But what he left unexamined was the grander ontological distortion inherent in *cartographization* – a process not merely of technical abstraction but of visual domination. The map, in this broader sense, is not simply a metaphor for law, but a world-making medium that has fundamentally shaped how the Earth – and legal authority over it – has been imagined, rendered legible, and governed. Today, it is difficult to conceive of the Earth outside of this habitual cartographic frame. Everyday vocabularies are saturated with it: we consult Google Maps,[18] we "map the field," we "get on the map." This ubiquity is not incidental. As Marshall McLuhan reminds us, the most influential media are those that shape human perception so completely as to become invisible:

The instance of the electric light may prove illuminating ... The electric light is pure information. It is a medium without a message ... unless it is used to spell out some verbal ad or name. This fact, characteristic of all media, means that the "content" of any medium is another medium. The content of writing is speech, just as the written word is the content of print, and print is the content of the telegraph ... What we are considering here, however are the psychic and social consequences of the designs or patterns as they amplify or accelerate existing processes. For the "message" of any medium or technology is the change of scale or pace or pattern that it introduces into human affairs ... Whether the light is being used for brain surgery or night baseball is a matter of indifference. It could be argued that these activities are in some way the "content" of the electric light, since they could not exist without the electric light. [I]t is the medium that shapes and controls the scale and form of human association and action ... Indeed, it is only too typical that the "content" of any medium blinds us to the character of the medium.[19]

17 de Sousa Santos, "Law: A Map of Misreading," 282.

18 See Ethan R. Merel, "Google's World: The Impact of 'Agnostic Cartographers' on the State-Dominated International Legal System," *Columbia Journal of Transnational Law* 54, no. 2 (2016): 424–72, at 424.

19 McLuhan, *Understanding Media*, 8–9.

McLuhan's illustration provides astute ways to see the deeper influence of law's cartographization, and how profound the map medium has been in structuring modern – and legal – spatial perceptions of the Earth. In a nutshell, the map and the history of cartography have had an effect analogous to McLuhan's electric light: a foundational – and ultimately ruling – medium that has for several centuries defined the visual possibilities of modern geographic "reality." As such, de Sousa Santos' earlier omission, in effect, obscured modern cartography's legacy as a *world-making medium*, which has influenced the visuality of, for example, geographers, social scientists and lawyers – to name only a few. What is more, cartographic mapping enabled Eurocentric and statist cartography to impose a visual hierarchy over nonhuman Earth, displacing planetary "reality" – to borrow from de Sousa Santos' phrasing – with a geometric Globe.

Yet, de Sousa Santos' blind-spot on the medium is not unique and, arguably, epiphenomenal. For instance, another exemplar is Richard T. Ford's reputed contribution on territorial jurisdiction. Similar to de Sousa Santos, maps feature prominently in Ford's explanation on how territorial jurisdiction was constructed and, ultimately, consolidated by mapping. He directly associated the ascendence of territorial jurisdiction with the rise of statist cartography: "territorial jurisdictions are relatively new ... New, because until the development of cartography, legal authority generally followed relationships of status rather than autochthony."[20] In fact, Ford emphasized that the concept of territorial jurisdiction was premised on a *cartographic view* of legal "space":

> A territorial jurisdiction categorizes the elements over which authority is to be exercised primarily by area ... It is abstractly and homogenously conceived ... By abstract I mean simply that the space of jurisdiction is conceived independently of any specific attribute of that space ... This empty space is a conception that is facilitated, if not made possible, by the modern, areal map. The map is the primary representation of abstract space ... Of course, other representations of abstract space are possible, but most refer to maps, such as notations in a treaty between nations that refers to a cartographic grid of latitude or longitude, or the language in a property title that refers to an official chart of plots.[21]

20 Richard T. Ford, "Law's Territory (A History of Jurisdiction)," *Michigan Law Review* 97, no. 4 (1999): 843–930, at 852–53.

21 Ford, "Law's Territory," 843.

Placing Ford alongside de Sousa Santos renders the medium unmistakable. The map emerges not only as an aid to legal thinking, but as a visual architecture that produces legal space as abstract, geometric, and divisible. And yet, it is within international legal thought specifically that this cartographic aura has become especially pronounced – and especially unexamined.

As explored in Chapter 2, Carl Schmitt's *The Nomos of the Earth* offered one of the few attempts to foreground the relationship between international legal order and the mapped world. Schmitt presented a grand narrative of International Law shaped by the confluence of two historic currents. One of ancient pedigree, and the other of modern transformation. He asserted that International Law was the inheritor of Europe's history and later mastery over land-appropriation on Earth. He underlined how that inheritance "constitutes the original spatial order, the source of all further concrete order and all further law."[22] In addition, Schmitt pointed to International Law's role in shaping a "new planetary consciousness of space," defined by a geometric "global spatial order":

> The first attempts in international law to divide the earth as a whole according to the new global concept of geography began immediately after 1492. These were also the first adaptations to the new, planetary image of the world. Apparently, they were initially nothing more than crude seizures of land as part of an immense appropriation. Yet, the struggle among European powers for land-appropriations made necessary certain divisions and distributions. These sprang from what I call *global linear thinking*, which represents a chapter in the historical development of spatial consciousness. It began with the discovery of a "new world" and the start of the "modern age," and kept pace with the development of geographical maps and of the globe itself. The word *global* captures the encompassing and planetary, as well as the external and superficial character of this type of thinking based on the equation of land and sea surfaces. The compound term "global linear thinking" seems very fitting. [...] No sooner had the first maps and globes been produced, and the first scientific concept of the true form of our planet and of the New World in the West been established, than the first global lines of division and distribution were drawn.[23]

[22] Schmitt, *The Nomos of the Earth*, 48.
[23] Schmitt, *The Nomos of the Earth*, 87–88.

Schmitt's narrative may be contestable, but his core insight remains vital: the map shaped not only the representation of legal space, but the *imagination* of it. He brings into focus how the map medium came to define perceptions of international legal order, and, consequently, impose a cartographic (visual) grammar for seeing legal space. Ironically, Schmitt's own framing idealizes the cartographic process by distinguishing "crude" land seizures from their refined, geometrically mapped successors. In doing so, he elevates the map to a medium of legal legibility – transforming appropriation into order, and conquest into law. Therefore, what Schmitt attempts to recount at base is the construction of a cartographic world order, and how the map medium became embedded historically within International Law and made imperative the seeing of a "territorialized" Earth or – better stated – Globe.

This sets the stage for some closing exemplars taken from treaty and case law, which help illustrate the extent cartographization influences international legal vision and doctrine – much like de Sousa Santos, Ford and Schmitt indicate. A number of references can be found across key doctrinal sources that associate International Law's visuality of legal space with the cartographic and mapped medium. Most explicit is the map-minded approach of the *Island of Palmas Case*, which asserted that states exercise exclusive sovereignty "in relation to a portion of the surface of the globe."[24] Further, the drafters of the *1933 Montevideo Convention* relied on that same cartographic backdrop vis-à-vis Article 9: "[t]the jurisdiction of [S]tates within the limits of national territory applies to all the inhabitants." Finally, there is the International Court of Justice in the *Frontier Dispute Case (Burkina Faso/Mali)*, which endorsed the mirror-like capacities of cartographic mapping to depict nature: "the technical reliability of maps ... has considerably increased, owing particularly to the progress achieved by aerial and satellite photography since the 1950s ... [T]he ... result is a more faithful rendering of nature by the map, and an increasingly accurate match between the two."[25] Yet the Court's language – "a more faithful rendering," "an increasingly accurate match" – is strikingly vague. "Progress achieved" relative to seeing what via the map?

[24] Island of Palmas (Netherlands/United States), Award of the Tribunal, April 4, 1928, II Reports of International Arbitral Awards 829, at 838–39.

[25] *Frontier Dispute* (Burkina Faso/Mali), Judgment, December 22, 1986, *ICJ Reports* 1986, 554, at 582–83, paras. 55–56.

What exactly is being matched? What "nature" is being rendered? What physicality is being visually captured? Such questions are seldom asked. There remains a curious reticence to discuss, engage or even mention the very notion of "legal space," even as legal institutions invest in its visual depiction. This silence is symptomatic of a deeper ontological contradiction: legal space is simultaneously treated as a given *and* as a representation, without clarifying whether those are separable categories.[26] As Christian Jacob reminds us, this confusion is foundational:

> The map generates an illusion of which it is itself the first victim, an illusion whose nature Franco Farinelli has so tersely defined: "The history of a geography is the history of the confusion between the model and the reality." ... What is a map? ... The map does not constitute an ahistorical and transcultural category. Instead, its viewer observes a variety of mechanisms, each of which is ordered by specific types of logic.[27]

Jacob's insight speaks directly to International Law's visual constitution. The "World Map" of states – ubiquitous in legal pedagogy and diplomatic representation – has become virtually synonymous with the discipline's very conception of the world. Yet this was never the outcome of spatial inevitability. Rather, it was the product of a protracted historical process in which the cartographic medium naturalized a visual grammar of authority, rendering the Earth governable by projecting a geometric imaginary upon it. This is the force of *cartographization*: a historical and ontological process through which the map reshaped cosmological, political, and legal perceptions of space. Over time, this projection solidified into a dominant worldview – one that constrains alternative ways of seeing, thinking about, and normatively engaging the Earth. The effect is not merely a disciplinary blind spot, but an ontological narrowing of what legal space is imagined to be.[28]

[26] For example: *Maritime Delimitation in the Black Sea* (Romania v. Ukraine), Judgment, February 3, 2009, *ICJ Reports* 2009, 61; *Territorial and Maritime Dispute* (Nicaragua v. Colombia), Judgment, November 19, 2012, *ICJ Reports* 2012, 624; *Temple of Preah Vihear* (Cambodia v. Thailand), Judgment, June 15, 1962, *ICJ Reports* 1962, 6.

[27] Christian Jacob, *The Sovereign Map: Theoretical Approaches in Cartography throughout History*, trans. Tom Conley (Chicago: University of Chicago Press, 2006), 11.

[28] See Rob Kitchin and Martin Dodge, "Rethinking Maps," *Progress in Human Geography* 31, no. 3 (2007): 331–44.

This begs a further question: how has this mapped *status quo* sustained its visual authority and dominance? If legal space is neither inherently territorial nor geometric, what explains the endurance of this cartographic imaginary? A cartographic worldview of legal space cannot be assumed as a natural given; it must be situated within a broader history of spatial representation, in which the Earth was conceptually and visually substituted by the spherical geometric Globe.[29] Understanding its persistence requires examining the processes through which this model of the world came to dominate the legal imagination and, in Christian Jacob's terms, to replace reality itself.

3.1.2 Prometheus Retold: Power and Why Its Typologies Matter

One impetus for focusing on the map medium is to reflect on cartographization's influence over the *seeing* of international legal space. Another is to address power's role in constructing, disciplining, and sustaining that perceived cartographic "state of nature." Put differently, the aim is to recognize that international legal space is richer – both in practice and theory – than the cartographic hegemony on which International Law has long relied, often without scrutiny. Acknowledging this influence and dominance forces a further question: has the discipline, across its diverse approaches, chronically overlooked the visual and conceptual infrastructure that underwrites and legitimates the doctrine of territoriality as the primary form of legal space?

If the story of international legal space is retold in terms of worldmaking and the influence of cartographization, it becomes difficult to continue introducing International Law through the habitual fiat captured by McCreary and Lamb: "The principles of international law hold as canonical fact the division of the world's landmass into discrete territorial sovereignties with defined boundaries and clear jurisdiction

[29] See Peter Sloterdijk, "Geometry in the Colossal: The Project of Metaphysical Globalization," *Environment and Planning D: Society and Space* 27, no. 1 (2009): 29–40, at 33: "as soon as the form of the sphere could be constructed in geometrical abstraction and gazed upon in cosmological contemplation, there arouse forcefully the question of who should rule over the represented and produced sphere."

over domestic affairs."[30] Established canon looks less self-evident once one grasps that cartographization moulded the Earth's territorial division into a subsequent legal fact. The stakes for international lawyers are considerable. As McLuhan's media theory reminds us, the map represents a prior normative source that has shaped the discipline's perception of both the physical Earth and legal space. In effect, a *cartographic canon* has defined how legal space and "reality" must be seen and known. Whether implicitly or explicitly, a governing cartography has long influenced the asserted "order" of what legal space should "look like" in the absolute. J. B. Harley captures this dynamic:

> Maps are never value-free images; except in the narrowest Euclidean sense they are not in themselves either true or false. Both in the selectivity of their content and in their signs and styles of representation maps are a way of conceiving, articulating, and structuring the human world which is biased towards, promoted by, and exerts influence upon particular sets of social relations. By accepting such premises it becomes easier to see how appropriate they are to manipulation by the powerful in society. … I view maps as a kind of … cartographic language. Language – perhaps more aptly a "literature" of maps – urges us to pursue questions about changing readerships for maps, about levels of carto-literacy, conditions of authorship … and also about the nature of the political statements which are made by maps … [L]iterary criticism can help us identify the particular form of cartographic "discourse."[31]

It makes good sense, therefore, to take into account how cartographic history and discourse came to precondition and determine orthodox norms of international legal space. To treat the map as an unacknowledged ruler of that space is to see the territorialized worldview of International Law as a product of cartography's visual hegemony over planetary space. However, in order to pursue that examination genuinely, international lawyers must make an un-canonical move: *unbracket* the concept of power to explore its typological nature, and learn how different kinds of power came to naturalize a statist cartography of legal space. The stumbling block is that scholars, policy-makers and practitioners turn intuitively to an essentialized

[30] Tyler McCreary and Vanessa Lamb, "Reflections on a Political Ecology of Sovereignty," in *Locating Nature: Making and Unmaking International Law*, ed. Usha Natarajan and Julia Dehm (Cambridge: Cambridge University Press, 2022), 134.

[31] Harley, "Maps, Knowledge, and Power," 53–54.

definition of power, formulated as follows: *the ability of A to use material resources to get B to do what B would not do otherwise.*[32] Generations of international lawyers have relied – implicitly or explicitly – on this formulation when contrasting law with power, a move long embedded in the discipline's self-image. As Oscar Schachter explains:

> International lawyers ... recognize, of course, that power is a pervasive factor in human affairs and especially in the behavior of states. However, many see power as antithetical to law, in particular as inimical to the conditions of equality and reciprocity essential to a legal order. The weakness of international law is often attributed to power politics and, more basically (in Raymond Aron's words), to the anarchical international order where might makes right. The mistrust of state power by international lawyers goes back some four centuries, when sovereign states were emerging in Europe, asserting their power through edicts and military force. The founding fathers of international law – Vittoria, Suarez, Grotius – condemned sovereigns for using their power in violation of the *jus inter gentes*. However, a century or so later, sovereign power found its intellectual supporters in Hobbes, Spinoza and jurists who concluded that state power was necessary to maintain order in a Europe ravaged by religious wars and peasant rebellions.[33]

Further, a sizable number of thinkers and textbooks have defined and discussed power relative to this formulation,[34] and scarcely a month passes in current affairs without some visible illustration of it.[35]

[32] David A. Baldwin, *Power and International Relations: A Conceptual Approach* (Princeton: Princeton University Press, 2016), 12: "Dahl's (1957) definition of power in terms of A's ability to get B to do something that B would not otherwise do has been both widely accepted and widely criticized. Although alternative definitions abound, none has been so widely accepted as this one."

[33] Oscar Schachter, "The Role of Power in International Law," *Proceedings of the Annual Meeting (American Society of International Law)* 93 (1999): 200–05, at 200.

[34] Baldwin, *Power and International Relations*, 2: "Despite the numerous political thinkers who have used the concept of power down through the ages, including Thucydides, Kautilya, Aristotle, Machiavelli, and Hobbes, little attention was devoted to explicating the concept by anyone other than Hobbes before the twentieth century."

[35] For example, Russia's invasion of Ukraine. See Dara Massicot, "What Russia Got Wrong: Can Moscow Learn from Its Failures in Ukraine?," *Foreign Affairs* 102, no. 1 (2023): 78–90.

Further, when E.H. Carr[36] and Hans Morgenthau[37] initially articulated disciplinary Realism within IR, they each did so by endorsing this approach as the most accurate and relevant way to understand power on an international scale. This essentialist emphasis had two notable effects in that, first, Realism and its narrow definition of power dominated disciplinary IR for several decades and, second, contending approaches – including International Law[38] – reacted by distancing their alternative perspectives from the notion of "power" permitting a narrow definition to occupy the concept uncontested. What emerged was a chronic dynamic where IR scholars – and international lawyers – were schooled to choose between Realism's essentialized conception versus a competing alternative. Although counter-point concepts did emerge, which attempted to nuance hard-core benchmarks, that is "soft power"[39] or "soft law."[40] This still

[36] See E. H. Carr, *The Twenty Years' Crisis, 1919–1939: An Introduction to the Study of International Relations*, 2nd ed. (London: Macmillan, 1974), 109: "The supreme importance of the military instrument lies in the fact that the ultima ratio of power in international relations is war. Every act of the state, in its power aspect, is directed to war, not as a desirable weapon, but as a weapon which it may require in the last resort to use."

[37] See Morgenthau, *Politics Among Nations*, 32:

> When we speak of power … we have in mind not man's power over nature, or over an artistic medium, such as language, speech, sound, or color, or over the means of production or consumption, or over himself in the sense of self-control. When we speak of power we refer to the mutual relations of control among holders of public authority and between the latter and the people at large.

[38] See Hersch Lauterpacht, "On Realism, Especially in International Relations," in *International Law, vol. 2: The Law of Peace, Part 1: International Law in General*, ed. Elihu Lauterpacht, Q.C. (Cambridge: Cambridge University Press, 2009), 57:

> The primacy of national power and national interest, as against the appeal to ideologies and principles, have been invoked, once more, as pre-eminently expressive of realism. However, it is equally legitimate to argue that the opposite of such approach is truly realistic; that ideas and ideals are the truly abiding basis of power and national interest; that, as abundant experience shows, States which act upon and acquire a reputation for acting on principles of law and ethics, are in a better position to achieve long-range aims of national life than States pursuing so-called realistic policies contemptuous of these principles.

[39] Joseph S. Nye Jr., "Soft Power," *Foreign Policy* 80 (1990): 153–71.

[40] Kenneth W. Abbott and Duncan Snidal, "Hard and Soft Law in International Governance," *International Organization* 54, no. 3 (2000): 421–56.

unfolded within a competitive context where scholars largely chose a correct side or disciplinary team.[41]

Yet, power exists in multiple dimensions and with manifold interconnections, which do not operate in competition or in isolation. As once noted eminently by Gallie: power is an "essentially contested concept."[42] Power can be observed in different forms, relations and with varied effects, which are difficult to collapse into a single and essentialized definition.[43] Further, as Barnett and Duvall underline, some types of power are not actor-oriented at all, and operate via structures and discourses that go beyond the proprietorship or control of any individual actor – no matter how materially or coercively powerful:

> One certainly needs to know about the ability of actors to use resources to compel others to change their foreign policies, and in the contemporary period transnational activists have been able to shame multinational corporations and abusive governments to alter their economic and human rights policies, respectively. Any discussion of power ... must include a consideration of how, why, and when some actors have "power over" others. Yet one must also consider the enduring structures and processes of global life that enable and constrain the ability of actors to shape their fates and their futures ... The starting point for opening the conceptual aperture is to identify the critical dimensions that generate different conceptualizations of power. In general terms, power is the production, in and through social relations, of effects that shape the capacities of actors to determine their circumstances and fate.[44]

Barnett and Duvall highlight the polymorphic and typological nature of power, which any singular definition ultimately suppresses. Their generic definition enables us to grasp epistemic, normative, and legal structures as impactful forms of power. Yet a cognitive obstacle persists: most international lawyers are reluctant to see or describe their work as relying on any theory of power. For many, the very question

[41] For example, see: John J. Mearsheimer, *The Tragedy of Great Power Politics* (New York: W. W. Norton, 2001), 422.

[42] W. B. Gallie, "Essentially Contested Concepts," *Proceedings of the Aristotelian Society* 56 (1956): 167–98; see also Stefano Guzzini, "Structural Power: The Limits of Neorealist Power Analysis," *International Organization* 47, no. 3 (1993): 443–78, at 446–47.

[43] See Chris Brown, *Understanding International Relations*, 5th ed. (London: Macmillan International Higher Education, 2019), 85–86.

[44] Michael Barnett and Raymond Duvall, "Power in International Politics," *International Organization* 59, no. 1 (2005): 39–75, at 41–42.

would trigger bewilderment – a posture fueled partly by reaction to Realism's essentialized definition and, as Schachter noted, by the discipline's self-identification as antithetical to power. There is also the deeper legacy of legal liberalism, which, as Koskenniemi explains, frames international law as inherently nonpolitical:

> I have not met an international lawyer who would have said: "Look, here is my liberal theory of politics. The international law which I teach is based on that theory" ... And yet, I know of no modern international lawyer who would not have accepted some central tenet in it ... Self-determination, independence, consent and, most notably, the idea of the Rule of Law, are all liberal themes. They create distinctly liberal problems: How to guarantee that States are not coerced by law imposed "from above"? ... How to guarantee State "freedom" while providing the conditions for international "order"? ... It is difficult to understand "liberalism" as materially controlling because it does not accept for itself the status of a grand political theory. It claims to be unpolitical and is even hostile to politics.[45]

Yet any meaningful contrast to power still requires some specification of what "power" refers to as an antithetical concept. The aim of countering or balancing also implies at least some background theory of how power operates. The paradox is that the discipline's formal distancing from power has effectively led to its informal submission to an underdeveloped, unspoken theory of power: *A* getting *B* to do what *B* would not otherwise do. This lacuna has impoverished the theoretical field, limiting the discipline's capacity to engage with epistemic and normative structures – most notably cartographic ones – as significant forms of power operating on and through law. As J. B. Harley illustrates with reference to McLuhan, the map's pervasive power escapes scrutiny because it is presumed to be a passive mirror rather than a blueprint for a cartographic planet:

> What have been the effects of this "logic of the map" upon human consciousness, if I may adapt Marshall McLuhan's phrase ("logic of print") ... It is the disjunction between those senses of place and many alternative visions of what the world is, or what it might be, that has raised questions about the effect of cartography in society ... One of these "liabilities" is that maps, by articulating the world in mass-produced and stereo-typical images, express an embedded social vision ... The question has now become:

45 Koskenniemi, *From Apology to Utopia*, 5.

do such empty images have their consequences in the way we think about the world? Because all the world is designed to look the same, is it easier to act upon it without realizing the social effects? ... The history of maps suggests ... that maps embody specific forms of power and authority ... In colonial North America, for example, it was easy for Europeans to draw lines across territories of Indian nations without sensing the reality of their political identity. The map allowed them to say, "This is mine; these are the boundaries." ... While the map is never the reality ... it helps to create a different reality. Once embedded in the published text the lines on the map acquire an authority that may be hard to dislodge. Maps are authoritarian images. Without our being aware of it maps can reinforce and legitimate the status quo ... Where it seems to be neutral it is the sly "rhetoric of neutrality" that is trying to persuade us.[46]

Looping back to our query on the dominance of the cartographic worldview, Harley suggests dominance flows from the map medium's power – in Gianfranco Poggi's words – "to turn nature against itself ... in order to make it serve human interests."[47] Specifically, the cartographic medium came to capture how the Earth *is and should be seen*. To connect this further to the chapter's opening: the map medium established a dominant *practice of seeing* the Earth or, more specifically, a visual model on *how to see* and relate all social ideas, identities, experiences and projects vis-à-vis the planet – including legal ones.

The significance of this feat is Promethean in character. In Greek mythology, Prometheus stole fire from the Olympian gods to enable human beings to burn parts of nature to survive and, ultimately, to control the whole of nature. In a similar way – though not with fire – the cartographic globe appropriated and modified the image of the physical Earth, becoming the visual model upon which social, political, and legal relations were reconstituted, rearranged, and formally structured. All the while, its mapped "reality" was held to mirror the very essence of the Earth and nature, rather than to represent an anthropic simulacrum.[48] This was a cartographic and visual conquest essential for the later imposition of a Eurocentric and ahistorical map

[46] Harley, "Deconstructing the Map," 13–14.

[47] Gianfranco Poggi, *Forms of Power* (Cambridge: Polity, 2001), 3.

[48] See Timothy Mitchell, *Carbon Democracy: Political Power in the Age of Oil* (New York: Verso, 2013), 233: "Nature is unable to speak for itself ... The facts of nature speak only with the help of measuring devices and tools of calculation."

of territorial demarcation across the globe,[49] which – as will be surveyed shortly – was normalized through the rise of "scientific cosmology"[50] and the geometric "science of space."[51] For these reasons, anyone questioning the veracity and dominance of the cartographic worldview risked folly, because it meant confronting not the visual medium or model but rather – what seemed popularly – the truest and most progressive *sight* of the Earth itself. As David Shim illustrates with the making of satellite "pictures" of the *Blue Marble*:

> People come to know the world – and its space and places – through visual imagery. Unknown locations are made familiar through visual representation ... The relationship between ... imaging and (spatial) imagination is complex and mutually reinforcing: images shape and at the same time are shaped by imaginations. The satellite picture of NASA's Blue Marble or popular night-time images of the world are cases in point. While the view from outer space forms spatial imaginations of the globe, particular imaginations also (in)form its visual representation. According to the creator of the Blue Marble, for instance, the Earth was made to look realistic – or, more precisely, as he himself would put it, "at least how I *imagined* the Earth would look." After all, satellite images are based on data; what we see and – therefore believe to – know ... is not the capture of physical referents similar to the practice of "classic" photography where the shutter is triggered, but it is the result of editing and synthetic imaging processes. The Blue Marble ... is thus a composite view of about 10,000 satellite

[49] See Jerry Brotton, *Trading Territories: Mapping the Early Modern World* (London: Reaktion Books, 1997), 14:

> Maps, charts and globes ... disseminated vital conceptual information on the changing territorial and commercial shape of the world they depicted ... such geographical artefacts became prized possessions, not only keeping their owners informed of the latest discoveries and commercial ventures, but also providing them with a sense of security as to their identity within such an ever-changing world. ... [This] production of maps and charts ... [became] the practical bedrock for all subsequent printed cartography over much of the globe for the next 200 years.

[50] See Allan, *Scientific Cosmology and International Orders*, 12–13: "cosmological ideas arising from the scientific tradition ... are powerful because they render some goals, interests, and purposes as natural or inevitable and others as unthinkable or illegitimate ... [C]osmologies and purposes do not float freely. They must be carried by concrete associations that possess the military, economic, and epistemic power to reproduce and disseminate ways of seeing the world."

[51] Henri Lefebvre, *The Production of Space*, trans. Donald Nicholson-Smith (Oxford: Blackwell, 1991), 1–2.

> scenes collected over the course of 100 days ... [S]atellites seem to be capable of what can be called "extra-discursivity": they are apparently well-positioned to ... operate outside of any sphere of (subjective) influence ... While, as shown above, a logic of inclusion and exclusion – what to scan/show, what not to, how – underlies a satellite's vision (revealing the politics of ... site/sight of the image itself).[52]

Shim's example points to how prevailing visual representations and imaginations ultimately construct and sustain a dominant worldview. Much like the creator of the Blue Marble, we can anticipate many international lawyers would rely on similar "realistic" images of what the Earth *looks* like – even though few, if any, have gazed directly at the Earth itself. This speaks to the prolonged influence of the map medium in shaping a seemingly inherent worldview and, notably, what Shim notes as the *politics of site/sight*. It is a politics reflected, for example, in four centuries of mappings that have governed the visuality of places, beings and entities relative to a cartographic globe. As discussed thus far, International Law has relied on that politics – consciously or not – by virtue of the visual and conceptual resources that cartographization provided to reimage the Earth as a territorially demarcated Globe.

Barnett and Duvall's typology of power offers a useful framework for unpacking the politics of *site/sight* that Shim identifies. In particular, Barnett and Duvall approach power with a taxonomy of four general types: Compulsory, Institutional, Structural and Productive.[53] For our purposes, it is the latter two types and their interplay – structural and productive – that appear most insightful on the politics of site/sight and the lasting dominance of the cartographic medium. Barnett and Duvall explain structural and productive power as follows:

[52] David Shim, "Remote Sensing Place: Satellite Images as Visual Spatial Imaginaries," *Geoforum* 51 (2014): 152–60, at 159.

[53] See Barnett and Duvall, "Power in International Politics," 43:

> Effective taxonomic exercises must try to "carve nature at its joints" to derive critical, mutually exclusive, and exhaustive distinctions ... The first type is power as relations of interaction of direct control by one actor over another – Compulsory Power; the second is the control actors exercise indirectly over others through diffuse relations of interaction – Institutional Power; the third is the constitution of subjects' capacities in direct structural relation to one another – Structural Power; and the fourth is the socially diffuse production of subjectivity in systems of meaning and signification – Productive Power. These different conceptualizations provide distinct answers to the fundamental question: in what respects are actors able to determine their fate, and how is that ability limited or enhanced through social relations with others?

> Structural power concerns structures ... that define what kinds of social beings actors are. It ... not only constitutes actors and their capacities, it also shapes their self-understanding and subjective interests ... In other words, structural power can work to constrain some actors from recognizing their own domination ... Capital-labor and master-slave are obvious examples ... As Steven Lukes observed: "is it not the supreme and most insidious exercise of power to prevent people, to whatever degree, from having grievances shaping their perceptions, cognitions, and preferences in such a way that they accept their roles in the existing order of things?" In this way, structural power operates even when there are no instances of A acting to exercise control over B. [...][54]
>
> [P]roductive power concerns discourse, the social processes and systems of knowledge through which meaning is produced, fixed, lived, experienced, and transformed. Discourses are understood here not as dialogues among specific actors in terms of Habermasian notions of communicative action. Instead ... discourses are sites of social relations of power because they situate ordinary practices of life and define the social fields of action that are imaginable and possible ... [P]roductive power concerns the boundaries of all social identity, and the capacity and inclination for action ... Some of the best example of the analysis of productive power ... refer to the discursive production of the subjects, the fixing of meanings, and the terms of action ... Basic categories of classification, like "civilized", "rogue", "European", "unstable", "Western", and "democratic" states, are representative of productive power, as they generate asymmetries of social capacities.[55]

Two points stand out from these definitions. First, one can observe the world-making character of structural power, which contrasts with the narrower, institutional understanding that international lawyers typically associate with "structure" or "structural." Here, structural power involves more than constraining or incentivising action – as the *institutions-as-structure* approach would suggest. It reaches deeper, constituting actor cognition and self-understanding of the world-at-large, informed by hierarchical relations, domination, and the perceived "order of things." In this light, the cartographic medium – and its ubiquitous World Map – functions as structural power by shaping the Earth's visuality and identity. It is upon this visual structure that the normative and formal edifice of International Law has been built.

Second, the definition of productive power captures the "extra-discursive" influence the map medium exercises visually over all forms

[54] Barnett and Duvall, "Power in International Politics," 52–53.
[55] Barnett and Duvall, "Power in International Politics," 55–56.

of social relations – political, economic, and legal. While Shim introduced the concept of *extra-discursivity* in relation to satellite imagery, this quality also characterizes cartographic maps, which enjoy privileged status as supposedly accurate depictions of the natural, normal, or "real" world. Such maps situate and demarcate boundaries that shape spatial identities, perceptions of place, and the limits of possible action. Moreover, the map is popularly associated with the production of geographic knowledge, spatial clarity, and situational awareness. Further, the map medium is tied in popular perception with the production of geographic knowledge, spatial clarity, and the provision of "situational awareness."[56]

Barnett and Duvall's definitions thus highlight an interplay between structural and productive types of power in the making of geographic – and ultimately legal – *sight*. It is an interplay *structured* – within Barnett and Duvall's meaning – by centuries of world-making maps that consolidated the cartographic medium's primacy over political and legal imaging of the Earth. The fundamental implication, as Bruno Latour illustrates in the following extract, is that the medium exerts power not merely as an interpretative tool or symbolic language for geographic knowing but, pivotally, as the hegemonic framework for seeing a cartographic world order:

> If postcolonial studies have succeeded in provincializing Europe, it still exerts one imperial dominion in its full and undisputed splendor, namely this strange idea that the Globe is the equivalent of the natural world [...] In other words, a natural Globe still offers the "ground map" which allows any localization to occur ... Nobody can stake a claim to a power without its position being *relativized* and instantly situated, while the system of coordinates that allows for such a localization is *absolute* and remains in the background, fully invisible ... All loci might be different, but they are all visualized and pointed to on the same grid. They all differ from one another, but in the same predictable way: by their longitude and latitude. What is amazing if you look at geopolitical textbooks, is that, apparently, the Globe remains universal, unproblematic ... But for me, this is just the position that marks, without any doubt, the imperial dominion of the European tradition that is now shared, or so it seems, by

[56] See Susanne Krasmann and Christine Hentschel, "'Situational Awareness': Rethinking Security in Times of Urban Terrorism," *Security Dialogue* 50, no. 2 (2019): 181–97, at 185: "Situational awareness is about presence in the here and now, which entails a particular mode of capturing time and space."

everyone else. [...] On such an empire – the empire of cartography, the world order, the all-encompassing Globe – the sun never sets. [...] [I]t has become clear that in addition to the land grabbing that has authorized the seizure of the Earth in the past by the competing imperial European power, there is still present a much deeper "*land drawing*" that has expanded naturalism everywhere. While the first colonial expansion is clearly visible, criticized and – only partially – counter-acted, this other land grab remains invisible.[57]

Latour's emphasis on *land drawing* underlines our distinctly cartographic and "map-minded age,"[58] where the map medium instills an essentialized model for visualizing, thinking about, and situating knowledge on nearly every aspect about the Earth.[59] Further still, geometric shapes and aesthetics attached to the map medium have naturalized a visual grammar, where the Earth's image is overlaid by a mathematical division of its land surface or, in more technical terms, the coordinate-based grid system.[60] As Jordan Branch underlines, that coordinate form and structure has become inseparable vis-à-vis the Earth's perceived physicality: "while nearly every technology of mapmaking continues to evolve, the foundational structure provided by the coordinate grid remains the same."[61] Notably, highly normative and Orientalizing place-frames used by many international lawyers, like *first–third world*, *developed-undeveloped* nations, *core-periphery*, or *global north/south*, all derive from this hegemonic image of a coordinate-based globe as Earth.

As Latour noted, the map medium's dominance has avoided problematization or even notice. In part, that flows from a long-running and consistent thesis across disciplinary Geography, IR, and Sociology,[62] which Saskia Sassen has summarized as the need to "neutralize state capture of the major historiographies since the 1600s as well as capture

[57] Latour, "*Onus Orbis Terrarum*," 308–09. [58] Rankin, *After the Map*, 1.

[59] Harley, "Maps, Knowledge, and Power," 53–55; Harley, "Deconstructing the Map," 1–5; see also Rankin, *After the Map*, 1, 24–26.

[60] Latour, "*Onus Orbis Terrarum*," 313–14.

[61] Branch, *Cartographic State*, 52.

[62] Robert D. Sack, *Human Territoriality: Its Theory and History* (Cambridge: Cambridge University Press, 1986); Robert D. Sack, *Homo Geographicus: A Framework for Action, Awareness, and Moral Concern* (Baltimore: Johns Hopkins University Press, 1997); Timothy Mitchell, *Rule of Experts: Egypt, Techno-Politics, Modernity* (Berkeley: University of California Press, 2002); Harley, "Maps, Knowledge, and Power," 24.

by abstractions such as society or economy."[63] However, if we return to McLuhan's earlier insight, this state capture thesis likely confuses a key distinction between the medium and its content. As McLuhan explains: "the content of a medium is like the juicy piece of meat carried by the burglar to distract the watchdog of the mind ... The effects of technology do not occur at the level of opinions or concepts, but alter sense ratios or patterns of perception steadily and without any resistance."[64] Taken together, McLuhan's and Latour's interventions point to the *visual capture* achieved by the cartographic medium – one that enabled the state's inscription as a geographic entity.[65] This capture continues today through the enduring dominance of the World Map of states and its geometric visualization of international authority. It is this combined structural and productive power that has fixed the state and territory as the professed *res extensa* of geographic "reality."

In sum, understanding the cartographic medium through the lens of structural and productive power reveals how International Law's visual and conceptual architecture has been shaped by forces operating beyond individual actors or formal institutions. The coordinate-based Globe has not merely represented the Earth; it has constituted the very conditions under which legal space can be imagined, articulated, and governed. This dual power – structural in its constitution of spatial identity, and productive in its fixation of meaning – has entrenched a Eurocentric, state-centric worldview as the default ontology of International Law. To interrogate this worldview is not simply to challenge a representational device, but to question the perceptual regime that has defined the limits of legal possibility. It is from this vantage point that we can better understand how the cartographic imagination has shaped, and continues to constrain, the ways in which international lawyers see and order the world.

3.2 *Cartogenesis*: The Cartographic Construction of Globality

The term *cartogenesis* captures a form of medium power and world-making that far exceeds the familiar claim that maps are instruments for making sense of physical reality. Despite popular anecdotes that

[63] Sassen, *Territory, Authority, Rights*, 402.
[64] McLuhan, *Understanding Media*, 19. [65] Branch, *Cartographic State*, 50–57.

maps constitute humanity's oldest communicative form, their actual history is comparatively marginal. As J. B. Harley reminds us, maps occupy only a "small part" of humanity's communication about space and "did not become everyday objects in many areas of the world until the European renaissance."[66] If this historical smallness is correct, what does it mean for International Law, a discipline that takes for granted the predominance of the cartographic medium and worldview?

Several points help us consider alternative ways of conceiving law and authority beyond the cartographic medium. First, the cartographic medium and worldview emerged only gradually from early modern European history.[67] As Luca Muscará explains:

> Until the 15th century, maps were relatively rare, mostly "coastal maps for navigation, schematic land itineraries, and symbolic representations of religious time and space" ... Although the city, usually enclosed by walls, dominated its countryside, there was no linear boundary defining its territory. The rediscovery of Ptolemy, and the related invention of the linear perspective ... promoted a new Age of Exploration, which, sponsored by the rulers of the time, eventually would contribute to the birth of the territorial state. Still, a place-based view of sovereignty continued to dominate over a space-based one ... [U]ntil the 17th century, maps did not include political borders of the ruling powers. With the exemption of some coastal fortifications, Europe was not divided by fixed political boundaries. The main frontier for the traveler was the language spoken in a particular place, which could hardly be conceived in linear terms.[68]

This genealogy underscores that cartographic representation was not primary but layered atop earlier textual media that privileged naming and describing places without depicting the spaces in between.[69] The conventional story, told in evolutionary terms, casts this shift as an inevitable leap from medieval to modern cognition: a textual Middle Ages hampered by technological immaturity, and a cartographic modernity unleashed by the scientific revolution and the printing press.

[66] Harley, "Deconstructing the Map," 1. [67] Branch, *Cartographic State*, 135.

[68] Luca Muscarà, "Maps, Complexity, and the Uncertainty of Power," in *Handbook on the Geographies of Power*, ed. Mat Coleman and John Agnew (Cheltenham: Edward Elgar, 2018), 367.

[69] Branch, *Cartographic State*, 48–49, 125–31.

Yet such narratives obscure more than they reveal. They impose neat dichotomies – medieval/modern, textual/cartographic – that flatten medieval spatial literacy into deficiency. They also naturalize the Enlightenment's portrayal of the cartographic medium as the decisive agent of progress in geographic knowledge. In doing so, they efface what was in fact a richer and more complex topological awareness, one in which place carried social depth and relational significance that planar cartographic visualization could never capture. As Jordan Branch observes:

> Two key features of the medieval view of space can be discerned: first, the world was understood as a series of unique places rather than as a geometric area or expanse; and, second, space was conceived in terms of time as much as distance ... Medieval Europeans perceived the world as a series of places, each with its own, possibly unique, characteristics. Ricardo Padron sums this up well: "For the medieval imagination, places were charged with a positive sense of thickness, stability, and indivisibility. Space, by contrast, was nothing but the empty 'in between.'"[70]

From this perspective, medieval Europe's textual medium was not a primitive substitute for cartography but a different literacy altogether – capable of inscribing nongeometric relations essential to both premodern and modern authority. The *mappaemundi* exemplify this sensibility: nongeometric maps that combined chorographic and theological normativities in order to depict a world that was as moral and cosmological as it was geographic (see Figure 3.1).[71] These maps made explicit the hybrid nature of spatial representation, revealing that all mapping – then as now – encodes normative as well as physical orderings.

It was this hybrid tradition that was progressively effaced as statist cartography ascended between the sixteenth and nineteenth centuries. The rise of the cartographic globe and the standardized World Map established a new visual hegemony in which territory and borders appeared self-evident, while the overt connection between normativity and representation was obscured. Earlier practices of seeing the world – and the alternative understandings of Earth they embodied – were crowded out. As Jens Bartelson notes, globe-making involved not just construction but deletion:

[70] Branch, *Cartographic State*, 48.
[71] Brotton, *A History of the World in Twelve Maps*, 84–85, 87–91.

Figure 3.1 The Hereford Mappa Mundi is the largest surviving (European) medieval world map. Oriented with East at the top, it places Jerusalem at the center and integrates biblical history, classical geography, and mythological creatures alongside known lands and peoples: *Hereford Mappa Mundi*, 1276–1283, made by Richard of Haldingham (DeAgostini/Getty Images) www.gettyimages.be/detail/nieuwsfoto%27s/hereford-mappa-mundi-1276-1283-made-by-richard-of-nieuwsfotos/500642963?adppopup=true

[T]he construction of a global space made it possible to divide that space into portions by simple geometrical methods ... Those who tried to justify the creation of states and empires faced the formidable task of reinterpreting and re-contextualizing the rich world of signs, symbols and metaphors that had been handed down to them from the ancients and medieval Christianity, and which had been filtered through Renaissance attempts to appropriate the same sources in support of city-states. Since these symbols and metaphors originally had been tailored to fit boundless forms of political community, the task at hand was to restrict their range of applicability ... In order to achieve this, certain things had to be remembered in order to bestow the emergent territorial order with intelligibility and legitimacy. Other things had to be forgotten, and for much the same reasons.[72]

Cartogenesis thus names this double movement: the construction of a global space through geometric division, and the erasure of alternative spatial imaginaries that did not conform to it. International Law is one of cartogenesis's principal inheritors. The discipline naturalized the cartographic grid as its visual infrastructure, internalizing borders, territories, and states as ontological givens rather than historical products. This is what I earlier described as International Law's "cartographic unconscious": a deep but unacknowledged dependence on cartographic ways of seeing. By obscuring the selective remembering and forgetting that enabled cartography's rise, the discipline has treated the World Map as a neutral backdrop rather than as a historically situated medium of power.

Seen in this light, cartogenesis was not simply a technical achievement in geographic representation but a formative episode in the constitution of international legality itself. It provided the visual grammar through which the world could be divided, classified, and rendered governable, making law appear global, universal, and objective – while concealing the normative choices, erasures, and exclusions that such a vision required. Yet once we recognize cartogenesis as a contingent and power-laden process of world-making, a further question arises: how might legal space be seen – or reenvisioned – beyond the constraints of cartographic ordering?

3.3 Conclusion: Seeing the Rule of (Cartographic) Law

We thus arrive at a fundamental question: if International Law's modern authority has been scaffolded by *cartogenesis* and sustained

[72] Bartelson, "Social Construction of Globality," 227–28.

through its cartographic unconscious, how can legal space now be seen – or reenvisioned – beyond the constraints of cartographic world ordering? How should an international lawyer approach her or his next encounter with an iconic World Map? A promising path opens once we break with the presumption that structured – again in Barnett and Duvall's connotation – the map-minded age, but which now bleeds relevance: "to map [is] to think."[73] A contemporary amendment might be: *To map is to inscribe.*

The history of spatial practices and representation has never been, and will likely never become, static – with all due respect to Francis Fukuyama. Yet, International Law's unexamined dependence on the cartographic medium has induced a myopia toward geopolitical and geo-economic practices that are increasingly cartographically unrepresentable. Algorithmic networks, digital infrastructures, and transboundary economic flows are, at best, only crudely traceable through conventional mapping. Their spatial nature is often nonplanar and noncontiguous, such that their scales and jurisdiction-like qualities are better apprehended through other media and representational forms of legal spacing.

In this respect, the cartographic worldview is already being challenged by the resurgence of alternative media. Textual, digital, and algorithmic forms increasingly provide the operative registers through which international authority is exercised. Some might even describe this shift as the emergence of a "quantum map" of the legal globe[74] – one in which space is encoded and governed through dispersed inscriptions rather than fixed borders. Within international security, for instance, a digitized list medium structures a global web of public and private watch jurisdictions. These lists index and regulate risk profiles for suspected persons and entities, effectively ruling over the right to life, liberty, and property for millions worldwide.[75] Similarly, the

[73] On the importance of spatial inscription, see: Tania Murray Li, "What Is Land? Assembling a Resource for Global Investment," *Transactions of the Institute of British Geographers* 39, no. 4 (2014): 589–602.

[74] For insight into the potential significance of quantum theorizing for international law: see Alexander Wendt, *Quantum Mind and Social Science: Unifying Physical and Social Ontology* (Cambridge: Cambridge University Press, 2015).

[75] See Marieke de Goede, "Blacklisting and the Ban: Contesting Targeted Sanctions in Europe," *Security Dialogue* 42, no. 6 (2011): 499–515.

rise of transnational contracts has enabled global corporate entities – long the invisible elephants of cartographic mapping – to inscribe vast cross-border dominions known as global value chains.[76] These contractual jurisdictions shape flows of production, trade, profits, and – of recent controversy – taxes, yet remain largely obscured in public discourse by the benign semantics of "partnerships."

In short, the cartographic medium that created and dominated the modern visualization of international authority now faces a challenge to its visual grammar unmatched since the Mercator Projection became a political and geographic fact. Recognizing these developments helps move spatial thinking and legal visualization beyond the isomorphic illusion the World Map has long represented in international legal theory. It reframes law's *cartographization* not as the culmination of legal spatial history but as one influential episode within it. International legal space should instead be understood as continuously unfolding, shaped by the changing media through which geopolitical, geo-economic, and geo-legal relations are seen and known.

As Chapter 4 will explore, the challenge for international lawyers is how to embrace new practices of seeing in ways that register these shifting spatialities. This is not a call to declare the obsolescence of the cartographic map but to widen the perceptual repertoire through which authority is apprehended. The question becomes whether our students, and the publics who fund and legitimize our work, will identify us as curators of a cartographic age – or as practitioners engaging with the considerably evolved spacing of authority in the twenty-first century. This requires attentiveness to what Chapter 4 will describe as the move from jurisdictions to *juriscapes*: an expanded spatial lexicon for understanding law's operations across complex, overlapping, and often trans-territorial domains.

Seen this way, the critique of statist cartography is not an invitation to abandon the World Map but to situate it as one artefact among many in a longer history of world-making – an artefact whose power, as Nicholas Onuf reminds us, lies in the fact that "the metaphor *world*

[76] See Gail Lythgoe, "Contracts: Reterritorializing the (Global) Exercise of Authority," *International Journal of Law in Context* (2025): 1–19; Thomas Dietz, "Relational Contracts 2.0: Efficiency and Power," in *The Politics of Private Transnational Governance by Contract*, ed. A. Claire Cutler and Thomas Dietz (Abingdon: Routledge, 2017), 115–30.

is exceptionally evocative and usefully ambiguous." The task ahead is to reequip international legal theory with the conceptual range to register both the persistence of that metaphor and the emergence of new spatial forms – *juriscapes* – that demand recognition in the evolving grammar of international legal space.

4 *From Jurisdictions to* Juriscapes

Toward a Transformative Theory of Territorialization

The state is invisible; it must be personified before it can be seen, symbolized before it can be loved, imagined before it can be conceived ... the image is prior to understanding.

Michael Walzer, "On the Role of Symbolism in Political Thought," *Political Science Quarterly*

The "rule of law" is about rule. It is an association less emphasized whenever the former – banner – concept is proclaimed. That omission brings forth implications which extend far beyond semantics. In terms of legal theory, for instance, the gap is notable should one grasp that there are no inherent boundaries attaching to either the "rule of law" or rule. Indeed, there are additional concepts one may attach to fill the void, such as empire, the corporation, the union, the state, territoriality or jurisdiction. However, these concepts are no more determinative, since they still rely on assumptions and theories that seek to govern – what Anthony Giddens has called generically – "spatial extension".[1] Indeed, Giddens' generic term falls outside regular legal vocabulary, but its basic meaning is still accessible and relevant for any lawyer: What is the domain of law's rule? What is the spatial extent or consistency of any system of law? How may rules apply in terms of scale? These are more than theoretical questions, because they are enacted every day in juridical practices across a variety of international or transboundary legal problems.

The intuitive reflex instilled in most law schools from the first year is that territorial states determine law's spatial extension via an exclusive sphere of jurisdiction. This is treated as textbook fact. Yet practical fact – or what sociologists call *social facticity*[2] – often diverges from

[1] Anthony Giddens, *A Contemporary Critique of Historical Materialism* (Berkeley: University of California Press, 1981), 45.

[2] See John Searle, *The Construction of Social Reality* (London: Penguin, 1995).

the cartographic image of state territoriality and jurisdiction. Law's rule sometimes aligns with that cartography, and sometimes it does not. This is why the notion of *extraterritoriality* has long served as a doctrinal patch: an exclusive cartography of law has never been descriptively precise.[3] Even when territoriality appeared fixed, the familiar "World Map" of states dissolved whenever metaphorical buttons like *terra nullius*, *nationality*, *the protective principle*, or *universality* were pressed.[4] International lawyers have long known that legal cartography is, in Brian Harley's words, "seldom what cartographers say it is."[5]

This chapter extends that insight, applying it to the foundational categories of territoriality and jurisdiction. The goal is not to discard these terms, but to reposition them. This is hardly radical: historically, spatial extension has been a persistent practical dilemma for lawyers. It is rooted in the ascriptive status of all boundaries – a quality shared across disparate medieval and modern forms of territorial rule.[6] Medieval spacing ascribed boundaries based on *consanguinity* (kin-based parameters), while modern spacing has been ascribed based on *contiguity* (areal and geometric parameters).[7] Both enacted social constructions of space, but justified their boundaries as grounded in inherent "physical" qualities, whether bloodlines or geophysical lines. As Friedrich Kratochwil reminds us, "This river or that mountain range are not a boundary, but serve as a boundary."[8] Spatial demarcation is never purely descriptive. It is a legal and political act of *ascription*.

3 Friedrich Kratochwil, "Of Maps, Law, and Politics: An Inquiry into the Changing Meaning of Territoriality," *DIIS Working Paper* 2011:03 (Copenhagen: Danish Institute for International Studies, 2011), 8.

4 See Karin Mickelson, "The Maps of International Law: Perceptions of Nature in the Classification of Territory beyond the State," in *Locating Nature: Making and Unmaking International Law*, ed. Usha Natarajan and Julia Dehm (Cambridge: Cambridge University Press, 2022), 159–78.

5 Harley, "Deconstructing the Map," 1.

6 See Friedrich Kratochwil, "Sovereignty as Dominium: Is There a Right of Humanitarian Intervention?" in *Beyond Westphalia? State Sovereignty and International Intervention*, ed. Gene M. Lyons and Michael Mastanduno (Baltimore: Johns Hopkins University Press, 1995), 21–42.

7 John Gerard Ruggie, "Territoriality and Beyond: Problematizing Modernity in International Relations," *International Organization* 47, no. 1 (1993): 139–74, at 146.

8 Kratochwil, "Of Maps, Law, and Politics," 9.

Read in this light, the epigraph signals a more basic condition of legal spatiality: Authority does not simply operate across space, it must first be rendered intelligible within it. Territoriality and jurisdiction have long functioned not only as legal techniques, but as visual and conceptual media through which international law learns to apprehend rule. Before space can be governed, it must be imagined; before jurisdiction can be exercised, it must be made visible. The images through which legal authority is symbolized – maps, borders, bounded jurisdictions – thus do not follow understanding, but actively shape it, conditioning what international lawyers are able to see as legally real in the first place.

Recognizing the performative, rather than descriptive, nature of boundaries also reveals something deeper: The medium through which international lawyers have pictured legal space – statist cartography – rests on a historically specific theory of space. That theory privileges contiguity, treats it as natural, and folds it into jurisdiction. It has proven so durable that it has come to shape what Kenneth Burke would call the *circumference of vision* (Chapter 2) – the range of what the discipline deems relevant or even thinkable.

Legal space has always extended through material means other than strictly bounded territory: through markets, infrastructures, communication networks, contractual regimes, and regulatory lists. These modes of spatial extension are increasingly central to legal ordering on a global scale, yet they remain undertheorized in doctrinal vocabulary because they escape the visual and conceptual logic of traditional jurisdiction. What is at stake, then, is less the *accuracy* of our maps than the *adequacy* of our concepts. The dominant medium through which legal authority has been visualized – statist cartography – rests on a theory of space that is both historically specific and increasingly out of joint with the material and institutional practices of legal rule. The problem is not simply that there are exceptions to the rule of territorial jurisdiction; it is that statist jurisdiction itself – viewed as a medium of legal seeing – is built on an ahistorical theory of spatial extension.

One predictable rebuttal is that fixed territoriality, like all working norms, comes with its exceptions. But this binary of "rule" and "exception" risks obscuring a deeper problem. Territorial jurisdiction is not merely a neutral descriptor with occasional anomalies; it is the product of a governing image – an historical inheritance of geometric and cartographic world-making – that has become naturalized in international legal thought.[9] This chapter argues for a conceptual shift: from *jurisdictions* to *juriscapes*. Jurisdictions refer to fixed, bounded zones of legal competence. Juriscapes, by contrast, denote complex, overlapping, and trans-territorial spatial formations through which legal authority moves, settles, and operates. They offer a more dynamic and plural account of law's spatialities – one that aligns better with how global extensions of authority and power are increasingly exercised across networks, infrastructures, and distributed regimes.

To critique jurisdiction's cartographic underpinnings is not to diminish the importance of territoriality, but to transform the theory that sustains it. Territorial jurisdiction has functioned as a powerful image – as Walzer observes, "the image is prior to understanding" – shaping not only how international lawyers picture authority but how they reason about it. The work ahead lies in developing a spatial vocabulary capacious enough to account for the diverse ways in which law materializes across and beyond state borders, and to unsettle the assumption that contiguity is law's inevitable spatial form. The rest of this chapter traces the conceptual scaffolding of that assumption and prepares the ground for an alternative in the form of *juriscapes*.

4.1 The Problem of Cartographic Theory as Practice

The challenge becomes acute when set against the realities of the present. Our human and geological world is changing – rapidly, materially, and spatially. The inherited image of legal rule, once relatively stable within the frame of statist cartography, is increasingly misaligned with the conditions it is meant to address. Transboundary flows – of people, data, pollutants, capital, pathogens, and threats[10] – now operate according to spatial logics that give diminishing regard to the taken-for-granted map of the territorial state. They carve out

[9] I am indebted to Jim George's inspiring use of "theory as practice" in the early 1990s to critique the predominance of Realism and Neo-Realism in IR theory. See: Jim George, *Discourses of Global Politics: A Critical (Re)Introduction to International Relations* (Boulder: Lynne Rienner, 1994).

[10] See Gavin Sullivan, *The Law of the List: UN Counterterrorism Sanctions and the Politics of Global Security Law* (Cambridge: Cambridge University Press, 2020).

Figure 4.1 Turning in circles – recent scholarly “turns” in international legal theory

irregular, overlapping, and often invisible geographies.[11] Climate change, cyberattacks, melting ice caps, viral and financial contagion, mass migration, energy insecurity, and networked extremism each produce spatial forms that exceed both the representational capacities of cartographic maps and the jurisdictional reach premised upon them. These developments sharpen the tension between the scale and morphology of contemporary global problems and the still-dominant cartographic presumptions embedded in law’s spatial architecture.[12]

Each of these interventions has sought to capture emergent forms of legal ordering that escape classical categories. They introduce new spatialities – of flows, fragments, plural sites, informal authority, and infrastructural rule. And yet, despite their diversity, these approaches often share a striking ambiguity: They refrain from directly confronting the continued centrality of statist cartography. Rather than displacing the cartographic core, they tend to orbit around it – adapting language to new forms of governance (e.g., regimes, networks, post-nationalism), while leaving the foundational spatial assumptions of territorial jurisdiction largely unchallenged (see Figure 4.1).

[11] See R. B. J. Walker, *After the Globe, Before the World* (London: Routledge, 2010), 19.

[12] See Bruno Latour, *Down to Earth: Politics in the New Climatic Regime* (Cambridge: Polity, 2018).

This tension reveals the limitations of what might be called *cartographic theory as practice*: the embedded assumption that law operates within fixed, contiguous, state-centric space, as visualized in the dominant World Map of states.[13] That assumption, long naturalized within international legal reasoning, continues to anchor canonical imaginaries of territory and jurisdiction – even as its descriptive power wanes. In response, a number of scholarly "turns" have emerged in international legal theory over recent decades. These include Global Administrative Law (GAL),[14] the Fragmentation of International Law (FRAG),[15] Global Legal Pluralism (GLP),[16] Informal International Lawmaking (IN-LAW),[17] and, more recently, Infrastructuring International Law (INFRA).[18]

This tendency to "turn" without displacing reflects a deeper structural hesitance – a reluctance to recognize that concepts like territoriality and jurisdiction remain anchored in an ahistorical theory of spatial extension. At stake is what historical sociologists describe as the *reification illusion*: the assumption that boundaries are self-constituted and autonomous, rather than socially and

13 I am indebted to Jim George's inspiring use of "theory as practice" in the early 1990s to critique the predominance of Realism and Neo-Realism in International Relations theory. See: Jim George, *Discourses of Global Politics: A Critical (Re)Introduction to International Relations* (Boulder: Lynne Rienner, 1994).

14 Nico Krisch, "Introduction: Global Governance and Global Administrative Law in the International Legal Order," *European Journal of International Law* 17, no. 1 (2006): 1–13; Benedict Kingsbury, "The Concept of 'Law' in Global Administrative Law," *European Journal of International Law* 20, no. 1 (2009): 23–57.

15 Gunther Teubner, *Constitutional Fragments: Societal Constitutionalism and Globalization* (Oxford: Oxford University Press, 2012); Margaret A. Young, ed., *Regime Interaction in International Law: Facing Fragmentation* (Cambridge: Cambridge University Press, 2012).

16 Paul Schiff Berman, *Global Legal Pluralism: A Jurisprudence of Law beyond Borders* (Cambridge: Cambridge University Press, 2012); Peer Zumbansen, "Defining the Space of Transnational Law: Legal Theory, Global Governance, and Legal Pluralism," in *Beyond Territoriality: Transnational Legal Authority in the Age of Globalization*, ed. Gunther Handl et al. (Leiden: Brill, 2013), 53–86.

17 Pauwelyn et al., *Informal International Lawmaking*; Joost Pauwelyn et al., "When Structures Become Shackles."

18 Benedict Kingsbury, "Infrastructure and InfraReg: On Rousing the International Law 'Wizards of Is'," *Cambridge International Law Journal* 8, no. 2 (2019): 171–94; Benedict Kingsbury and Nahuel Maisley, "Infrastructures and Laws: Publics and Publicness," *Annual Review of Law and Social Science* 17 (2021): 353–73.

historically ascribed.[19] In the legal context, this illusion manifests in the persistent treatment of jurisdictional boundaries as fixed givens, rather than the products of institutionalized practices, political struggles, and shifting power dynamics.

Yet as previously discussed, legal boundaries are rarely static or immutable. They are subject to ongoing processes of formation, deformation, and reformation – always embedded in wider social structures and driven by various configurations of power, as explored in Chapter 3. The historical record offers ample evidence: From consanguineous medieval spacing to areal-contiguous modern territoriality, boundaries have always been enacted and *ascribed* through prevailing logics of inclusion, exclusion, and rule. Contemporary spatial institutions such as international airports illustrate this vividly – functioning as complex, layered artefacts of legal spatialization that mutate cartographic jurisdiction.[20]

Acknowledging the reification illusion is thus a critical step toward reconceptualizing territoriality and jurisdiction. It permits international legal theory to move beyond what John Gerard Ruggie termed a *system maintenance logic* – in which statist territoriality is preserved as a structural constant – toward a *morphogenetic* or transformative logic that recognizes the potential for fundamental change in legal spatial ordering.[21] Invoking such a logic also exposes a liberal presumption often embedded, if tacitly, in international legal thought: that statist territoriality and jurisdiction represent a kind of historical apex or terminus.[22] This presumption is questionable. No form of territorial rule has ever been permanent or self-contained.[23] Territorialization

[19] John M. Hobson, "What's at Stake in 'Bringing Historical Sociology Back into International Relations'? Transcending 'Chronofetishism' and 'Tempocentrism' in International Relations," in *Historical Sociology of International Relations*, ed. Stephen Hobden and John M. Hobson (Cambridge: Cambridge University Press, 2002), 6–8.

[20] See William Walters, "Aviation as Deportation Infrastructure: Airports, Planes, and Expulsion," *Journal of Ethnic and Migration Studies* 44, no. 16 (2018): 2796–813; Peer Schouten, "Security as Controversy: Reassembling Security at Amsterdam Airport," *Security Dialogue* 45, no. 1 (2014): 23–39.

[21] John Gerard Ruggie, "What Makes the World Hang Together: Neo-Utilitarianism and the Social Constructivist Challenge," *International Organization* 52, no. 4 (1998): 855–85, at 874.

[22] Jens Bartelson, *Becoming International* (Cambridge: Cambridge University Press, 2023), 5.

[23] Bartelson, *Becoming International*, 10.

has always been, as Robert Sack explains, a socially contingent and effortful process: "territories require constant effort to establish and maintain. They are the results of strategies to affect, influence, and control people, phenomena, and relationships ... Circumscribing things in space, or on a map, as when a geographer delimits an area ... becomes a territory only when its boundaries are used to affect behaviour by controlling access."[24]

In this light, territoriality and jurisdiction are better understood as evolving institutions – shaped by changing spatial dynamics, material conditions, and boundary practices. The theoretical "turns" in international legal scholarship have done important work to illuminate this complexity. But few have directly interrogated the conceptual core of the international legal imaginary: the statist nucleus around which so much doctrinal and institutional reasoning still orbits. This chapter argues that the time has come to address that conceptual core directly. Territorialization must be rethought not as a given, but as a malleable socio-legal process – one subject to historical contingency, institutional reworking, and conceptual revision. Doing so opens space for a new spatial lexicon, capable of grasping law's operations not just within jurisdictions, but across *juriscapes*: dynamic, overlapping, and trans-territorial configurations of legal rule.

4.2 Theorizing *Juriscapes*

This chapter proceeds from a different starting point. My central claim is that the reification of state territoriality and jurisdiction stems not from legal doctrine alone, but from the way statist cartography has visually captured and stabilized institutional perceptions of territorial rule. This visual capture, however, has never been uniform, complete, or historically static. It began with the cartographic revolution of the fifteenth and sixteenth centuries and evolved through hundreds of years of cumulative map production,[25] gradually constructing a visual and ontological "reality" of a world composed of states.[26] Through

[24] Sack, *Human Territoriality*, 19.

[25] Peter Sloterdijk, *Globes: Macrospherology: Spheres II*, trans. Wieland Hoban (Cambridge: MIT Press, 2014), 785.

[26] John Pickles, *A History of Spaces: Cartographic Reason, Mapping, and the Geo-Coded World* (London: Routledge, 2004), 4–5.

this long sedimentation, *cartographic theory as practice* helped shape a state-centric planet into institutional existence – an existence which, in turn, informed the formalization of International Law.

But to assume that this visual capture has consistently mirrored boundary practices on the ground is to mistake representational power for legal accuracy. Statist territoriality and jurisdiction have functioned more as ideal types, derived from geometric science and cartographic reasoning, than as stable institutional facts. They were never immune to morphogenetic pressures – historical transformations in the spatial logics and practices of law's rule. This realization compels the development of a more expansive theory of territorialization, one that (a) critically engages the historical limitations of the statist frame, and (b) incorporates morphogenetic logics that account for how spatial authority is produced, contested, and reshaped over time.

This chapter aims to fill these voids with a transformative theory of territorialization and – by extension – jurisdiction. I develop an intermediate approach that links legal theorizing more directly to how international space is perceived canonically, and in turn reacquaints international legal theory with the myriad of practices involved in the extension of – formal and informal – territorialization. The objective is to leverage greater inductiveness and nuance into what has been International Law's typically *systems maintenance* approach in defining territorialization. To do so, I propose a conceptual counterpart for jurisdiction: *juriscapes*. The term builds, in part, on earlier conceptualizations and theorizing about non-state forms of transborder authority, concepts such as network society,[27] regionalization, debordered territory,[28] connectography,[29] and liquid authority.[30] Yet, the heterodox concept for *juriscapes* also draws from a number of critical insights regarding how territorialization and territorial rule may be theorized alternatively (see Figure 4.2).

[27] Manuel Castells, *The Rise of the Network Society*, vol. 1 of *The Information Age: Economy, Society and Culture* (Oxford: Blackwell, 1996).
[28] Sassen, "When Territory Deborders Territoriality," 23.
[29] Parag Khanna, *Connectography: Mapping the Global Network Revolution* (New York: Random House, 2016).
[30] Nico Krisch, "Liquid Authority in Global Governance," *International Theory* 9, no. 2 (2017): 237–60.

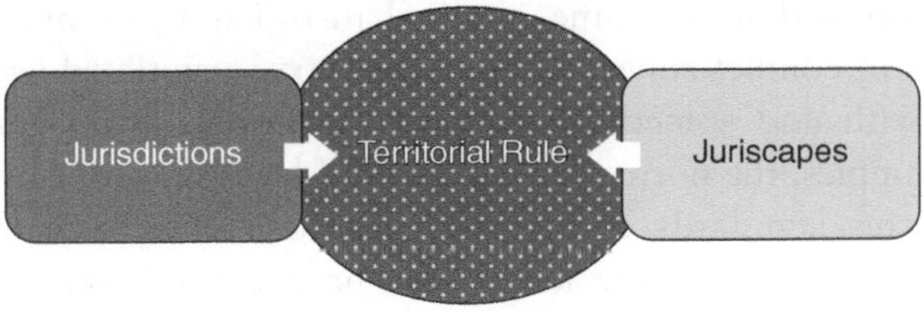

Figure 4.2 Diagram of jurisdictions/juriscapes

First, the suffix *-scape* is borrowed from anthropological and globalization scholarship on the historical production of geographies[31] – particularly on how mutable landscapes of actors (state, non-state, sub-state), practices, and technologies construct ways of seeing, knowing, adapting, and extending territorial rule.[32] Relative to *jurisdiction*, the suffix *-scape* can complement our understanding of *-diction*,[33] since such landscapes often influence the very vocabulary of formal law and, in turn, shape the spatial extension of legal authority in applied contexts. In this sense, *juriscapes* are not fixed containers but dynamic socio-legal terrains that condition what can be legally said, claimed, or enforced across space.

To put it metaphorically, if jurisdictions appear as geometrically bounded polygons on a map, *juriscapes* resemble the legal topographies and topologies that give those polygons texture, slope, and depth – like plots of farmland in a floodplain, terraced slopes in a highland valley, or an irregular mosaic of fields stretching across a mountain range. These are not merely geological features but socio-legal formations: shipping lanes that function as de facto regulatory corridors cutting through high seas; investment treaty networks creating overlapping zones of arbitral authority that mutate national borders; digital platforms whose content-moderation regimes operate transnationally but unevenly, producing enclaves of permissibility and

[31] Arjun Appadurai, *Modernity at Large: Cultural Dimensions of Globalization* (Minneapolis: University of Minnesota Press, 2010), 33–36; Andreas Philippopoulos-Mihalopoulos, *Spatial Justice: Body, Lawscape, Atmosphere* (London: Routledge, 2015).

[32] For example: Nicholas Blomley, *Rights of Passage: Sidewalks and the Regulation of Public Flow* (London: Routledge, 2011); Sarah Marusek, "Lavascape: Legal Spectacle at Kīlauea," *Social Semiotics* 29, no. 3 (2019): 351–67.

[33] A noun pertaining to the choice or use of words.

prohibition within the same nominal jurisdiction; or humanitarian corridors in conflict zones, where temporary, negotiated legal spaces coexist with and sometimes override territorial sovereignty. In all these examples, the normative contours of legal space (i.e., governing rules, norms, standards, and metrics) are shaped less by the geometric line on a map than by the sedimented practices, infrastructures, and institutional logics that constitute a *juriscape*. And unlike geological contours, these socio-legal forms are more plastic – capable of rapid reconfiguration in response to political shifts, technological change, or emergent crises.

Second, juriscapes align with core commitments in human and critical geography: namely, to render visible the complexity of spatial practices that cannot be reduced to the division of the Earth into discrete statist units.[34] This matters for international legal theory today as, for instance, it faces an amalgam of mega-cities, transborder corridors, and regional gateways, which are grafting multiple, complex, and overlapping geographies of rule over land and seas.[35] The notion of grafting is chosen specifically in order to depict statist territoriality and jurisdiction as *rootstock* (legal) infrastructures, from which grow novel boundary practices and forms of exclusion/inclusion that resemble – what horticulturalists would call – a *scion*.

That *rootstock/scion* analogy (see Figure 4.3) can help us visualize a spectrum of territorial rule shaped by spatial continuities and discontinuities, underlining how all grafts of authority rarely rupture from what preceded: scions (juriscapes) draw force and resources from grafted rootstocks, while the rootstock (i.e., state territories and jurisdiction) also possesses inverse capacities to influence how a scion

[34] See Kitchin and Dodge, "Rethinking Maps"; Nicholas Blomley, "The Spaces of Critical Geography," *Progress in Human Geography* 32, no. 3 (2008): 285–93; Valentina Carraro, "The C-word: How Critical Cartography, Critical GIS and Critical Data Studies Can Repoliticise Disaster-Related Maps," *Disaster Prevention and Management* 32, no. 3 (2023): 1–12; Virginija Popvaite, "Navigating Maps in the Arctic: Tracing More-than-Human Interactions of Mapping Practices in Norwegian Rescue Services," *Polar Geography* 46, no. 3 (2023): 190–206.

[35] See Keller Easterling, *Extrastatecraft: The Power of Infrastructure* (London: Verso, 2016); Saskia Sassen, "The New Global Market for Land," in *Expulsions: Brutality and Complexity in the Global Economy* (Cambridge: Belknap Press of Harvard University Press, 2014), 80–116; John Urry, *Offshoring* (Cambridge: Polity, 2014).

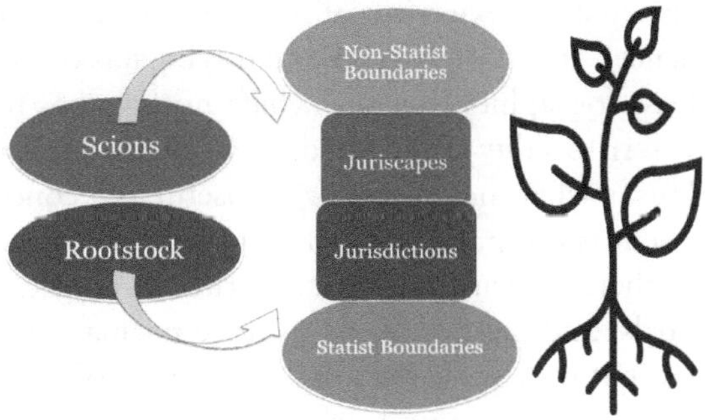

Figure 4.3 Rootstock/scions spectrum of territorial rule

unfolds and travels.[36] This grafted way of seeing territorial rule contrasts with a functionalist tradition that has shaped the discipline's self-perception and worldview, notably through textbook dichotomies such as international/transnational law, formal/informal international law, soft/hard law, or public/private governance. A focus on territorial rule rather than just territorial jurisdiction allows us to consider the broader spectrum of practices through which legal authority is scaled, projected, and sustained – especially across hybrid or trans-territorial boundary practices.

Third, the suffix *-scape* is also informed by work in IR on the importance of underlying assumptions for key norms and rules in International Law. In this sense, *-scape* refers to a scene of common assumptions integral for the functioning of any legal framework. IR scholars employ a more specific concept to encompass that dynamic, a grand social bargain.[37] It emphasizes how institutions in International Law, such as the United Nations Charter, International Humanitarian Law, or the World Trade Organization, need actors to believe in common presumptions that undergird governing norms and rules. Applied to state territoriality and jurisdiction, one key bargain has been *cartographic theory as practice*, and the presumption that territorial rule is represented spatially – and credibly – via statist boundaries.

However, as discussed earlier, state territorialization has always extended through a variety of non-statist boundaries as well, which is

[36] Tung-Hui Hu, *A Prehistory of the Cloud* (Cambridge: MIT Press, 2015), 7–8.
[37] Ian Clark et al., "Crisis in the Laws of War? Beyond Compliance and Effectiveness," *European Journal of International Relations* 24, no. 2 (2018): 319–43, at 330.

one reason why rules on exterritoriality have generated such an extensive jurisprudence. An innate tension and fraying has occupied the core of this grand (cartographic) bargain, which notably has informed and justified state territoriality and jurisdiction as fundamental units of legal space. This is what makes *juriscapes* useful as a conceptual counterpart, because it is not premised or reliant upon *cartographic theory as practice*. Rather, it focuses on trans-territorial landscapes of rules, norms, standards, and metrics, so as to trace normative topographies and topologies that transverse the areal geometries of jurisdictions. As such, juxtaposing juriscapes with jurisdictions makes visible a wider spectrum of territorial rule beyond the narrowness of jurisdictional boundary lines, and enables – pivotally – a comparison of the extent to which these related geographies overlap or diverge over time and subject matter.

Importantly, this concept remains novel within international legal theory, and it requires some conceptual groundwork. The familiar move would be to return to the foundational term: *territory*. That method was noticeably prevalent at the turn of the millennium with multidisciplinary debates over the question of *deterritorialization*, which produced considerable literature and contention over whether processes of globalization had made the concept of state territory archaic – or to what extent at least.[38] However, those debates were grounded on the faulty premise that territory was conceptually descriptive rather than *ascriptive*, and this produced more scholarly heat than light since territory was more a conceptual construction than a reified thing to be pulled out. The binary focus on territory versus deterritorialization distracted from a much deeper issue, which returns us to the opening frame that began this chapter: the relationship between legal rule and *spatial extension*. How are the boundaries of legal rule extended? Or, more specifically, what theory of spatial extension has predominated legal understanding, and with what limits?

[38] Paul Virilio, *Speed and Politics: An Essay on Dromology*, trans. Mark Polizzotti (Los Angeles: Semiotext(e), 2006); Nikos Papastergiadis, *The Turbulence of Migration: Globalisation, Deterritorialization and Hybridity* (Cambridge: Polity, 2000); John Anderson, "The Shifting Stage of Politics: New Medieval and Postmodern Territorialities?" *Environment and Planning D: Society and Space* 14, no. 2 (1996): 133–53; Ó Tuathail, "Borderless Worlds? Problematizing Discourses of Deterritorialization"; Gearóid Ó Tuathail, "Political Geography III: Dealing with Deterritorialization," *Progress in Human Geography* 22, no. 1 (1998): 81–94.

The short answer is that international legal theory has long sidestepped this inquiry by taking state territoriality and jurisdiction as self-constituted – concepts grounded in legal semantics but underwritten by extra-legal spatial assumptions. But there is a longer answer: These assumptions derive from Cartesian geometry, which undergirded the rise of early modern mapping and its later political uses. That geometric legacy remains embedded, if obscured, in the centuries of cartographic knowledge that have shaped how lawyers see the Earth.

The remainder of this chapter explores these hidden foundations more fully. Section 4.3 examines the geometry of territorialization that still structures International Law's dominant theory of spatial extension. Section 4.4 investigates the historical divergence between statist jurisdictions and juriscapes, revealing the spatial continuities and discontinuities that define the past and future of territorial rule.

4.3 A Space Odyssey

Conceptions of human space have conditioned perceptions of the actual, the thinkable and the imaginable.[39] Spatial conceptions of territorialization and territorial rule have been no different. This is why such significance and apprehension has been attached historically to spatial representations of, for example, the polis, the empire, the state, the world, or the cosmos.[40] International lawyers have had a strong connection with that enduring preoccupation, because the discipline was founded on a teleology and presumption of the international as a spatial "unity."[41] Near the turn of the millennium, the proliferation of normative "regimes" prompted legal voices to start raising anxieties about that unitary essence being upended or "fragmented". A narrative of "danger"[42] emerged cautioning how the Westphalian order of *ejus regio, cujus religio* had become undermined by overlapping – and

[39] See Reinhart Koselleck, *The Practice of Conceptual History: Timing History, Spacing Concepts*, trans. Todd Samuel Presner and others (Stanford: Stanford University Press, 2002).

[40] See Benedict Anderson, *Imagined Communities: Reflections on the Origin and Spread of Nationalism* (London: Verso, 1991).

[41] Gilbert Guillaume, "The Future of International Judicial Institutions," *International and Comparative Law Quarterly* 44, no. 4 (1995): 848–62, at 849.

[42] Robert Y. Jennings, "The Role of the International Court of Justice," *British Yearbook of International Law* 68 (1997): 1–63, at 60.

competing – global "regimes" (such as human rights law, trade law), which displayed autonomy over their "fragments", "islands", or "projects" of normative domain, for example. More recently, the United Nations Secretary-General, Antonio Guterres, proclaimed that "forces of fragmentation" were "inching [the world]" ever close to a great fracture."[43] Such fragmentation anxiety even drew the earlier concern of the International Law Commission (ILC) in 2006, which precipitated the Report of the Study Group on "The Fragmentation of International Law" (the Report) chaired by Martti Koskenniemi.

However, the Report became remarkable for a motive few have underlined to date: it upheld a *systems maintenance logic*. Instead of examining the spatial presumptions defining a unity/fragmentation binary, the Report cast "fragmentation" less as a radical transformation and more an organizational challenge in need of fixing. It proposed a problem-solving strategy that involved – to use a familiar expression – more of the same: more coherence-making, creative management, and more "coordination and cooperation". In the words of the Report:

> The move from a world fragmented into sovereign States to a world fragmented into specialized "regimes" may in fact not at all require a fundamental transformation of public international law – though it may call for imaginative uses of its traditional techniques. There were always States that regarded international law as incompatible with their sovereignty. Similarly, there may today exist global regimes or rule-complexes that feel international law an alien intrusion ... If international law is needed as a structure for coordination and cooperation between (sovereign) States, it is no less needed in order to coordinate and organize the cooperation of (autonomous) rule-complexes and institutions.[44]

Conceptually, the Report's framing was revealing. Change was recast as continuity; dilemmas were reframed as phenomena; and global regimes were treated as no more than epiphenomena of International

[43] Patrick Wintour, "World Inching Ever Closer to a Great Fracture, Says UN Chief," *The Guardian*, September 19, 2023, www.theguardian.com/world/2023/sep/19/world-inching-ever-closer-to-a-great-fracture-says-un-chief

[44] International Law Commission, *Fragmentation of International Law: Difficulties Arising from the Diversification and Expansion of International Law. Report of the Study Group of the International Law Commission*, finalized by Martti Koskenniemi, UN Doc. A/CN.4/L.682 and Corr.1 (April 13, 2006), 246.

Law's inherent fragmentation and spatial rationality. Missing from this analysis was any sustained consideration of whether fragmentation might signal a deeper transformation in the configuration of legal space itself. Equally absent was any reflection on the descriptive adequacy of the metaphors at work, or on the extra-legal axiom underpinning the fragmentation discourse: that legal and territorial rule are inherently reducible to geometric forms. In short, the Report left intact a critical conflation – between legal space and geometric space – that has long underwritten the appearance of territorialization as a natural, geometric phenomenon rather than as an historically contingent and socially constructed process.

4.3.1 Fragments and Scions

Yet, consider this simple question: What is a "fragment"? To borrow from Felix Cohen's words, "nobody has ever seen" or touched an international legal fragment since its verifiable existence does not extend beyond the mind of legal scholars.[45] Moreover, dictionary definitions are vague: A fragment is defined as a piece or component separated from an original whole,[46] and derives from the Latin root *frangere* which means "to break into pieces." One scientific dictionary even uses the example of an exploding bomb to illustrate what a "fragment" is.[47] Accordingly, my simple question gains relevance, especially since the

[45] See Felix S. Cohen, "Transcendental Nonsense and the Functional Approach," *Columbia Law Review* 35, no. 6 (1935): 809–49; reprinted in *The Canon of American Legal Thought*, ed. David Kennedy and William W. Fisher III (Princeton: Princeton University Press, 2006), 176:

> When the vivid fictions and metaphors of traditional jurisprudence are thought of as reasons for decisions, rather than poetical or mnemonic devices for formulating decisions reached on other grounds, then the author, as well as the reader, of the opinion or argument, is apt to forget the social forces which mold the law and the social ideals by which the law is to be judged.

[46] A "fragment" is defined by *The New Oxford Dictionary of English* as: "A small part broken or separated off something: *The New Oxford Dictionary of English*, ed. Judy Pearsall (Oxford: Oxford University Press, 1998), s.v. "fragment."

[47] A "fragment" is defined by the *McGraw-Hill Dictionary of Scientific and Technical Terms* as: "A piece of an exploding or exploded bomb, projectile, or the like", *McGraw-Hill Dictionary of Scientific and Technical Terms*, 6th ed. (New York: McGraw-Hill, 2003), s.v. "fragment."

term fragmentation was widely adopted across international legal vocabulary and theorizing – and without much conceptual inquiry. The list of journal articles and edited volumes[48] dedicated to the term are extensive,[49] and fragmentation reached such acceptance that its use has transcended methodological lines in international legal academia.[50] What is more, acceptance of the term is traceable to a much earlier generation of legal realist scholarship, renowned for its critique of legal concepts as seemingly natural, preexisting, and separable from the social and political worlds.[51] The poetry of Oliver Wendell Holmes providing a lucid illustration of that absorption:

> The life of an individual is in many respects like a child's dissected map. If I could live a hundred years, keeping my intelligence to the last, I feel as if I could put the pieces together until they made a properly connected whole. As it is, I, like all others, find a certain number of connected fragments, and a larger number of disjointed pieces, which I in time place in their natural connection. Many of these pieces seem fragmentary, but would in time show themselves as essential parts of the whole. What strikes me very forcibly is the arbitrary and as it were accidental way in which the lines of junction appear to run irregularly among the fragments. With every decade I find some new pieces coming into place. Blanks which have been left in former years find their complement among the undisturbed fragments. If I could look back on the whole, as we look at the child's map when it is put together, I feel that I should have my whole life intelligently laid out before me.[52]

48 See Young, *Regime Interaction in International Law*.

49 Andreas Fischer-Lescano and Gunther Teubner, "Regime-Collisions: The Vain Search for Legal Unity in the Fragmentation of Global Law," *Michigan Journal of International Law* 25, no. 4 (2004): 999–1046; Joel P. Trachtman, "The International Law of Financial Crisis: Spillovers, Subsidiarity, Fragmentation and Cooperation," *Journal of International Economic Law* 13, no. 3 (2010): 719–42; William A. Schabas, "Synergy or Fragmentation? International Criminal Law and the European Convention on Human Rights," *Journal of International Criminal Justice* 9, no. 3 (2011): 609–32; Young, *Regime Interaction*; Teubner, *Constitutional Fragments*.

50 Martti Koskenniemi and Päivi Leino, "Fragmentation of International Law? Postmodern Anxieties," *Leiden Journal of International Law* 15, no. 3 (2002): 553–79.

51 Morton J. Horwitz, *The Transformation of American Law, 1870–1960: The Crisis of Legal Orthodoxy* (Oxford: Oxford University Press, 1992), 169.

52 Graham Greene, *Journey without Maps* (London: Penguin Books, 1980), opening quotation.

What this entails I argue – reusing my rootstock/scion imagery – is need for tracing and digging into antecedent assumptions that facilitated this uncritical acceptance. Indeed, my digging metaphor might be associated with Michel Foucault's "archaeology of knowledge,"[53] and it is in part. Specifically, Foucault's assertions that present-day knowledge is grounded on layers of earlier knowledge, which subsequently steer possible knowledge in a given culture and moment.[54] But, in contrast to archaeology, horticulture modifies that perspective somewhat: it looks at buried and unburied layers in a more organic, two-way, and continual living relationship. In methodological terms, this implies tracing and digging that explores the intertwines between novel and elder strata, which together coproduce axioms and conceptions regarding what are *thinkable*, that is, geometric forms of territorialization and territorial rule.

By extension, this means International Law must be understood as entwined with Eurocentric thought, because the discipline grew out of that rootstock of conceptual and theoretical presumptions. A metaphorical *scion* – among many – that emerged from and is still entwined with Eurocentric thinking on what the Earth *is* and *should be*. One need only think of a few exemplars, and their notable influences on international legal theory to envision the complexity and depth of these intertwines, such as Vitoria, Grotius, Pufendorf, Locke, Hume, Kant, and Bentham. This further connects with Koskenniemi's observations regarding early International Law historiographies: the first nineteenth-century texts on the history of International Law flatly assumed that "the history of international law simply *was* the history of humanity."[55]

As such, my prior fragment question was not that "simple" at all. Admittedly, a more polemical question intended to shed light on a rootstock of world-making assumptions that have enabled the fragment metaphor to penetrate so uncritically into international legal theory. In other words, an invitation to trace and dig into underlying theories and concepts that have influenced how international lawyers spatially see and – subsequently – theorize the extension of territorial

53 Michel Foucault, *The Order of Things: An Archaeology of the Human Sciences* (New York: Vintage Books, 1994).

54 Foucault, *The Order of Things*, 168.

55 Martti Koskenniemi, "Law, Teleology and International Relations: An Essay in Counterdisciplinarity," *International Relations* 26, no. 1 (2012): 3–34, at 4.

rule. And, returning to our discussion of the Report, to help grasp how it was possible that the ILC did not see or scrutinize what were nebulous spatial assumptions on the nature of international legal space. Where did that unquestioned acceptance come from? How was it possible that an ill-defined metaphor so shaped legal perceptions of territorial rule?

4.3.2 The Geometry behind Inter-State Rule

One reason the term "fragment" has escaped sustained conceptual scrutiny may lie in the kind of material resonance it offers to a disciplinary and vocational audience convinced by its own concreteness. There are two steps to this observation. The first relates to what social constructivists refer to as the mutual constitution of the subject and object: what we believe to be the world *out there* is in no small measure defined by our social beliefs and constructs, rather than simply given by nature.[56] Second, international lawyers often reinforce their own sense of conceptual certainty through what might be called a common-sense empiricism – pointing to the materiality of treaties, cases, courts, or clients as proof of the discipline's groundedness.[57] In this light, the use of the term "fragment" provides a quaint fit for a disciplinary and vocational identity assured by images of the tangible.

A further, more interdisciplinary, explanation points to a long history in the life of ideas. All knowledge claims build on inherited terms, concepts, and theories that set the limits of what can be thought and believed.[58] In the case of "fragmentation," the metaphor draws – perhaps unwittingly – on a deeper conceptual heritage in which social, legal, and earthly space came to be understood as

[56] Friedrich Kratochwil, "Constructivism: What It Is (Not) and How It Matters," in *Approaches and Methodologies in the Social Sciences: A Pluralist Perspective*, ed. Donatella Della Porta and Michael Keating (Cambridge: Cambridge University Press, 2008), 80–98, at 82; see also James W. Davis, *Terms of Inquiry: On the Theory and Practice of Political Science* (Baltimore: Johns Hopkins University Press, 2005), 10–60.

[57] Martti Koskenniemi, "The Fate of Public International Law: Between Technique and Politics," *Modern Law Review* 70, no. 1 (2007): 1–30, at 1–2.

[58] However, there are a diversity of approaches, and considerable debate, within the history of ideas on how to go about studying that context: assemblage theory, archaeology, genealogy, and even anti-genealogy.

reducible to a geometric object, capable of being captured on a planimetric map. This heritage is tied to scientific positivism and, more specifically, to the Cartesian axiom that space is fundamentally a geometric construct.

This spatial legacy helps explain why the fragment metaphor has been so readily accepted and so rarely interrogated in international legal theory. The geometric worldview it inherits continues to shape how territorialization is perceived, defining which forms of spatial extension are treated as *real* legal boundaries. State territoriality and jurisdiction gained much of their authority not only from political and doctrinal developments, but also from the convenience of their geometric regularity and aesthetics – a convenience that masks an enduring problem. Disciplinary International Law remains tethered to a *thinkable geography* scripted by the mapped rules of seventeenth-century Cartesian geometry: a worldview engineered through a particular geometric rationality, its artifice largely invisible because legal vocabulary treats territoriality and jurisdiction as self-evident descriptors rather than as historically contingent constructs.

Focusing on this *thinkable geography* allows us to return to, and press more deeply on, the statist nucleus of international legal theory discussed earlier in this chapter (Section 4.1). That nucleus has been reified over centuries by geometric world-making, sustained by the teleology of a geometrically perfected world. I emphasize the word *world* deliberately: Metaphors of the world, and of the globe, are central to how European modernity – and, by extension, International Law – has imagined space. At the core lies perhaps the most profound reification of Eurocentric thought: the *globalization* of Earth, or the framing of spatial comprehension through an absolute, spherical, geometric globe.

The story of how legal and social theory came to compress life on Earth into a geometric object has many strands. While this chapter cannot recount each in detail, a few developments are pivotal for understanding how a Cartesian view of legal geography became not only thinkable but naturalized within international legal theory. For many international lawyers, as for most social scientists, imagining space without reference to a geometric area remains a difficult exercise. Even in debates about the Digital or Platform Revolutions – covering the internet, information technologies, Artificial Intelligence, and social media – discussion frequently loops back to the metaphor of a "virtual world," regardless of any rhetoric about infinite connectivity or "de-territorialization."[59]

This persistence reflects more than geometric representation alone. It is tied to a longstanding social impulse to depict spatial perception through the planimetric map. Whether consciously or not, legal space has been governed by an underlying geometry – one that has profoundly influenced what is perceived as the proper order, scale, and shape of legality. To return to the rootstock/scion metaphor introduced earlier, the conflation of legal space with geometric and planimetric reality is the product of a centuries-long intertwining between International Law's disciplinary imagination and the geometric world-making that shaped modern cartography. The next step is to examine that historical intertwining more closely, to trace how it has conditioned the discipline's perception of legal geography and its boundaries – and, crucially, to consider what might be thinkable once those geometric presumptions are made visible.

4.3.3 Singularity: The Legacies of Brunelleschi and Copernicus

One way to grasp the social construction of geometric and planimetric reality is to revisit alternative historical and conceptual understandings of space. Doing so helps reveal how international legal history has been shaped by a rootstock of geometric science. Although modern narratives often credit the Ancient Greeks – particularly Euclid – with introducing a geometric understanding of space, it is worth stressing that the Greeks had no word equivalent to the modern term, "space."[60] Nor should we forget the long stretch of medieval European history that preceded both the Renaissance and modernity. As Camille observes, "there [was] no such thing as 'space' for medieval people" in the later European sense of a global abstraction.[61] Instead, as Jens

[59] Gunther Handl, "Extra-Territoriality and Transnational Legal Authority," in *Beyond Territoriality: Transnational Legal Authority in the Age of Globalization*, ed. Gunther Handl et al. (Leiden: Martinus Nijhoff Publishers, 2012), 3–34, at 3–4.

[60] Stuart Elden, "Missing the Point: Globalization, Deterritorialization and the Space of the World," *Transactions of the Institute of British Geographers*, n.s., 30, no. 1 (2005): 8–19, at 12.

[61] Michael Camille, "Signs of the City: Place, Power, and Public Fantasy in Medieval Paris," in *Medieval Practices of Space*, ed. Barbara A. Hanawalt and Michal Kobialka (Minneapolis: University of Minnesota Press, 2000), 1–36, at 9.

Bartelson explains, medieval conceptions were structured through a kind of graphic and didactic cosmography, combining the finite and the infinite within a bi-spherical cosmos and earth:

Medieval cosmology was based on a variety of sources, most of which distinguished between a celestial and a terrestrial region. While the former embraced everything from the moon to the limits of the universe, the latter included everything below the moon to the centre of the earth ... According to Genesis I, 9, the terrestrial region was in turn divided into two different zones, those of earth and water respectively. These zones were mutually exclusive, so where there was water, there could be no earth, and conversely.[62]

Juxtaposing this premodern worldview with the modern construction of global space underscores the transformation: the shift to equating space – and thus spatial representation – with a discrete object, specifically a "single sphere with one common centre of gravity."[63] Often overlooked in this shift is the catalytic role of the visual arts in preparing the ground for a new cosmology. In the early fifteenth century, Filippo Brunelleschi devised and applied *single-point perspective* – a method of representation that positioned the viewer at a fixed point and rendered the subject accordingly (see Figure 4.4).[64] This broke with the medieval European tradition of depicting objects from multiple sides or angles.

For European imperialism, the implications were extraordinary. It now became possible to represent and conceptually organize territorialization and territorial rule from *a single, dominant viewpoint*. This visual innovation formed part of the rootstock for Copernicus' early sixteenth-century claim of a *rotunditate absoluta*, establishing the Earth as a perfectly shaped sphere – at once knowable, navigable, and, for European empires, appropriable. Copernicus' model implied that social – and therefore legal – space could be conceived as similarly singular and absolute.[65] Lost in this transformation was the premodern openness to multiple, qualitatively distinct dimensions of reality, each with its own images, meanings, and scales.

62 Jens Bartelson, "The Social Construction of Globality," *International Political Sociology* 4, no. 3 (2010): 219–35, at 223–24.
63 Bartelson, "Social Construction of Globality," 225.
64 Samuel Y. Edgerton Jr., *The Renaissance Rediscovery of Linear Perspective* (New York: Basic Books, 1975), 9.
65 Arthur Jay Klinghoffer, *The Power of Projections: How Maps Reflect Global Politics and History* (Westport, CT: Praeger Publishers, 2006), 75.

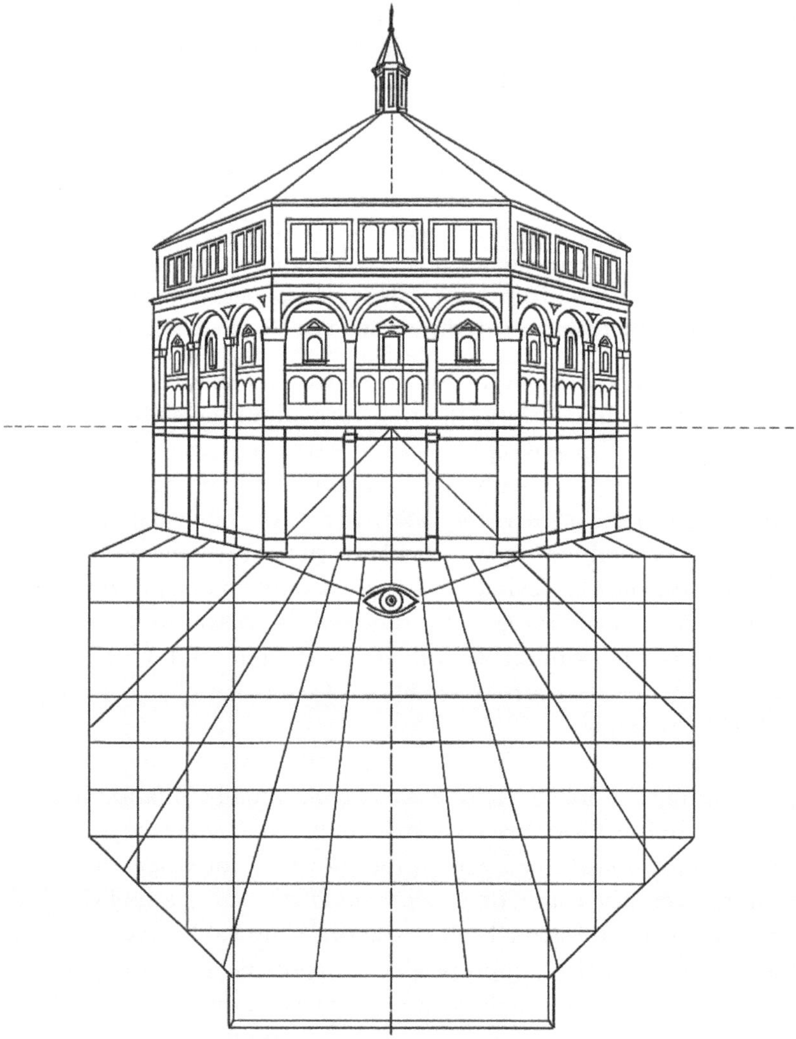

Figure 4.4 *Single-Point Perspective of the Florence Baptistry.* Author's own illustration, created with AI-assisted design tools, August 2025.

From Copernicus onward, space was conceived as absolute and singular, which in turn made it divisible – or, in the familiar metaphor, fragmentable (see Figure 4.5).[66] The combined legacies of

[66] John Rennie Short, *Making Space: Revisioning the World, 1475–1600* (Syracuse: Syracuse University Press, 2004), 84–85.

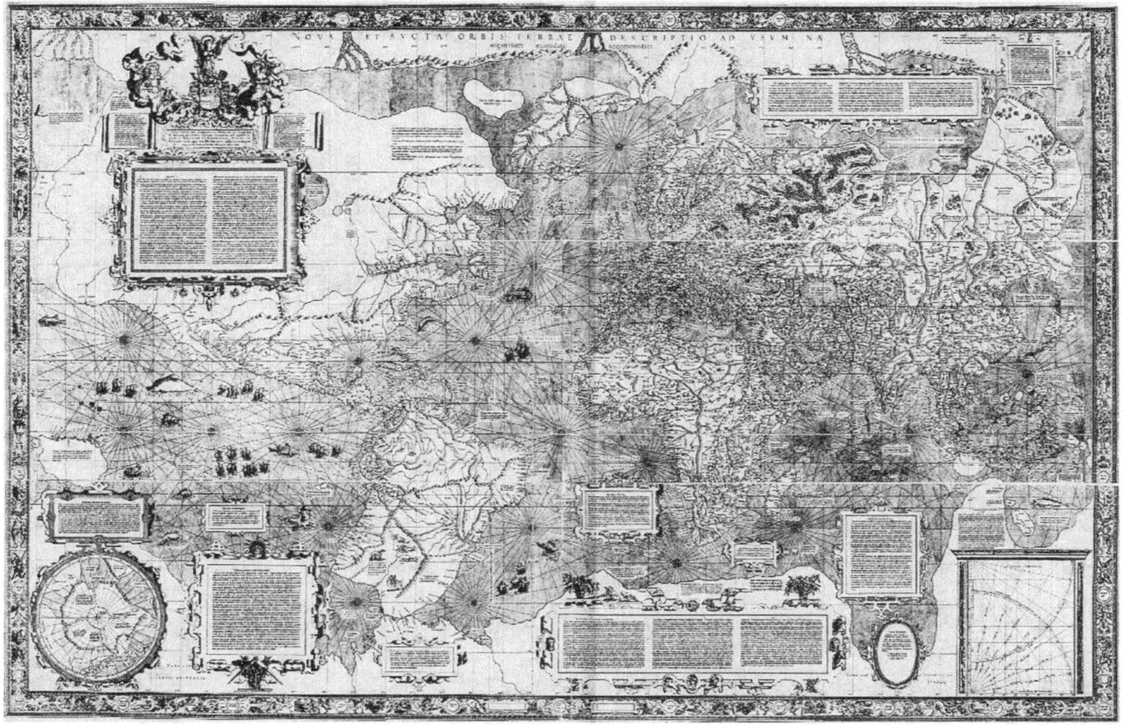

Figure 4.5 Gerardus Mercator, *Nova et Aucta Orbis Terrae* (World Map, 1569). Mercator projection of the globe – produced just over two decades after Copernicus' *De revolutionibus orbium coelestium* (1543) and assertion of the *rotunditate absoluta* of Earth. Public domain image (courtesy of Art Collection / Alamy). www.alamy.com/stock-photo-the-1569-map-by-gerardus-mercator-is-a-key-historical-document-in-137389212.html

Brunelleschi and Copernicus thus produced a radically new worldview centered on the visual and physical singularity of the terraqueous globe. With this certainty came geopolitical anxiety: the imperative to order the newly defined globe through geometric partitioning. Having displaced the sublime cosmos, the European globe now became the object of political and legal geometry. As Jerry Brotton explains, the race began to mold this "newborn" globe through acts of visual appropriation, notably the cartographic bisection of the *rotunditate absoluta*:

> Maps, charts and globes such as the Cantino Planisphere and Behaim's terrestrial globe disseminated vital conceptual information on the changing territorial and commercial shape of the world they depicted. Supplemented by the mass of travel narratives and diplomatic reports which emerged … such geographical artefacts became prized possessions, not only keeping their owners informed of the latest discoveries and commercial ventures, but also providing them with a sense of security as to their own identity within such an ever-changing world. […] [This] production of maps and charts … [became] the practical bedrock for all subsequent printed cartography over much of the globe for the next 200 years.[67]

Yet, the drive to geometrize the globe quickly ran into a problem. The Treaty of Tordesillas (1494) infamously sought to divide the world between Portugal and Spain by drawing a "straight line … north and south … from pole to pole … at a distance three hundred and seventy leagues west of the Cape Verde Islands."[68] Portugal was assigned the eastern hemisphere (Africa, Asia), Spain the western (the Americas). But it was later discovered that South America's eastward bulge extended beyond the Tordesillas line, granting Portugal control over what became Brazil.[69] The difficulty of partitioning a spherical globe exceeded the navigational and cartographic capacities of the time. More fundamentally, it revealed a deeper epistemic problem: the limitations of the rootstock knowledge upon which conquest cartography relied – namely, Euclidean geometry.

[67] Brotton, *Trading Territories*, 75, 83.

[68] Treaty of Tordesillas, June 7, 1494, The Avalon Project, Yale Law School, https://avalon.law.yale.edu/15th_century/mod001.asp (accessed August 23, 2025), clause 1.

[69] Sack, *Human Territoriality*.

4.3.4 Descartes and the Rise of Planimetric Earth

The legacies of Brunelleschi and Copernicus set the stage for René Descartes, whose seventeenth-century philosophical interventions would give *cartographic theory as practice* the appearance of mathematical and analytical precision. His work supplied the epistemic foundations for the scientific revolution in European philosophy and geometry, providing states with a powerful means to fortify a singular conception of territorialization through mathematical translation and *ascription*. Tracing this intellectual rootstock is essential for understanding why Cartesian geometry remains so consequential for the *thinkable* legal geography of today.

Although Euclid's contributions to geometry remained integral, they had to be reconciled with Copernicus' assertion of an absolute globe. Descartes was at the vanguard of this geometric renovation – a process later advanced by Spinoza, Leibniz, Newton, and Kant.[70] Two moves were pivotal. First, Descartes drew a sharp ontological distinction between thought (*res cogitans*) and the material world (*res extensa*),[71] giving space a Cartesian identity as material and absolute – independent of human thought and senses.[72] Second, he conceived this material world as arithmetically divisible and calculable, opening the way for geometry's algebraic translation (analytic geometry) and its appropriation by mathematics.[73] As Stuart Elden describes, Cartesian geometry overturned Aristotle's separation of geometry from arithmetic:

> For Aristotle, the key thing about the connectivity of units is that they are discrete, separate from each other. A sequence of numbers, for example, has a distance between each of them, we count one after the other, steps along the way. A line, in distinction, while it has points within it, cannot simply be reduced to a string of points. There is more to the line, because the connection of points is different from the sequence of numbers. Points, when they are connected, literally have the end of one as the beginning of the next, there is nothing between them ... Descartes [saw] geometry as equivalent

[70] Lefebvre, *The Production of Space*, 1–2.

[71] René Descartes, *Oeuvres de Descartes*, ed. Charles Adam and Paul Tannery (Paris: J. Vrin, 1964), vol. 7, 85–86.

[72] Geoff King, *Mapping Reality: An Exploration of Cultural Cartographies* (New York: St. Martin's Press, 1996), 140.

[73] King, *Mapping Reality*.

of algebra; it is the symbolic version of the world ... Descartes [saw] geometrical figures and, by extension, the world of which they are symbols, as numerically calculated.[74]

What Descartes thus made possible is what Henri Lefebvre calls the geometric "science of space,"[75] where the purpose of mapping shifted from the rich didactics of medieval cosmography to the mathematical rigor required for locating and asserting precise claims on a geometric surface. The Cartesian coordinate system allowed the spherical globe to be projected onto a flat surface, enabling "an exhaustive geographical inventory."[76] This geometric capacity overlapped with another seventeenth-century transformation: the emergence of the Westphalian states system. Westphalian sovereignty required monarchs to demonstrate control over their territories,[77] which demanded systematic knowledge and description of crown lands. The convergence of this political prerogative with Cartesian geometry contributed to the visual construction of jurisdiction – and, more importantly, to the appearance of territorialization as measurable ownership of Earth space.[78] This expression crystallized in the singular model of state territoriality.

Geometric cartography flourished under the patronage of Europe's Baroque dynasties, who sponsored cadastral surveys, military mapping, and advances in longitude measurement.[79] The genesis of this cartographic science was foremost directed at visual appropriation of the Earth's terrain through geometric representation[80] and planimetric measurement.[81] Compressing the spherical globe onto a gridded surface enabled the graphic production of territorial extension and rule, reducing the risk of another Tordesillas-style miscalculation and ushering in the wholesale geometrization of the Earth.[82] Cartesian geometry, geopolitics, and territorialization combined to produce a nascent anthropocentrism – displacing the "crudeness" of nature with the symmetry and perfection of linear borders and gridlines.

[74] Elden, "Missing the Point," 12. [75] Lefebvre, *Production of Space*, 3.
[76] Arturo Escobar, "Exploration, Cartography and the Modernization of State Power," in *State/Space: A Reader*, ed. Neil Brenner et al. (Oxford: Blackwell Publishing, 2003), 131–52, at 135.
[77] Escobar, "Exploration, Cartography".
[78] Jeremy Black, *Maps and History: Constructing Images of the Past* (New Haven: Yale University Press, 1997), 15.
[79] Black, *Maps and History*, 14–16.
[80] Paul Virilio, *L'Insécurité du territoire* (Paris: Stock, 1975), 120.
[81] Black, *Maps and History*, 16–17. [82] King, *Mapping Reality*, 142.

In this way, state territoriality and jurisdiction became legal concepts bound to the image and teleology of a "geometrically perfect world," echoing the Renaissance pursuit of "geometrically perfect towns" and landscapes.[83] A milestone was reached in 1659 with Europe's first modern, geometrically derived border – the Pyrenees boundary between France and Spain. The implications were even more visible in the colonial *new world*,[84] where planimetric reduction was perfected: the gridlines of latitude and longitude sliced through Indigenous homelands[85] in what became the continental United States[86] and across Africa.[87] *Thinkable geography* became entwined with the ambitions of Cartesian science, and with its blindness to the ecological and social violence such world-making entailed.

In short, a geometric worldview came to define what territorialization *is* and *should* look like – as geographic shape, aesthetic form, and legal fact – allowing *cartographic theory as practice* to "intelligently lay before us" a Planimetric Earth. Two pivotal observations follow. First, centuries of geometric world-making reified the image of a contiguous world map. Second, international lawyers largely accepted this inheritance ahistorically, building upon it normatively without scrutinizing its spatial presumptions.[88] Recognizing this geometric history as a rootstock of the discipline illuminates International Law's deep entanglement with the history of *cartographic theory as practice*. It also reveals a persistent blind spot: The geometric and cartographic capture of legal space has rarely been interrogated for its role in reifying a singular, mapped reality. As Brian Harley reminds us:

> Far from holding up a simple mirror of nature that is true or false, maps redescribe the world – like any other document – in terms of relations of power and of cultural practices, preferences, and priorities. What we read on a map is as much related to an invisible social world and to ideology as it is to phenomena seen and measured in the landscape … The fascination

[83] Abraham Akkerman, "Urban Planning in the Founding of Cartesian Thought," *Philosophy and Geography* 4, no. 2 (2001): 141–67.

[84] Klinghoffer, *Power of Projections*, 78–79.

[85] We should not forget that part of the violence of the colonial conquest and expansion was the imposition of colonial mapping over alternate Indigenous worldviews. See King, *Mapping Reality*, 142.

[86] See Sack, *Human Territoriality*, 127–68.

[87] See Makau W. Mutua, "Why Redraw the Map of Africa: A Moral and Legal Inquiry," *Michigan Journal of International Law* 16, no. 3 (1995): 1113–76.

[88] Escobar, "Exploration, Cartography," 147.

of maps as humanly created documents is found not merely in the extent to which they are objective or accurate. It also lies in their inherent ambivalence and in our ability to tease out new meanings, hidden agendas, and contrasting worldview from between the lines on the image … Like books, they are also products of both individuals minds and the wider cultural values in particular societies.[89]

4.4 Territorialization Revisited: The Gaze of Contiguity

Far from being a relic of a bygone era, the ideal of a "geometrically perfect world" remains embedded in the heritage of International Law. Centuries of geometric and cartographic world-making produced an iconic, mapped image of a Planimetric Earth – an ordered, sublime, and perfected entity. Upon this image, statist geography, territorialization, and jurisdiction took root as if they were natural extensions. These spatial conventions subsequently shaped the geographic premises that underpinned the discipline's formalization.

This geometric and linear conditioning did more than represent the world – it actively territorialized it. An unruly mass of ecosystems, species, peoples, places, and homes was reimagined as a gridded, measurable, and governable domain of discrete state units. This was a mobilization of unprecedented scale, turning nature into an object to be reorganized according to a singular, contiguous system of material culture.[90] The result was not only a practical ordering of space but also a world invested with immense symbolic and social authority. As Michael Walzer observes, state units became "fundamental to all thinking and doing, units of feeling around which emotions of loyalty and assurance … cluster."[91]

After successive centuries of such planimetric conditioning, a gridded and contiguous Earth became more than a political convention – it became the default way of seeing and imagining the legal world, of assuming how it *is* and how it *should be*. Against this backdrop, it is unsurprising that the metaphor of the "fragment" could slip so effortlessly into the vocabulary of the discipline, the profession, and even the ILC's *Report on the Fragmentation of International Law*.

89 Harley, "Deconstructing the Map," 8–9.
90 Chandra Mukerji, *Territorial Ambitions and the Gardens of Versailles* (Cambridge: Cambridge University Press, 1997), 37–38.
91 Walzer, "On the Role of Symbolism in Political Thought," 194–95.

4.4.1 Disciplinary Contiguity and Aristotle's Gaze

We now encounter a significant twist: The preceding analysis runs counter to a widespread conviction among international lawyers that the discipline operates as an autonomous practice, largely insulated from the sciences. Here, Kenneth Burke's notions of the gaze and *circumferential logic* (Chapter 2) become relevant once more – particularly his insight that the circumference of what is made visible shapes what is deemed relevant, and what remains unseen.[92] As discussed in Section 4.3, geometric and cartographic world-making provided the spatial premises that shaped thinkable legal geography and inevitably extended into the disciplinary world of International Law. Yet, as Martti Koskenniemi illustrates, altering the circumference of a discipline's vision can determine whether such scientific world-making is visible at all:

> Interdisciplinary vocabularies of "scholarship" and "science" miss what for most international lawyers is the most obvious aspect of our trade: namely, its craft-likeness, its being above all a practice. International law is not a social science. It is not a (theoretical) science at all – that is to say, it does not operate on the basis of demonstrable, even less empirical truths, nor with ideas about moral goodness. Legal "truth" or "goodness" is concerned with ... the correctness of the legal decision. This is a product of legal practice, argument, persuasion, not its precondition. Even as lawyers may use empirical arguments from "theory" and sometimes invoke moral sentiments, the practical reasoning – *phronesis* – that best characterizes what lawyers do cannot be reduced to either one or the other. What works depends on context.[93]

[92] Kenneth Burke, *A Grammar of Motives* (Berkeley: University of California Press, 1969), 84:

> In time[s] of adversity one can readily note the workings of "circumferential" logic, in that [persons] choose to define their acts in terms of much wider orbits than the orbit of the adversity itself. The "solace of religion", for instance, may have its roots not in a mere self-deception, whereby one can buoy [themselves] up with false promises or persuade [themselves] that the situation is not bad when it is so palpably bad; but it may stem from an accurate awareness that one can define human nature and human actions in much wider terms than the particularities of his immediate circumstances would permit; and this option is not an "illusion", but a fact, and as true as a fact as any fact in his immediate circumstances.

[93] Koskenniemi, "Law, Teleology and International Relations," 19.

Koskenniemi's distinction between law as "practice" versus science as "theory" is not uniquely his, but in fact reflects a gaze intuitive to many international lawyers.[94] What makes Koskenniemi's intervention noteworthy is his sensitivity to the power of the gaze, and especially how he maneuvers it to shape disciplinary *context*. In particular, he uses Aristotelian *phronêsis* to tactically widen the discipline's circumference of vision and, consequently, impart what seems a transhistorical partition between law and science. It provides a powerful rhetorical argument that uses an ancient scheme of knowledge classification, often seen as hereditary for modern Western thought, to convey an almost geological representation of disciplinary ordering, much in the way fault lines would appear on the terrestrial surface.[95]

However, that widening is selective and camera-like. To use an analogy, Koskenniemi takes a snapshot at a very wide circumference to include and leverage Aristotelian metaphysics, but this widening fades focus on the overlap of geometric and cartographic science with International Law's emergence. Koskenniemi, on the one hand, uses Aristotelian *phronêsis* to better situate International Law relative to the theory-testing of many – but not all[96] – social science disciplines.[97] Yet, on the other hand, that wide gaze produced a hyperopic image of International Law, blurring the more immediate relevance of geometric and cartographic world-making.[98]

94 See James Crawford, "International Law as a Discipline and Profession," *Proceedings of the American Society of International Law* 106 (2012): 471–82; Jan Klabbers, "The Bridge Crack'd: A Critical Look at Interdisciplinary Relations," *International Relations* 23, no. 1 (2009): 119–25; Philip Allott, "Review of Books," *British Yearbook of International Law* 80, no. 1 (2009): 409–25.

95 Metaphors of geology and topography are used vividly in the acclaimed book of Hans Lindahl, *Fault Lines of Globalization: Legal Order and the Politics of A-Legality* (Oxford: Oxford University Press, 2013).

96 The recent "practice" turn in disciplinary IR being just one good and relevant example, see: Emanuel Adler and Vincent Pouliot, eds., *International Practices* (Cambridge: Cambridge University Press, 2011).

97 See Donatella Della Porta and Michael Keating, eds., *Approaches and Methodologies in the Social Sciences: A Pluralist Perspective* (Cambridge: Cambridge University Press, 2008).

98 Notably, Koskenniemi's use of Aristotelian *phronêsis* also involved a circumferential logic because it focused on Aristotle's work in the *Metaphysics*, where he delineated, in descending hierarchy, between theoretical (theology, mathematics, and physics), practical (ethics and politics) and productive (fine arts, poetics, and engineering) subjects

The result is a disciplinary variant of the *reification illusion* (Section 4.1): A gaze that naturalizes the boundary between international lawyers and social scientists by mobilizing Aristotle's distinction, much as Kant's "geography of reason" once mapped the domains of thought into discrete intellectual territories.[99] This distributive mapping lends itself to a "common sense" division of labor in which courts, treaties, and cases appear to belong inherently to lawyers, just as terrestrial distribution belongs to geographers, matter to physicists, and outer space to astronomers.[100] Yet, as historical sociology reminds us, such divisions are neither fixed nor purely "objective": they shift as material conditions change and as cultural interpretations reshape the very qualities that disciplines claim as their own.[101]

This is why *contiguity* – in both spatial and disciplinary senses – has proved so powerful. As Koskenniemi demonstrates, the disciplinary gaze extends the rootstock of geometric world-making into perceptions of intellectual space, entwining the contours of the discipline with the spatial axioms of Cartesian science and, above all, with *cartographic theory as practice*. His account also shows how the assertion of disciplinary contiguity resists the encroachments of the "knowledge society," in which universities and disciplines no longer monopolize the terms of knowledge production.[102] In this context, defending disciplinary boundaries serves not only to demarcate International Law from adjacent fields but also to guard against the blending of once-bounded domains – whether through the rise

of knowledge. However, in *Nicomachean Ethics* (Book VI), Aristotle complicated matters considerably with his assertion that the human mind in action produced five *interrelated* categories of knowledge: technical (*technê*), scientific (*epistêmê*), practical (*phronêsis*), wisdom (*sophia*), and understanding (*nous*, *dianoia*). Aristotle's thinking on practical reason was extended beyond the gaze of the *Metaphysics*, *Aristotle, Nicomachean Ethics*, trans. Terence Irwin, 2nd ed. (Indianapolis: Hackett, 1999), book VI.

99 See Jeff Malpas and Karsten Thiel, "Kant's Geography of Reason," in *Reading Kant's Geography*, ed. Stuart Elden and Eduardo Mendieta (Albany: SUNY Press, 2011), 195–211; Immanuel Kant, *Critique of Pure Reason*, trans. Paul Guyer and Allen W. Wood (Cambridge: Cambridge University Press, 1998), A760/B788 ("On the Impossibility of a Sceptical Satisfaction of Pure Reason That Is Divided Against Itself").

100 Andrew Abbott, *The System of Professions: An Essay on the Division of Expert Labor* (Chicago: University of Chicago Press, 1988), 36.

101 Abbott, *System of Professions*.

102 Robert Frodeman, *Sustainable Knowledge: A Theory of Interdisciplinarity* (London: Palgrave Macmillan, 2014), 26–27.

of cross-disciplinary institutes or the funding priorities of agencies favoring hybrid research on, for example, Artificial Intelligence and Political Economy, Law and Climate Change, or International Law and International Relations.[103]

4.4.2 Territorial Contiguity and Schematic Control

Contiguity has imposed a geometric framing that is central to how territorialization is perceived and extended across social, scholarly, and physical geographies. Its diffusion into the mindset of disciplinary International Law has reinforced the presumption that statist territoriality is a manifest, autonomous, and fixed phenomenon. However, the narrowness of that gaze, obscuring the history of its emergence, created a sizeable theoretical void because the discipline's worldview of space was tied to – borrowing from Jens Bartelson – a "conceptual mummy."[104] In other words, a contiguous world looked self-evident since territoriality was detached from the history of geometric and cartographic world-making – both theoretically and canonically. Here the irony is clear. As James C. Scott reminds us, statist territorialization was part of a much larger social transformation – one that redefined the perception of space through a deliberate narrowing of circumferential logic:

> Certain forms of knowledge and control require a narrowing of vision. The great advantage of such tunnel vision is that it brings into sharp focus certain limited aspects of an otherwise far more complex and unwieldy reality. This very simplification, in turn, makes the phenomenon as the center of the field of vision more legible and hence more susceptible to careful measurement and calculation. Combined with similar observations, an overall, aggregate, synoptic view of a selective reality is achieved, making possible a high degree of schematic knowledge, control and manipulation[105]

That "tunnel vision" Scott describes brings into view a homogenizing purpose embedded within international legal space. The discipline's

[103] Oliver Kessler, "So Close Yet So Far Away? International Law in International Political Sociology," *International Political Sociology* 4, no. 3 (2010): 303–07.

[104] Bartelson, *Becoming International*, 10.

[105] James C. Scott, *Seeing Like a State: How Certain Schemes to Improve the Human Condition Have Failed* (New Haven: Yale University Press, 1998), 11.

image of Earth, that is, as a grid of geometric territorialities, is an exemplary illustration of such narrowing and simplifying for the purpose of attaining schematic control and manipulation. However, if pressed, few international lawyers would be comfortable with the assertion that their worldview is a product of "tunnel vision" or "selective reality". Quite the opposite, in fact, their reply would be this contiguous worldview merely reflects the established "bedrock" of territorial and thus legal reality. Yet, while rhetorically familiar, the curious thing about that bedrock metaphor is its impoverished geophysics: There is no such thing as a single type of bedrock, rather there are multiple kinds of bedrock formed with different densities, at different times, and in different ways.[106]

This geophysical primer provides an opening to leverage what has been a presumptive bedrock for the doctrinal field: the Earth's landmass is innately divided into contiguous, fixed, and mutually exclusive territorial units. I argue this seemingly timeworn principle is merely reflective of a periodic history, because a broader aperture shows plurality and intersectionality have often defined the spatial parameters of territorial rule over time. Moreover, if anything can be identified as transhistorical, it is that territorial rule has been shaped constantly by varying transboundary dynamics, geopolitical exigencies, and cross-cutting legal practices. As John Ruggie reminds us:

> There are at least three ways in which prior or other systems of rule have differed … from the modern territorial state.
>
> First, systems of rule need not be territorial at all. That is to say, the basis on which the human species is socially individuated and individuals, in turn, are bound together into collectivities can take (and historically has taken) forms other than territoriality …
>
> Second, systems of rule need not be territorially fixed. Owen Lattimore's work on nomadic property rights is of relevance here. Writing of Mongol tribes, Lattimore pointed out that no single pasture would have had much value for them because it soon would become exhausted. Hence, driven by what Lattimore called "the sovereign importance of movement … they laid claim to definite pastures and to the control of routes of migration between the pastures" …

106 See Timothy Darvill, *The Concise Oxford Dictionary of Archaeology*, 3rd ed. (Oxford: Oxford University Press, 2021), s.v. "bedrock": "Bedrock is not necessarily solid rock: gravels, sands, glacial tills, and many other kinds of relatively soft materials are … bedrock."

> Third, even where systems of rule are territorial, and even where territoriality is relatively fixed, the prevailing concept of territory need not entail mutual exclusion ... Briefly put, the spatial extension of the medieval system of rule was structured by a nonexclusive form of territoriality, in which authority was both personalized and parcelized within and across territorial formations.[107]

Scarcely has there been a one-size-fits-all model for territorial rule and even territorialization, rather an evolving history of concepts and arrangements adapted to differing social demands, interests, and imaginations over time. Further, Ruggie's insights provoke some apt questions: How did such a narrow circumference endure? What perpetuated disciplinary belief in territorial contiguity? Or, bluntly, what has tethered international lawyers to this spatial mummy?

Once again, there are short and long answers. But the short one this time is acutely short, and might grate some who still assert a fenced disciplinary geometry: power. Indeed, one may elaborate a bit: Territorial contiguity has been an *ascriptive* construction, produced socially and historically through different types of power. The long answer, foreseeably, then becomes a task of unpacking how that contested concept is used here. Especially since "power" is leveraged – going back to Scott's quote – to broaden the *schematics* of how international lawyers construe territorial rule and the seminal concept of territory – past, present and future. As such, the influence of these different types of power will be now explained in four concise steps, which cumulatively led to the privileging of contiguity as a given spatial feature of territorialization.

4.4.3 Kartenpolitik *and the Reign of Contiguity*

The four steps that follow will be familiar from Chapter 3's discussion of Barnett and Duvall's taxonomy of power, and in particular the interplay of structural, productive, compulsory, and institutional power.[108] First, territorial contiguity exemplifies *structural power*: It has defined – often unconsciously – how almost all forms of space and

[107] Ruggie, "Territoriality and Beyond," 149–50.
[108] Michael Barnett and Raymond Duvall, "Power in International Politics," *International Organization* 59, no. 1 (2005): 39–75, at 43:

place, social and physical, are perceived. Few appreciate that contiguity is not a transhistorical quality of legal space but an ascriptive model that has grown steadily in influence since the seventeenth century. That power-blindness deriving from how key legal terms, like sovereignty, territory, and property, have rarely been linked to geometric world-making and the way this made thinkable and embedded – in effect – the reign of contiguity. Or, to rework Koskenniemi's words, the way territorial contiguity made possible a *Kartenpolitik*: "[Maps] are *politics*; When [maps] change, things that previously could not be said are now spoken by [others] … With a change of [the map], new speakers become authoritative."[109]

Second, *productive power* explains how this *Kartenpolitik* arose in the first place. The key point is territorial contiguity arose as a potent tool of cultural appropriation and arguably conquest,[110] specifically used to enculture the Earth's surface into a puzzle board of statist territorial units. It delineated a "geo-body" that attached an essential form and geometry to the conceptual meaning of territorialization.[111] This gaze and visual expectation played an underlying – but no less fundamental – role in the discursive production and homogenization of statist legal geography. What is more, it entwined the imaginary of "nature" with a geometric and contiguous body of territorial space.[112]

> The first type is power as relations of interaction of direct control by one actor over another – Compulsory Power; the second is the control actors exercise indirectly over others through diffuse relations of interaction – Institutional Power; the third is the constitution of subjects' capacities in direct structural relation to one another – Structural Power; and the fourth is the socially diffuse production of subjectivity in systems of meaning and signification – Productive Power. These different conceptualizations provide distinct answers to the fundamental question: in what respects are actors able to determine their fate, and how is that ability limited or enhanced through social relations with others?

109 Martti Koskenniemi, "Miserable Comforters: International Relations as the New Natural Law," *European Journal of International Relations* 15, no. 3 (2009): 395–422, at 395. For an excellent introduction to critical cartography, see: Harley, "Deconstructing the Map."

110 See Rajkovic, "The Visual Conquest of International Law."

111 Thongchai Winichakul, *Siam Mapped: A History of the Geo-Body of a Nation* (Honolulu: University of Hawai'i Press, 1994).

112 Winichakul, *Siam Mapped*, 132–33:

> The naturalization, literally, of the geo-body can be done at one stroke since its material basis is the earth's surface. Its representations … maintain their referent and root in the earth or soil … The geo-body supplies the new

Yet, as Luca Muscarà underlines, contiguity was in fact foreign to the scion of statist territoriality and territorialization as it emerged in fifteenth-century Europe. Rather, contiguity was only grafted centuries later once *linear schematics* became integral to the ascription of territorial rule:

The 1648 Treaties of Westphalia are conventionally seen as the birth of the modern nation-state, defined by its territorial integrity, within a pluralist international system where each state is legally seen as equal. Still this view doesn't find the cartographic support it would require. Even if rulers had used maps and made political claims in the New World based on geometry since 1490s, "territory continued to be understood ... as a series of differentiated places" with their rights and privileges, following a jurisdictional, non-territorial notion ... where space is still a list of toponyms, not areas on a map ... The European vision of America as "empty space" made it easier to apply geometry to boundaries there, rather than the densely inhabited Europe. Formally ending the American Revolutionary War, the Treaty of Paris (1783) still had no maps ... Cartographies did supplement the settlements of the Congress of Vienna and the 1814–1815 Treaties of Paris. Political authority was now defined in terms of linear boundaries, making it unnecessary to list all rights and jurisdictions as in previous treaties, 'the linear boundary circumscribed the territorial claim completely.[113]

Third, *compulsory power* materialized contiguity as an ascribed physical and social reality. Contiguity was never an inherent feature of physical or legal geography – it was coercively engineered to satisfy the demands of geometric and cartographic world-making. That materialization involved a protracted history of social and political interventions by European rulers – spread over several centuries – which turned contiguous boundaries on maps into contiguous territorialities on the ground. It was a transformative process that – to use John Herz's words – was "neither easy, nor straight, nor short,"[114] since it involved remaking generic land to fit "within the languages of maps

objectification for the ... common soil and, reciprocally, acquires the human loyalty originally given to the soil ... Not only was the geo-body naturalized but it was also given what Clifford Geertz might call the primordial sentiment by the soil.

113 Muscarà, "Maps, Complexity, and the Uncertainty of Power," 369–70.

114 John H. Herz, "Rise and Demise of the Territorial State," *World Politics* 9, no. 4 (1957): 473–93, at 475.

so it could be carried on pieces of paper and made a public image."[115] As Jordan Branch explains, the upheavals and changes that ensued were nothing short of radical, since contiguity altered the meaning, inscriptions, and material practices behind territorial rule and, notably, statist territorialization:

> Frontier zones filled with enclaves and overlaps were "rationalized", or made linear ... This involved processes of fortification, internal homogenization and infrastructural development, and finally boundary demarcation. Cartography was an integral part of this process, although the visual language of maps preceded the implementation of territoriality by several centuries – in other words, existing customary authority structures within Europe were not immediately supplanted by map-based ideas. Once the ideational foundations of those traditional authorities were undermined by maps and their effects, however, old authorities were actively eliminated by centralizing powers ... The Swiss philosopher Emerich de Vattel, for example, wrote in the 1750s: "It is necessary to mark clearly and with precision the boundaries of territories." This was one of the first and most influential statements of ... boundary linearization. The ideas of territorial exclusivity were thus applied directly to boundary delimitation and demarcation.[116]

That salience of boundary linearization brings us, fourth and finally, to *institutional power*, as well as back to those prior questions that had spurred our series of steps. In a nutshell: How could such an ahistorical model of territorialization endure and persist across disciplinary theorizing and practice? I argue Koskenniemi's earlier demarcation (Section 4.4.1) once again becomes pertinent and useful, because it reveals

[115] Chandra Mukerji, "The Political Mobilization of Nature in Seventeenth-Century French Formal Gardens." *Theory and Society* 23, no. 5 (1994): 651–57, at 675:

> We tend to think of territoriality as a state of mind, a way of feeling about a portion of land, but the territoriality that developed ... was, first of all, a form of material practice, a way of acting on the land ... Land was politically mobilized as territory ... using engineering skills to reshape it and in the process alter its meaning. Land was measured and fitted within the languages of maps so it could be carried on pieces of paper and made a public image; it was marked and bounded with military fortresses so its breadth would be visible and its relations to state power tangible; it was suffused with humanly engineered waterways and roadways that gave it internal orderliness and tied it to an economic rationality ... Land was not just seen in a new way ... it was handled differently, and this made it represent simultaneously a new materialism and new political trajectory.

[116] Branch, *The Cartographic State*, 92.

something profound about institutional power even within the corpus of critical legal scholarship. Koskenniemi's demarcation relied on – albeit implicitly – a cultural and institutional norm deriving directly from geometric and cartographic world-making: boundary linearization. Its leveraging was more than a move of productive power, it was simultaneously a stroke of institutional power because boundary linearization had normative standing and influence in International Law – seemingly since Vattel.[117] As such, the norm possessed a seminal influence over how rule and territorialization *could be* perceived spatially and, in turn, made legally thinkable. What is more, as Thongchai Winichakul points out, boundary linearization also came with a conceptual teleology of profuse significance, because it projected contiguity as a manifest form and destination in the genesis of geo-institutional spaces:

> It has become an adequately meaningful sign in itself, not necessarily with a further reference to the territoriality of [a] nation. It no longer belongs to the cartographer, who has lost control over it completely. Independent of the object as well as its human creator, it becomes a common property ... [I]t is an object of reference in itself and can create more meanings and values beyond its origin ... [I]t monopolizes the means of human conceptualization ... to reign comfortably over the domain of knowledge.[118]

Accordingly, Koskenniemi's linearization between law and science was about more than just proper taxonomy. It reflected the way contiguity – in the words of Winichakul – had become "an object of reference in itself," framing and capturing the discipline's worldview of territorial, social, and even scholarly spaces. This is unsurprising since geometric and cartographic premises had preceded and preconditioned the discipline's formalization, and thus in turn nurtured the optics of international lawyers – much like most Europeans. That process driven by the types of power we traced earlier, and how they came to naturalize a contiguous worldview of the earth, rule, disciplinarity and, especially, territorialization. In sum, Koskenniemi's boundary linearization was about more than substantive differentiation, it enacted a teleology that permeated the discipline's institutional picture of spatial reality. A contiguous teleology that drew its lineage from the mapped world made by Cartesian science and

117 See John R. Searle, "Creating Institutional Facts," in *The Construction of Social Reality* (New York: Free Press, 1995), 31–58.

118 Winichakul, *Siam Mapped*, 138–39.

history, and much less Aristotelean metaphysics as Koskenniemi had claimed rhetorically.

Of course, one may rebut that Koskenniemi's delineation was more specific, because it focused on a narrower circumference of what international lawyers *do* in everyday legal praxis versus everyday scientific praxis, that is, the former focused on "rhetorical truths", while the latter "empirical truths."[119] However – broadening that aperture – even legal *doing* is performed in everyday settings of defined space and time, and thus reliant on (e.g., scientific) premises that shape empirical perceptions of what is here (space) and now (time) in any context of praxis. Consequently, the rootstock of geometric and cartographic science still influences those empirical perceptions of space and time during everyday legal praxis.

Therefore, I argue, something deeper also motivated the linearization of law as an autonomous "rhetorical practice." A historical trajectory that the discipline often addresses and concedes in terms of its Eurocentric "past," but usually with a restrained scrutiny into how that rootstock "past" lives – and arguably thrives – within a Cartesian-inspired spacing which continues to influence international legal theory and, notably, territorialization. As Arjun Appadurai reminds us, contiguity dominates the legally thinkable foremost because it is an extension – and scion – of the trajectorism that International Law emerged from spatially, and to this day the discipline remains entangled with conceptually, institutionally and – deeper still – teleologically:

> Trajectorism is a deeper epistemological and ontological habit, which always assumes that there is a cumulative journey from here to there … as natural as a river and as all-encompassing as the sky. Trajectorism is the idea that time's arrow inevitably has a telos, and in that telos are to be found all the significant patterns of change, process, and history. Modern social science inherits this telos and turns it into a method for the study of humanity … What I have called trajectorism is thus … a transverse spatial enactment of a defective vision of temporality in which time's arrow always has a single direction and a known destination. That destination is the world written in the image of Europe.[120]

[119] For a discussion of science as a rhetorical practice, see Bruno Latour, *Science in Action: How to Follow Scientists and Engineers through Society* (Cambridge: Harvard University Press, 1987).

[120] Arjun Appadurai, *The Future as Cultural Fact: Essays on the Global Condition* (London: Verso, 2013), 223–25.

4.5 *Juriscapes*: Theorizing Territorialization beyond Contiguity

That widened circumference of vision reveals how the ascription – and, arguably, "mummification" – of contiguity within International Law is bound to the trajectorism Appadurai describes. Territorial contiguity has not merely functioned as a spatial descriptor, but as an "arrow" animating a canonical worldview of legal space and territorial rule. Understanding statist territorialization, therefore, requires acknowledging the telos and directionality that trajectorism imparts – one that has insulated and reified contiguity as if it were an innate feature of legal rule.

This recognition helps explain how the geometric and cartographic premises underpinning modern legal geography have evaded sustained conceptual scrutiny. *Cartographic theory as practice*, operating as a subterranean rootstock within international legal thought, has been obscured from both the curriculum and the discipline's theoretical self-image. By broadening the circumference of vision as Appadurai does, what emerges is a more teleological but no less morphogenetic constitution behind international legal space, which the reign of spatial contiguity has obscured from the discipline's curriculum and, importantly, scope of theorizing.

Returning to our focal question – how could such an ahistorical model of territorialization endure? – the answer now appears straightforward: Contiguity has homogenized the social and legal imagination to such an extent that its conceptual and institutional standing feels, in Appadurai's terms, "as natural as a river and as all-encompassing as the sky." This helps account for the persistence of the "Territorial Trap" identified in Chapter 2, and why much cross-disciplinary work has either interrogated territory as a spatial concept or explored *deterritorialization* as an alternative. Saskia Sassen's work remains a touchstone here, not least in her argument that territory has "debordered" from its conventional alignment with territoriality:

> The question of a bordered territory as a parameter for authority has today entered a new phase ... State borders, with all their continuing formal weight and practical flexibility, are merely one of several key elements in a larger operational space that ... today deborders the interstate system ... It is a debordering that constitutes new types of bordered spaces inside national territory itself. These may be internal to a state's territory or cut across state

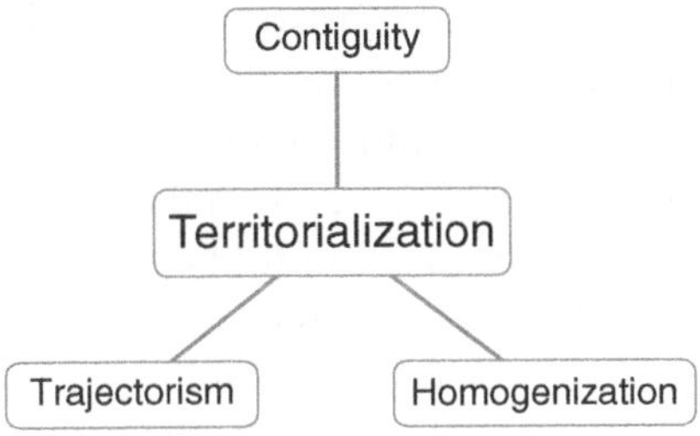

Figure 4.6 The meta-triad behind statist territorialization

borders. To give them conceptual visibility I argued that they are a distinct, albeit partial jurisdiction not generated by or dependent on the state itself ... They signal that territory, as an analytic category, cannot be confined to its national instantiation, even if this is the dominant one. This confinement keeps this category from working analytically. Conceived of as a complex capability, it can be shown to have more meanings than are signalled by prevalent notions of territoriality.[121]

Yet, through Kenneth Burke's *circumference of vision*, it becomes clear that the deeper constraint lies not in territorialization per se, but in the contiguous premise and trajectorism sedimented within it.[122] James C. Scott's reminder about the "tunnel vision" of schematic control also applies: Homogenization is not an accidental by-product, but a function of how territorialization has been disciplined into a singular, mapped archetype. This meta-triad of contiguity, trajectorism, and homogeneity did not appear instantaneously or concurrently (see Figure 4.6), rather it became assembled over time as statist territorialization emerged and became ever more fused with geometric and cartographic world-making. Conceptually, one may envision and trace that longer and morphogenetic process via a spectrum, where the Eurocentric notion of territorial rule and territorialization migrated gradually from heterogeneous and transversal spacing – which was topological and ascribed through lists of toponyms – to a contiguous and homogeneous archetype – shaped by an underlying *cartographic theory as practice*.

121 Sassen, "When Territory Deborders Territoriality," 38–39.
122 See Antje Wiener, "Enacting Meaning-in-Use: Qualitative Research on Norms and International Relations," *Review of International Studies* 35, no. 1 (2009): 175–93.

The risk in narrating this trajectory is to read it as an irreversible arrow – precisely the trap Appadurai warns against. In other words, whether territorial contiguity and homogenization are read as a singular destination, or as one historic exemplar reflective of conceptual and spatial changes inherent to the unfolding history of territorial rule and territorialization. That latter stance feeds into my motivation for proposing *juriscapes* as a conceptual counterpart vis-à-vis statist territoriality and jurisdiction. The theoretical purpose of *juriscapes* is to leverage the discipline's circumferential logic on spatial extension, and animate a more morphogenetic and thus transformational understanding of legal rule and, especially, territorialization.

As a dialectical counterpart, *juriscapes* seeks to disrupt the meta-triad sustaining *cartographic theory as practice*. It reorients inquiry from the binary of "is territoriality still relevant?" toward examining how boundary practices migrate – sometimes subtly, sometimes radically – between heterogeneous and homogeneous spatial orderings. This approach anticipates the emergence of novel geographies of legal rule that are neither contiguous nor uniformly homogeneous, and which resist easy reconciliation with the planimetric map. It offers a conceptual means to break down a *systems maintenance* approach that has predominated international legal theory, and thus led to the "circling" of novel theoretical and empirical insights around an ascribed statist nucleus (Section 4.1).

In sum, a widening gap is opening between the orthodoxy of territorial contiguity and the evolving realities of legal rule, where productive, institutional, structural, and compulsory forms of power remain dynamic, continually redrawing both the formal and informal boundaries of jurisdiction – regardless of whether those boundaries are contiguous. It is precisely into this gap that Chapter 5 turns, applying the *juriscapes* lens to empirical sites where legal authority is asserted, contested, and reconfigured. There, we will see how cartographic legacies still shape the optics of legal actors, even as emergent practices generate spatial orders that elude contiguous mapping – revealing forms of jurisdiction that are less territorial "containers" than pointillistic, networked, and topologically complex fields of legal rule.

5 Vidi et Vici

The Rise and Decline of Cartographic Rule

Cargo is an unlikely protagonist in the vocabulary of Public International Law. The term is more at home in private, trade, and commercial law, and many international lawyers might pass entire careers without uttering it. Yet cargo has an underexamined legacy in the origins of International Law. Europe's pursuit of cargo was a central impetus behind the cartographic world-making that defined how the discipline came to *see* – and order – the planet. My emphasis on cargo may seem bold, even counterintuitive, given how International Law's spatial imagination is more tied to this immobile noun: *land*. This reflects the rootstock of European legal philosophy, shaped by Vitoria,[1] Locke,[2] and Kant's[3] veneration of proprietary land through the concepts of property and possession. Land has held an iconic, even sublime, place in European legal imaginaries, a centrality captured by Carl Schmitt with unmistakable geopoetic force:

1 Francisco de Vitoria, "De Indis," in *Political Writings*, eds. Anthony Pagden and Jeremy Lawrance (Cambridge: Cambridge University Press, 1991), 290; Amaya Amell, *Francisco de Vitoria and the Evolution of International Law* (Lanham: Lexington Books, 2021), 85.

2 John Locke, *Two Treatises of Government*, 1823 ed., available at www.efm.bris.ac.uk/het/locke/government.pdf, Second Treatise, §33, 118; See James Tully, *A Discourse on Property: John Locke and His Adversaries* (Cambridge: Cambridge University Press, 2009), x:

> since the early nineteenth century … Locke's theory of property has played a major and contradictory role in western political thought. The early English and French socialists took it as the major philosophical foundation of modern socialism: the workers' right to the product of their labour and possession regulated by need. In the twentieth century the tables were turned; Locke became the spokesman for limited private property and, more recently, for unlimited private property.

3 See Jeffrey Edwards, "The Unity of All Places on the Face of the Earth," in *Reading Kant's Geography*, ed. Stuart Elden and Eduardo Mendieta (Albany: SUNY Press, 2011), 233–63; see also Arthur Ripstein, *Force and Freedom: Kant's Legal and Political Philosophy* (Cambridge: Harvard University Press, 2009), 95.

> The constitutive process of a land-appropriation is found at the beginning of the history of every settled people, every commonwealth, every empire ... [L]and-appropriation ... constitutes the original spatial order, the source of all further concrete order and all further law. It is the reproductive root in the normative order of history ... The traditional history of international law is ... a history of land-appropriations.[4]

But let us pause at Schmitt's passage for a moment. What if Schmitt's assertion puts the proverbial cart before the horse? What if the "reproductive root" is not land's proprietary essence, but the systems of knowledge that make land appropriable in the first place?[5] There is nothing inevitable about land appropriation[6] – unless one privileges a Eurocentric history of spatial practice.[7] What has been naturalized is a proprietary worldview: a teleology that made appropriation seem intrinsic to land, reinforced by geometric, planar, and cartographic depictions. As discussed in Chapter 4, boundaries acquire their "natural" geophysical and legal meanings through acts of social ascription. International Law is deeply entwined with that essentialized view of land as inherently proprietary.

So what does all this have to do with *cargo*? Quite a lot. To borrow a familiar investigative maxim: *Follow the ball.*[8] The rise of statist

[4] Schmitt, *The Nomos of the Earth*, 48.

[5] See Carol M. Rose, "Property as Storytelling: Perspectives from Game Theory, Narrative Theory, Feminist Theory," *Yale Journal of Law and the Humanities* 2 (1990): 37, 38: "[H]owever much these early modern theorists hoped to ground political economy as a science, one notices that their discussion of property at some point take a striking turn towards a narrative or 'diachronic' explanatory mode, treating property regimes as if they had origins as if they developed over time ... Locke used this narrative approach in his famous discussion of property in the Second Treatise of Government ... Locke's choice of a narrative mode is all the more striking because he appears to have been indifferent to the factual accuracy of the story as a genuine history."

[6] Agnew, "The Territorial Trap," 53, 55.

[7] See Marie-Eve Loiselle, *Building Walls, Constructing Identities: Legal Discourse and the Creation of National Borders* (Stanford: Stanford University Press, 2025), 30–31.

[8] See Michael Serres and Bruno Latour, *Conversations on Science, Culture, and Time*, trans. Roxanne Lapidus (Ann Arbor: University of Michigan Press, 1995), 108:

> Configurations and fixed places are important when the players don't move – just before the game begins, or when certain established positions are called for at various points in the game – scrimmages or line-outs. They begin to fluctuate as soon as the game begins, and the multiple and fluctuating ways

cartography coincided with – and was propelled by – Europe's early modern pursuit of cargo. The connection is even visible in the word itself. *Cargo* derives from *carraca* (Spanish) or *carrack* (English): a large, multi-masted sailing ship of the fifteenth and sixteenth centuries with a dedicated cargo hold (*nau* in Portuguese).[9] Christopher Columbus' flagship in 1492, the *Santa Maria*, was a 100-ton *carraca*. Vasco da Gama's expedition eastward in 1497 was also led by a *carraca*, the 120-ton *São Gabriel*.[10] That conjunction the *carraca* symbolizes is noteworthy because these vessels were both instruments of geographic exploration and of imperial appropriation – of mobile and immobile wealth alike.[11] The European desire to *know* the wider world converged with a drive to dominate the flows of commodities and goods.[12] Put simply: Follow the cargo, and you follow the rise and decline of cartographic rule.

This historic intertwining of cargo and cartographic world-making is rarely acknowledged in accounts of how the imperial teleology of appropriation shaped the mapping that public international lawyers inherited – and continue to work upon. Statist cartography was designed to facilitate appropriation on a planetary scale, parceling

of passing the ball are traced out. The ball is played, and the teams place themselves in relation to it, not vice versa. As a quasi object, the ball is the true subject of the game. It is like a tracker of the relations in the fluctuating collectivity around it.

9 See Malyn Newitt, *Navigations: The Portuguese Discoveries and the Renaissance* (London: Reaktion Books, 2023), 35: "Fourteenth- and fifteenth-century ship design was endlessly adapted to meet the different needs of warfare, cargo-carrying and navigation in the rough seas of the Atlantic."

10 Newitt, *Navigations*, 199.

11 As Beatriz Pastor Bodmer explains in *The Armature of Conquest: Spanish Accounts of the Discovery of America, 1492–1589* (Stanford: Stanford University Press, 1992), 38:

> The image of vast expanses of unknown lands, inhabited by prosperous, civilized, peace-loving people with a long tradition as tradesmen not only corresponded to Marco Polo's version of Asia but reflected the need for trade and new markets that Columbus's project promised to satisfy … After obtaining the support of the king and queen, he signed a contract under which he was granted important privileges but which also committed him to the achievement of certain results … By accepting the vessels and provisions from such investors, Columbus committed himself to find in the Indies or any other lands he discovered everything he had promised.

12 Nicolás Wey Gómez, *The Tropics of Empire: Why Columbus Sailed South to the Indies* (Cambridge: MIT Press, 2008), xiv.

land, water, and life into geometric units amenable to commodification. In this process, a planimetric and proprietary worldview came to be seen as a *natural* attribute of the Earth's physicality. The cartographic premises of International Law were thus constructed within a social order that had already encoded appropriation into a naturalized, two-dimensional vision of the planet.

Looping back to Schmitt, his emphasis on land appropriation obscures how ontology disciplines perceptions of spatial order – including his own *concrete view*. The "concreteness" of land was itself a product of productive power (Chapter 3): a late fifteenth-century convergence of profit-consciousness, cargo-seeking, and scientific-cartographic representation.[13] The planispheres and "World Maps" that followed represented not neutral knowledge, but regulated visions of the Earth in service to imperial aims: to see, traverse, and ultimately *claim* an appropriable planet. This cartographic rule projected *approprio-centrism* – the presumption that every space could and should be appropriated – onto every feature and particle of the Earth's materiality.[14]

Fast forward to the present, and the so-called end of geography declared by Daniel Bethlehem (Chapter 2) signals a profound ontological problem for that cartographic world. Statist cartography is faltering in its "world-configuring function"[15] in the face of unruly

[13] See Branch, *The Cartographic State*, 100:

> The European expansion of commercial activity and political power that began with the late fifteenth-century Iberian voyages to both east and west was tied closely to cartographic developments. These links went well beyond simply using maps in navigation ... new mapping techniques were central to how European political actors supported their claims to new territories, trade routes, or commercial privileges ... It was the need to divide, claim, and assign dominion over the unknown spaces of the New World that drove the first use of the abstract mathematical and geometric methods that were newly available for understanding and claiming territories.

[14] This reflecting what Peter Jackson calls maps of meaning, Peter Jackson, *Maps of Meaning: An Introduction to Cultural Geography* (London: Unwin Hyman, 1989), 185–86: "Like any cartographic image, 'maps of meaning' codify knowledge and represent it symbolically. But, like other maps, they are ideological instruments in the sense that they project a preferred reading of the material world, with prevailing social relations mirrored in the depiction of physical space."

[15] See Étienne Balibar, *Politics and the Other Scene*, trans. Christine Jones et al. (London: Verso, 2002), 79.

mobilities – capital, fentanyl, migrants, trade, viruses – and proliferating, fluid boundaries. Today's legal geographies are increasingly overlapping, polysemic, and heterogeneous. Material appropriation, wealth accumulation, and coercive power now operate through elastic, para-jurisdictional networks. This is significant not only for international lawyers but across legal disciplines, each of which has long relied on the meta-presumption that statist cartography is a given, transhistorical representation – a scientifically vetted "mirror of nature." Yet no human, social, or cultural geography is ever given or transhistorical. Change is the only constant, and it is often diachronic. In contemporary terms: there is no "future-proofing" a geographic worldview – only a shifting spectrum of spatial relevance and social weight.

Accordingly, this chapter relates the histories of imperial cargo and statist cartography to unpack a cartographic world that few lawyers appreciate was, in essence, an ontological means of planetary appropriation. Using cargo as the thematic thread, it pursues two related aims: (1) to show how mapped rule first emerged alongside the imperial pursuit of global cargo; and (2) to explain how mapped representation is now destabilized by geopolitical and geo-economic practices organized around electronic coordinates and intermodal cargo. The analysis proceeds with the awareness that geographic boundaries – like law – have always been engineered by someone, for some purpose, and under some patronage.[16] Scientific maps are no exception.

The first part resituates statist cartography as the outgrowth of a knowledge system that, between the fifteenth and nineteenth centuries, structured the possibilities for seeing, knowing, and acting upon the Earth – sponsored by profit consciousness and cargo seeking, scaled to Europe's global circumnavigation and proprietary claims. The second part turns to the present, where this mapped world is being disrupted by a new global logic of profit consciousness and appropriation. Here, the emblematic technology is no longer the *carraca* but the standardized *shipping container* – millions of them circulating in a planetary network. This shift marks the transition from an imperial cartographic planet to a pointillistic geography that empowers transterritorial appropriation and rule, yet resists easy translation into the representational claims of incumbent cartography.

[16] Pickles, *A History of Spaces*, 107–08.

5.1 The "Business of Seeing" and Ruling

International lawyers, like all observers, are governed by practices of seeing. The worlds we claim to see and act upon are never encountered in a raw, unmediated form; they are filtered through concepts, maps, models, tools, and frameworks. They constitute the practices of seeing which make the world "what we see it to be" in any given moment and context. As Nicholas Onuf underlines: "the worlds that we make for ourselves ... look the way that they do because of the ways that we go about the business of seeing ... Different worlds call for, and depend on, different ways of world-making. Scholars have always raised questions about accepted ways of seeing."[17]

This connection between perception and legal ordering has received renewed attention in international legal scholarship. David Kennedy has underscored how lawyers and other experts each struggle to impose their own professional image of "the world" onto contemporary political and legal realities.[18] Martti Koskenniemi – working more historically – has traced how the "international" has been shaped by legal imagination, framed and constrained by prevailing vocabularies and established assumptions.[19] These interventions are important because they foreground a dimension that doctrinal practice too often brackets out: the intimate connection between how international lawyers *see*, the worlds they *imagine*, and the worlds they then *act upon*.

This is not entirely new ground. Kennedy and Koskenniemi's insights echo Benedict Anderson's earlier appeal – directed at historians, sociologists, and anthropologists – to treat nations as "imagined communities."[20] By extension, international lawyers themselves form an imagined community,[21] shaped by dominant images, pictures, maps, and theories that cohere into a collective vision of – borrowing John Ruggie's phrase – "what makes the world hang together."[22]

17 Onuf, *Making Sense, Making Worlds*, 26–27.

18 David Kennedy, *A World of Struggle: How Power, Law, and Expertise Shape Global Political Economy* (Princeton: Princeton University Press, 2016), 90–93.

19 Martti Koskenniemi, *To the Uttermost Parts of the Earth: Legal Imagination and International Power, 1300–1870* (Cambridge: Cambridge University Press, 2022), 1–3.

20 See Anderson, *Imagined Communities*.

21 Anderson, *Imagined Communities*.

22 See Ruggie, "What Makes the World Hang Together?".

This governing imagination is not a side effect of professional life; it is constitutive of the discipline's sense of its object.

Yet such a prospect – that international lawyers are governed by ways of seeing and imagining – sits uneasily with a longstanding formalist project within the field.[23] Doctrinal labor has often been oriented toward professionalizing International Law's boundaries: defending its relevance *internally* against other branches of law and *externally* to the social sciences and to society at large.[24] This will to professionalize empowered a largely European oligarchy of international lawyers to fence the discipline's subject matter, casting themselves as surveyors of inter-state rules, rights, and obligations. In this self-image, the lawyer becomes a kind of legal geologist – mapping normative topologies and topographies, charting fault lines, and diagnosing tectonic shifts when conflicts erupt.

Sticking with this geological metaphor, such surveying presumes a relatively fixed, inherent, and timeworn terrain of legal order.[25] Or, as Carl Schmitt phrased it, a *nomos* of the Earth *seen*, imagined, and believed to provide "an original distribution of land."[26] But this raises a crucial question: what is an "original" distribution, and according to whom? The perception of space – whether land, sea, disciplinary boundaries, or national frontiers – is always mediated socially and symbolically.[27] The so-called Archimedean point from which such distributions are *seen* is itself constructed, not discovered. What Schmitt, and many international lawyers after him, neglect is that land appropriation is inseparable from the social processes of inscription and land drawing, not from any transhistorical lines of geophysical division. As Tania Murray Li has observed: "[land] is an assemblage of

23 Thomas Skouteris, "The Force of a Doctrine: Article 38 of the PCIJ Statute and the Sources of International Law," in *Events: The Force of International Law*, ed. Fleur Johns et al. (London: Routledge, 2011), 72–75.

24 See H. L. A. Hart, *The Concept of Law*, 2nd ed., ed. Joseph Raz and Penelope A. Bulloch (Oxford: Oxford University Press, 1997); Joseph Raz, *The Authority of Law: Essays on Law and Morality* (Oxford: Clarendon Press, 1983); Jean d'Aspremont, *Formalism and the Sources of International Law: A Theory of the Ascertainment of Legal Rules* (Oxford: Oxford University Press, 2011).

25 See Anne Orford's critique of how international lawyers have ceased to reflect on spatial ordering: Anne Orford, "Regional Orders, Geopolitics, and the Future of International Law," *Current Legal Problems* 74, no. 1 (2021): 149–76.

26 Schmitt, *The Nomos of the Earth*, 68.

27 See Lefebvre, *The Production of Space*, 1–23.

materialities, relations, technologies and discourses that have to be pulled together and made to align."[28]

In other words, particular actors, identities, interests, images, and theories assemble the very *possibility* of seeing and knowing a given world. Such a "knowledge space" is animated by specific world-making aims, a preferred depiction of material reality, and social judgments about what counts as *real* perception. The ultimate effect, as Jean-Jacques Rousseau warned, is to render an act of social land drawing as though it were a mirror of nature, masking an arbitrary appropriation as timeless truth:

> The first man who, having fenced off a plot of land [*enclose un terrain*], thought of saying, *this is mine*, and found people simple enough to believe him, was the real founder of civil society ... Beware of listening to this impostor: You are lost if you forget the fruits of the earth belong to all and that the Earth [*Terre*] belongs to no one.[29]

Seeing, then, is never neutral. It is a practice embedded in structures of power, designed to make certain worlds imaginable and others invisible. The "business of seeing" in International Law has always been bound up with the business of ruling.

5.1.1 Knowledge and Disciplinary World-Making

This brings us back to the *reification illusion* discussed in Chapter 4 – an essential communicative and performative effect that sustains any world-making project. The same illusion is visible in how many imagine the "map" of university disciplines as if it reflected an inherent geography of knowledge.[30] Yet the label *discipline* does not signify a physical geography. Rather, it denotes a bounded economy of scholarly labor – an artefact of modern institutional organization – which only became globally predominant around the mid-twentieth century.

28 Tania Murray Li, "What Is Land? Assembling a Resource for Global Investment," *Transactions of the Institute of British Geographers* 39, no. 4 (2014): 589–602, at 589.

29 Jean-Jacques Rousseau, "Discourse on the Origin and Foundation of Inequality," in *The Discourses and Other Early Political Writings*, ed. and trans. Victor Gourevitch (Cambridge: Cambridge University Press, 1997), 164.

30 Andrew Abbott, *The System of Professions: An Essay on the Division of Expert Labor* (Chicago: University of Chicago Press, 1988), 36.

In other words, the perceived geography of disciplines reflects less an inherent division of knowledge and more a world reified through the vision of the discipline as a self-contained, essential unit of knowledge.[31]

The historical details of this transformation exceed the scope of the present chapter, but one feature is worth underscoring: Appropriation has also shaped disciplinary world-making, albeit through a different kind of figurative vessel. In the late nineteenth century, American universities began creating departments and awarding "disciplinary degrees."[32] Curricula were restructured so that a disciplinary "major" became the organizing principle for university education. Over time, these discipline-denominated degrees became standardized and spread internationally, structuring enrolment patterns and professional training worldwide.[33] Today, millions of students are annually "disciplined" by universities in this way.

This process had two major ontological implications for scholarship. First, it brought an end to the Renaissance's encyclopedic vision of knowledge as a universal, listed whole. Under disciplinization, each field had to achieve visibility and relevance to maintain its cartographic position on the university (or campus) map.[34] Second, the survival of each discipline came to depend on cultivating the perceived value of both its knowledge and its diploma as coveted assets for social appropriation.[35] Knowledge thus assumed a more spatial and jurisdictional quality, as disciplinization effectively mapped a seemingly self-evident geography of disciplines.[36]

Yet this disciplinary geography is as illusory as it is real – the very hallmark of the reification illusion. Each discipline is constituted by scholars, students, and practitioners who continually reproduce its identity, curricula, and methods, thereby constructing *their own world* of knowledge.[37] In doing so, they generate a *discipline effect*:

31 Michèle Lamont, "On Disciplinary Cultures," in *How Professors Think: Inside the Curious World of Academic Judgment* (Cambridge: Harvard University Press, 2009), 53–57.
32 Andrew Abbott, "The Context of Disciplines," in *Chaos of Disciplines* (Chicago: University of Chicago Press, 2001), 123–25.
33 Abbott, "The Context of Disciplines," 127.
34 Abbott, "The Context of Disciplines," 126.
35 Abbott, *System of Professions*, 55–56.
36 Andrew Abbott, "Things of Boundaries," *Social Research* 62, no. 4 (1995): 857–82, at 860.
37 For more on world-making, see: Onuf, "Worlds of Our Making," 21–39.

a cognitive form and collective belief that the discipline possesses a social reality, a "thingness," and a pre-given body of knowledge mapped through its propinquity – much like contiguity in territorial mapping.[38]

In truth, the nature and boundaries of disciplines are historically contingent, mutable, and porous. A discipline is not a transhistorical container but a late modern medium for ordering the scholarly world. Like other modern social entities, disciplines leave an enduring legacy of reifying consciousness and imagined thingness[39] – projecting the perception of a coherent, enduring world of knowledge.[40] In this, they share notable affinities with other world-making projects, especially in their ability to consolidate a ruling spatial image across internal and external audiences.

The result is paradoxical: University maps are read as if they displayed inherent disciplinary divisions, yet few appreciate the degree of artifice involved in producing and sustaining that divided perception of knowledge.[41] The established picture of disciplines as geometrically bounded spaces did not emerge from a transhistorical scheme of knowledge differentiation. It arose from a mapped medium and imaginary that has shaped the modern *seeing* of geophysical, social, and scholarly spaces alike.[42] This is part of a wider territorialization of vision – an appropriating medium that has reduced much of social perception to cartographic form.[43] As David Turnbull observes:

> The most common metaphor for scientific knowledge or theories [is] the map ... Virtually every domain ... is now found to have a spatial dimension through the process of mapping. In the social sciences, spatial explanations are complementing the historical; in the cultural and literary arenas,

38 Lamont, *How Professors Think*, 53–57.
39 Abbott, "Things of Boundaries," 860.
40 See Lefebvre, *Production of Space*, 82–83.
41 Abbott, "Things of Boundaries," 867–69.
42 Hilary Putnam, *Reason, Truth and History* (Cambridge: Cambridge University Press, 1981), 49: "the world consists of some fixed totality of mind-independent objects. There is exactly one true and complete description of 'the way the world is'. Truth involves some sort of correspondence relation between words or thought-signs and external things and sets of things." See also Martin Jay, *Downcast Eyes: The Denigration of Vision in Twentieth-Century French Thought* (Berkeley: University of California Press, 1993), 14.
43 Robert Frodeman, *Sustainable Knowledge: A Theory of Interdisciplinarity* (Basingstoke: Palgrave Macmillan, 2014), 18–22.

cartographic and spatial tropes abound. The spatialization of knowledge is one of the defining characters of … modernism.[44]

While Turnbull casts this dynamic in terms of modernism, the underlying point is more general: The mapping metaphor has become pervasive across scholarly and cultural domains, shaping the way knowledge itself is imagined. The dynamic of disciplinary mapping is therefore neither isolated nor unique. It belongs to a broader habit of translating complex, heterogeneous realities into ordered, bounded spaces – whether those spaces are intellectual, social, or territorial. The cartographic imagination that disciplines the university is structurally akin to the cartographic imagination that has long disciplined International Law. Both operate through practices of abstraction, projection, and boundary-drawing, presenting socially produced geographies as natural and inevitable.

In the case of International Law, statist cartography emerged as one of the most consequential of these mapping projects. As Turnbull suggests of knowledge more generally, maps do not simply describe; they impose spatial form. Statist maps, like disciplinary maps, were thus performative – producing the very order they claimed to depict. And like the disciplinary "campus map," the World Map of states has sustained its authority by embedding itself in the professional common sense of those who navigate and reproduce it. This parallel underscores that the history of statist cartography is also a history of disciplinary world-making: A system of knowledge that enabled jurists to see, know, and act upon the Earth in ways that reinforced imperial appropriation and the juridical order built in its wake.

5.1.2 *Cargo and Imperial World-Making*

Recognizing that all geographies are social representations and historical productions raises several key questions: How did this particular mapped worldview come into being? What historical context defined its initial emergence, and with what social motivations? What combination of actors, practices, and technologies – produced this mapped perspective and entrenched its predominance?

44 David Turnbull, "Cartography and Science in Early Modern Europe: Mapping the Construction of Knowledge Spaces," *Imago Mundi* 48 (1996): 5–24, at 6.

The familiar response to such questions is often a celebratory "parade" of canonical maps: Ptolemy's grids, Vespucci's New World projections, Waldseemüller's naming of America, Piri Reis's Ottoman charts, Agnese's atlases, Münster's cosmographies, Mercator's cylindrical projections, and Ortelius's *Theatrum Orbis Terrarum*.[45] But, like most parades, this sequence is designed to inspire awe and imaginative escape while distracting from the political economy in which it was embedded. In this case, it diverts attention from the profit-conscious and cargo-seeking teleology that propelled the making of a cartographic worldview. The deeper story is how mobile and immobile appropriation drove the depiction of the planet as if it were mapped *by nature*, erasing ontological distinctions between brute materiality, social representation, and the map as a medium. As the section title suggests, this was quite literally a "business of seeing," where European imperial appropriation and cargo-seeking intersected with the emergence of mapped rule.

5.1.2.1 The *Carraca*, Ptolemy, and the Birth of a Mapped World

This is why the *carraca* emerges with such significance for the making of mapped images that public lawyers still rely upon today. The curious thing is the direct connection between the *carraca*, cargo, and cartography has been in plain sight as far as recorded history is concerned.[46] However, what likely obscured visibility was that related pieces of knowledge were fragmented across disciplinary boundaries, which meant heavy interdisciplinary investment was required to draw-out connections and underline pertinence. Investment that, notably, ran the risk of undermining a vulnerable – liberal – separation between international public versus international private law.

[45] John P. Snyder, *Flattening the Earth: Two Thousand Years of Map Projections* (Chicago: University of Chicago Press, 1993), 53–54.

[46] See Sarah A. Radcliffe on geography's "sanctioned ignorance" in *Decolonizing Geography: An Introduction* (Cambridge: Polity, 2022), 82: "Whether in the sixteenth or twenty-first centuries, colonial-modern structures of power result in highly-selective and skewed collections of knowledge and relations with the world … The postcolonial theorist Gayatri Spivak critiques this outcome, suggesting that globally powerful actors are in a position to *ignore* other knowledges because of the latter appear to be irrelevant to the world."

In short: World Maps emerged to serve an imperial aim – depicting an unfolding non-European world in a medium that could facilitate profit-consciousness, appropriation, and cargo extraction.[47] Whether explicitly or implicitly, that cartographic legacy continues to shape how international lawyers perceive "legal geography," with too little reflection on the normativity embedded in those perceptions. To "tour" those motives, as Michel de Certeau has emphasized, serves to illuminate normative "itineraries" that mapped the world, which the map's tableau gradually "pushes away" into pre-history: "the map … eliminates little by little … the practices that produce it."[48]

Touring those practices reveals the "gluing" of legal perception to a planetary conquest enacted by imperial mapping. Yet, it is a metaphorical gluing few lawyers have noticed or sought to interrogate, despite the capture it has exacted over legal perceptions of geography. What gluing, concretely? It relates to a history you are likely familiar with from "formal schooling,"[49] but with the problem that such teaching typically delivers an abridged version. In other words, we return to the earlier mentioned *Santa Maria*, focusing on its significance not as a "ship of discovery" but as a *carraca*, designed for long-haul transportation of extracted cargo from distant shores.

47 Branch, *Cartographic State*, 106: "After their 'discovery' and increasing exploitation in the 1490s and early 1500s, the Americas were not easily incorporated into European geographic and cosmological thinking … Ptolemaic mapping, in fact, offered a particularly useful means of integrating these and other discoveries into the existing knowledge and belief structure of Europeans."

48 Michel de Certeau, *The Practice of Everyday Life*, trans. Steven Rendall (Berkeley: University of California Press, 1984), 120–21:

> [W]e can compare the combination of "tours" and "maps" in everyday stories with the manner in which, over the past five centuries, they have been interlaced and then slowly dissociated in literature and scientific representations of space. In particular, if one takes the "map" in its current geographical form, we can see that in the course of the period marked by the birth of modern scientific discourse (i.e., from the fifteenth to the seventeenth century) the map has slowly disengaged itself from the itineraries that were the conditions of its possibility … [T]he important thing here is the erasure of the itineraries … The map … pushes away into its prehistory or in its posterity, as if into the wings, the operations of which it is the result or the necessary condition. It remains alone on the stage. The tour describers have disappeared.

49 Koskenniemi, *To the Uttermost Parts of the Earth*, 1.

One of the defining impacts of the "voyages of discovery"[50] is what David Harvey labels time-space compression.[51] At first, this term appears overwhelmingly technical, but a closer look reveals similarity with what many lawyers do in practice vis-à-vis making legal sense of complex spatial arrangements, whether in, for example, multinational contracting, maritime disputes, or transnational litigation.[52] Harvey defined the term as follows: "processes that so revolutionize the objective qualities of space and time that we are forced to alter ... how we represent the world to ourselves."[53] Prior to the voyages of discovery, European understandings of – what we today call – "space" were defined by a patchwork of definite and reverent places, imagined as discrete human worlds and related via cosmologies that answered to "some external authority, heavenly hosts, or more sinister figures of myth and imagination."[54] As Jens Bartelson helps illustrate:

From a biblical perspective, the ocean literally marked the end of the known and inhabitable world. The Latin and Greek terms most frequently used to describe this world was *orbis terrarum* or *oikoumene*. The former referred to the three interconnected continents – Europe, Asia, and Africa – which were surrounded by an impenetrable ocean beyond which life was thought to be unlikely or even impossible. At the center of the *orbis terrarum* was Jerusalem to be found, The Holy City. Ideally, the borders of the *orbis terrarum* ought to coincide with those of the *oikoumene*: even though primarily a geographical concept, the *oikoumene*, "in its most essential meaning, can be defined as a region made coherent by the intercommunication of its inhabitants, such that ... no tribe or race is completely cut off from the people beyond it". But beyond the *oikoumene* no human life was to be found. Both concepts thus restricted the habitat of humanity to the northern hemisphere, since the southern hemisphere consisted of a torrid zone, at the end of which the quasi-mythological Antipodes were to be found. The question whether the latter really existed and were inhabited, and if

[50] The label, "voyages of discovery," is Eurocentric and colonial in origin and application, and is tied to the colonial *doctrines of discovery* that designated non-European lands on the Earth's surface as *terra nullius* or nobody's land. See Radcliffe, *Decolonizing Geography*, 15, 115.

[51] David Harvey, *The Condition of Postmodernity* (Oxford: Blackwell, 1990), 240.

[52] See A. Claire Cutler and Thomas Dietz, eds., *The Politics of Private Transnational Governance by Contract* (London: Routledge, 2017).

[53] Harvey, *Condition of Postmodernity*, 240.

[54] Harvey, *Condition of Postmodernity*, 240–41.

inhabited, whether by men or by monstrous races, was subject to considerable debate during the Middle Ages.[55]

The rediscovery and Latin translation of Ptolemy's *Geographia* in 1406 set in train a radical reconstruction of those European views,[56] notably because it suggested the Earth should be *seen* as a gridded space rather than a collage of distinct places.[57] Specifically, the *Geographia* insisted on an "astronomer's vision", which meant all places could be located on an abstract grid by viewing the stars above.[58] It offered a mode of geographic representation that plotted static locations on the Earth's surface. Furthermore, Ptolemy's grid made possible a *compression* of the whole world using a mathematical framework (equipollent-coordinate logic), fixing all places with coordinates and thus more calculable distances.[59]

This Ptolemaic grid was an extraordinary instrument of productive power (see Chapter 3) and world-making in multiple senses.[60] First, it negated a long-held Aristotelean belief – sustained by medieval *mappaemundi* and portolan charts – that the Mediterranean basin marked an inherent confine for human life: "The sea surrounds the earth like the

55 Bartelson, "The Social Construction of Globality," 223–24; see also Wey Gómez, *Tropics of Empire*, xv.

56 Francisco Contente Domingues and Luís Filipe Barreto, "The Recovery of Ptolemy's Geography in Renaissance Italy and Its Impact in Spain and Portugal in the Period of the Discoveries," in *Geography, Cartography and Nautical Science in the Renaissance*, ed. W. G. L. Randles (Aldershot: Ashgate, 2000), 145–51.

57 This finite nature of places is describes as follows Harvey, *Condition of Postmodernity*, 240–41:

> In the relatively isolated worlds ... of European feudalism, place assumed a definite legal, political, and social ... autonomy ... inside roughly given territorial boundaries ... The finite centred qualities of place ... matched time-honoured routines of daily life set in the infinity and unknowability of "enduring time"... Medieval parochialism and superstition were paralleled by an "easy and hedonistic psycho-physiological" approach to spatial representation. The medieval artist 'believed that he could render what he saw before his eyes convincingly by representing what it felt like to walk about, experience structures, almost tactilely, frame many different angles'.

58 Denis Cosgrove, *Apollo's Eye: A Cartographic Genealogy of the Earth in the Western Imagination* (Baltimore: Johns Hopkins University Press, 2001), 105.

59 Philip E. Steinberg, "Sovereignty, Territory, and the Mapping of Mobility: A View from the Outside," *Annals of the Association of American Geographers* 99, no. 3 (2009): 467–95, at 477.

60 Pickles, *History of Spaces*, 83, 90.

horizon, and ships cannot cross it, and it is unknown where it ends."[61] As Jean Bodin noted – a century after *Geographia*'s publication – charts inspired by Ptolemaic space extended navigation such that European ships could "traverse the whole earth every year in frequent voyages and lead colonies into another world ... in order to open up ... an abundant and profitable commerce ... as if in one and the same city-state."[62] Second, the grid diminished the ontological distinction between land and sea, rendering the ocean not as a forbidding void but as a traversable surface akin to land – a space for commercial routes and imperial acquisitions. Maritime corridors and distant ports became mappable commodities in themselves. Third, Ptolemy's system equipped the rising territorial state with a tool for projecting its authority onto a "terraqueous globe."[63] World Maps and spheres could now depict imperial ambitions with mathematical precision, lending them the veneer of scientific objectivity. In this way, coordinates became not only navigational aids but also instruments of geopolitical inscription, embedding imperial claims within an ostensibly neutral geometric order.

This convergence of maritime technology (*carraca*), navigational science (Ptolemaic coordinates), and imperial ambition generated more than just improved seafaring capacity – it laid the groundwork for what would become statist cartography, the dominant optic through which International Law would *see* and organize the planet. By rendering the globe as a measurable, gridded totality, the Ptolemaic framework offered early modern European states not only a tool for navigation, but a universal representational language for spatial claim-making. In practice, the grid served as both a medium of projection – displaying expansive territorial ambitions – and a means of inscription, embedding those ambitions into the very geometry of the Earth's depiction. The map thus ceased to be merely a record of space; it became an instrument of spatial rule.

The *carraca*'s long-range cargo capacity amplified this process. It transformed distant, previously inaccessible coasts into integral nodes in emerging global circuits of trade and extraction. The capacity to transport substantial quantities across oceans meant that mapped

[61] Donald S. Johnson, *Phantom Islands of the Atlantic: The Legends of Seven Lands That Never Were* (Fredericton: Goose Lane Editions, 1994), 38.

[62] Jean Bodin, *Method for the Easy Comprehension of History*, trans. Beatrice Reynolds (New York: W. W. Norton, 1969), 301.

[63] Bartelson, *Becoming International*, 34.

points – ports, anchorages, trading posts – could be rapidly transformed into sites of enduring imperial presence. In effect, the grid and the ship coproduced a spatial reality in which possession and movement became mutually reinforcing logics: fixed coordinates justified claims, while mobile cargo sustained them. As imperial powers refined this practice, the cartographic image of "the world" began to naturalize a proprietary worldview. Every coastline, island, and inland region could be slotted into a preexisting geometric schema, ready to be claimed, divided, and ruled. Over time, this representational logic – rooted in the interplay of technological possibility and imperial desire – became so deeply embedded in legal and political reasoning that it appeared self-evident.

For International Law, this matters profoundly. The discipline inherited not simply a set of maps, but an entire epistemic apparatus that equated the visibility of a place on a map with its susceptibility to legal appropriation. Jurisdictional thinking, as it evolved in the early modern period, became conditioned gradually by the pairing marriage of imperial teleology with cartographic claiming. To *see* space in legal terms increasingly meant to see it as the map saw it: contiguous, divisible, and subject to bounded allocation.

By the nineteenth century, this optic was firmly entrenched. Statist cartography, perfected through centuries of maritime expansion and colonial conquest, became the default representational mode of the international legal order. The world was *pictured* – and therefore governed – through a grid that had originated in the confluence of ancient astronomical theory, Renaissance mathematical abstraction, and the brute commercial imperatives of the cargo ship. The irony is that this supposedly timeless and objective image of "the world" was in fact the historical artifact forged in the holds of the *carraca*, plotted on Ptolemaic coordinates, and financed by the relentless pursuit of cargo. What International Law came to treat as a given was, in truth, a carefully engineered representational regime, designed to facilitate and legitimize a planetary appropriation project.

5.1.2.2 The *Casas*, the Planispheres, and Cassini's Globe

Maps – whatever their technical sophistication – only become *world-making* when they attain the status of common knowledge, commanding widespread credibility as the frame within which "the world" is seen and known. As David Turnbull explains, this feat of social perception is as difficult to achieve in practice as it reads in theory: "Maps connect heterogeneous and disparate entities, events, locations and phenomena, enabling us to see patterns that are not otherwise visible ... They connect ... the social order with an apparently natural order, maps 'naturalise the arbitrary.'"[64] The depth of that challenge likely explains why dedicated bureaucracies emerged in imperial Portugal and Spain at the start of the sixteenth century (post-Columbus), which were tasked with producing and regulating what amounted to the first institutionalized mappings of the wider world.[65] These institutional bureaucracies were located in Lisbon (*Casa da Mina*) and Seville (*Casa de la Contratación*) respectively, housed in the Boards of Trade but labelled notably as "hydrographic" – and not cartographic – offices.[66]

The official mandate of both *Casas* was to manage a rapidly expanding world of cargo, carried by rival fleets of *carraca*.[67] In concrete terms, their hydrographic work aimed to protect trade monopolies and secure import taxes from the New World and East Indies.[68]

64 Turnbull, "Cartography and Science in Early Modern Europe," 7.

65 I use the term "mappings" loosely in this subsection because the *Padreo Real* and *Padron Real* were not geometric maps, since they were not based on a grid or organized formally by coordinate geometry and mathematical calculation. At best, they were hybrid and evolving Portolan Charts that mixed navigational experiences and local knowledges with Ptolemaic insight.

66 Branch, *Cartographic State*, 105:

> The mapping of oceanic voyages and discoveries thus quickly captured the attention of the governments of Portugal and Spain, both which created institutions for consolidating, managing, and securing cartographic knowledge: the Casa da Mina in Lisbon and the Casa de la Contratación in Seville ... In particular, both institutions were meant to create, update, and keep secret "master maps" of their respective overseas empires.

67 See Edward L. Stevenson, "The Geographical Activities of the Casa de la Contratación," *Annals of the Association of American Geographers* 17, no. 1 (1927): 39–59, at 41:

> All maritime affairs, in the broadest sense of the term, fell to its jurisdiction in the passing years, including the direct regulation of overseas trade and commercial relations, the examination of pilots and masters and the granting of license to them, the charting of all the new regions from the detailed geographical records which it was demanded should be most carefully made and fully reported by those who had visited them, the formulation and the supervision of laws of navigation with an especial reference to the navigation of the western seas.

68 Stevenson, "The Geographical Activities of the Casa de la Contratación," 41.

In practice, however, their remit was far broader and – by contemporary standards – deeply interdisciplinary. The voyages of discovery generated valuable cargo as well as large amounts of prized information from the "discovered" world, with the latter coming in diverse fragments that somehow had to be assembled and comprehended. The *Casas* operated like early modern intelligence agencies dedicated to schematize spatial information for the exclusive benefit of the crown, in an evolving context where spatial knowledge about the wider world had become highly strategic for the accumulation of trade (i.e., cargo), wealth, and power.[69] As Philip Steinberg summarized aptly, Portuguese and Spanish conquerors celebrated less that "they had found a distant land" and much more how "they had discovered a way to get there."[70]

The big challenge, however, was schematizing "how to get there" entailed much more than simply collating information. There was little prior experience or knowledge on how to rationalize spatial knowledge about a finite globe, and especially without the geopoetry of mythology or religion that previously had been used to make world images stick emotively. What is more, the information the *Casas* received were a complex mass of rough sketches, vague logbooks, cluttered diaries, diverse instrument notes, contrasting testimonials, and – myriad – theories as well as tales,[71] which all had to be reconciled and processed in some way into licensed charts, standardized tables, and

[69] See Newitt, *Navigations*, 83, 242; see also Bailey W. Diffie, "Foreigners in Portugal and the 'Policy of Silence,'" *Terrae Incognitae* 1, no. 1 (1960): 23–32.

[70] Steinberg, "Sovereignty, Territory, and the Mapping of Mobility," 481.

[71] See Stevenson, "The Geographical Activities of the Casa de la Contratación," 42:

> Information had been received of the use of many charts by different masters, charts differing, the one from the other in the record of the geographical location of lands and islands in the Indies, it was further ordained that a general or model map should be; made to be called a *Padron Real* or Pattern Map, and to that end the several officials of the Casa were directed to call together all pilots of marked ability to assist in its construction. Pilots were not to be permitted to make use of any other map than this, and they were directed, upon finding new islands or lands, new ports or bays, or any other thing-currents, or tides, head-land or mountains-which might serve the purpose of subsequent identification of localities, to enter the same in the copy of the Padron Real which they carried, reporting all such entries made on return to Seville, but nothing should be inserted that was not properly attested and sworn to. This decree seems to mark the real beginning of an interesting development in Spain's orderly handling of her New World affairs.

certified instruments.[72] In effect, the Portuguese and Spanish crowns had initiated an unprecedented mega-project of ontological proportions, which aimed to accumulate and regulate all contemporary knowledge regarding the globe's surface.[73] But, as David Turnbull explains once more, the scale of literal world-making that this had necessitated would involve: "a complex degree of heterogeneous engineering ... that brought together a range of experts (cosmographers, astronomers, navigators and pilots, ship's masters, instrument makers and cartographers) and a variety of instruments, navigational techniques, tables and methods of calculation, as well as the diverse observations and practical experiences of all kinds of mariners."[74]

Ultimately, the two rival *Casas* succeeded in producing and safeguarding what were de jure the first respective "maps of empire" (*Padreo Real* and *Padron Real*), but in terms of productive and institutional power (discussed in Chapter 3) those maps amounted to so much more. De facto they represented the first institutionalized mappings of the geophysical world, which were artefacts legitimated by crown authority for the purpose of standardizing metrics, rules, and expectations on *how to see* spatial relations within a single representation.[75] Accordingly, these unique normative and institutional qualities not only made such mappings highly valuable in their day and thus fiercely guarded.

That secrecy was not impenetrable. In 1502, Alberto Cantino, a diplomatic agent of the Duke of Ferrara, allegedly smuggled a

[72] Joaquim Alves Gaspar, "Blunders, Errors and Entanglements: Scrutinizing the Cantino Planisphere with a Cartometric Eye," *Imago Mundi* 64, no. 2 (2012): 181–200, at 184.

[73] See Stevenson, "The Geographical Activities of the Casa de la Contratación," 41:

> its jurisdiction is as large as its territory is boundless; its authority is so extraordinary that it has supplied the place of a Council, and has acted as such not only in reference to revenues and military affairs, with orders passing directly from the King to it; its wealth is such that none in Europe can compare with it; its credit so high that no private person could equal it; its pre-eminence is such that it had the appointment of all officers including admirals of the Royal fleet, and the civil magistrates; it gave passes to ships sailing to all ports, and the dispatching of advice boats with only its own owners.

[74] Turnbull, "Cartography and Science in Early Modern Europe," 9.

[75] See John Law, "On the Social Explanation of Technical Change: The Case of the Portuguese Maritime Expansion," *Technology and Culture* 28, no. 2 (1987): 227–52, at 244.

copy of the *Padreo Real* from Lisbon.[76] The resulting *Cantino Planisphere* is of exceptional historical importance – not least because the original Portuguese imperial charts were destroyed in the 1755 Lisbon earthquake (see Figure 5.1). It provides one of the few surviving examples of how the Iberian crowns sought to consolidate a singular, standardized image of the entire world. The work of the *Casas* symbolized the start – in Europe – of an institutional history of geographic representation and "metrication,"[77] which culminated in 1696 with Jacques Cassini's cartographic engraving *Planisphère Terrestre*. Cassini's World Map being notably distinguished as a scientific and cartographic milestone, because its gridded mapping was the product of geometric data taken from over forty astronomical stations.[78]

Yet institutionalization marks only one threshold in the making of a world-image. It speaks to state or elite perception, not to the embedding of that image in the wider social imagination. Here it is vital to distinguish, as argued in Chapter 3, between *institutional power* – which shapes incentives within formal structures – and *structural power* – which produces pervasive social facts. Structural power operates at the level where a representation becomes the unexamined "order of things" in Foucauldian terms.[79] The planispheres of the *Casas* were thus an inaugural step in a longer historical process by which successive generations of maps came to structure not only the perceptions of imperial states but also the assumptions of broader publics. The question, then, is how this elite image of "the world" was able to permeate beyond imperial courts and become common social knowledge, gaining widespread credibility and social belief? Especially in light of the pluralistic and cosmological worldviews

[76] Gaspar, "Blunders, Errors and Entanglements," 181–82:

> The Cantino planisphere, now in the Biblioteca Estense Universitaria in Modena, Italy, is a manuscript nautical chart comprising six rectangular pieces of parchment mounted on a large sheet of canvas and measuring overall about 220 × 105 centimetres. On the back is an inscription, presumably written by Alberto Cantino: "Navigational chart of the islands recently (discovered) … in part of the Indies: from Alberto Cantino to Duke Hercole."

[77] Gaspar, "Blunders, Errors and Entanglements," 181–82.

[78] See Dalia Deias, "A Vanished Curiosity from the Observatoire of Louis XIV: The *Parterre géographique*, a Tool Both of Precision and of Representation," *Archives Internationales d'Histoire des Sciences* 72, no. 196 (2022): 74–96.

[79] See Barnett and Duvall, "Power in International Politics," 55–56.

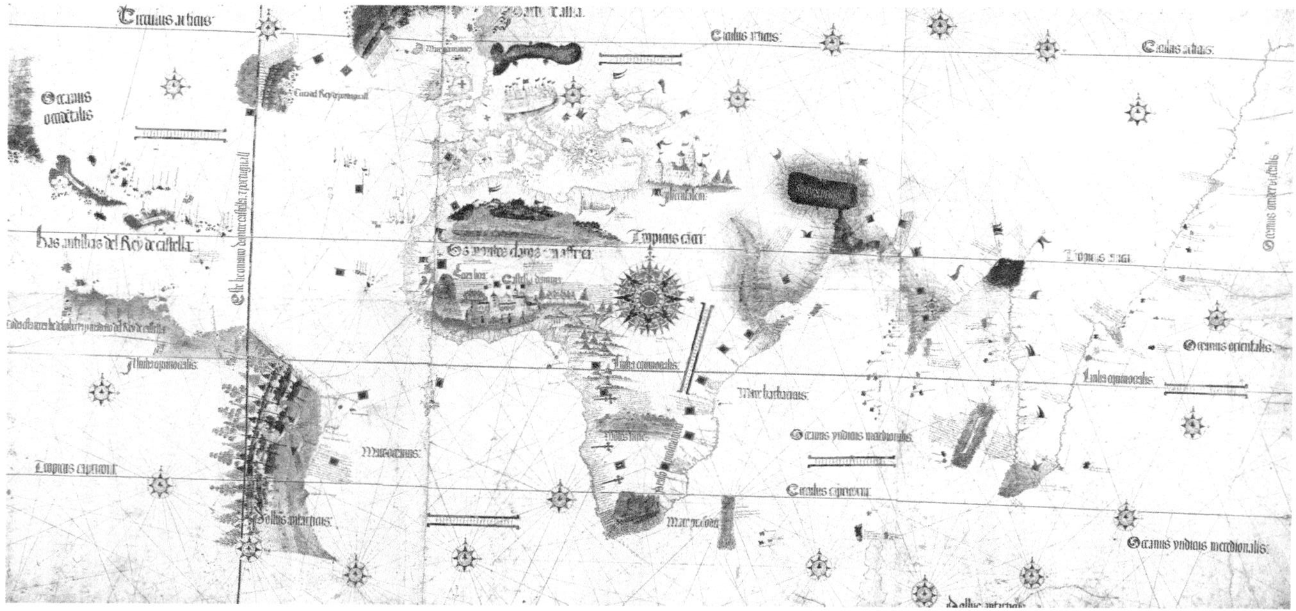

Figure 5.1 *Cantino Planisphere* (1502), *Unknown cartographer*. Biblioteca Estense Universitaria, Modena. Earliest surviving world map showing Portuguese discoveries. (World History Archive / Alamy) www.alamy.com/stock-photo-the-cantino-planisphere-or-cantino-world-map-is-the-earliest-surviving-57362096.html

that had dominated European early modern imaginations, where the uniqueness of discrete places, and not abstract space, defined common perception.

5.1.2.3 Perspectivism, the European "Eye," and Mapped Totality

Several historical factors were involved, but my answer takes a narrower focus via the Latin title of this chapter – *Vidi et Vici*. Perhaps some thought the title was just a play on words of Julius Caesar's historic pronouncement regarding Asia Minor: *Veni, Vidi, Vici*. Yet, my title has another comparative intent, which is potentially more subversive. The title probes a generic similarity between the meaning of Caesar's ancient phrase and Europe's modernist mission: the ordering and conquering of the wider world by Europeans. The teleology of appropriation and cargo seeking, along with the planispheres and maps, effectively represent scions of that modernist mission and, arguably, Caesarian rootstock. A mission notably governed by a key visual principle: the "perspective" of the individual's "seeing eye" defines the ordering (and conquering) of nature and the world.[80]

Perspectivism emerged from fifteenth-century Florence (see Chapter 4) and came to dominate European perception for four centuries. It privileged the individual's capacity to produce – from a fixed vantage point – a geometrically ordered, rational, and singular representation of perceived reality.[81] What made perspectivism transformative was not merely its impact on painting or architecture, but its extension into commerce,

[80] See John Berger, *Ways of Seeing* (London: BBC Books, 1972), 16:

> The convention of the perspective, which is unique to European art and which was first established in the early Renaissance, centres everything on the eye of the beholder. It is like a beam from a lighthouse – only instead of light travelling outward, appearance travel in. The convention called those appearances reality. Perspective makes the single eye the centre of the visible world.

[81] See A. Mark Smith, *From Sight to Light: The Passage from Ancient to Modern Optics* (Chicago: University of Chicago Press, 2015), 299:

> At an operational level, mirroring appears to have been crucial to the development of linear perspective in the early 15th century by the Florentine artist, architect, Filippo Brunelleschi (1377–1447). According to several early accounts, Brunelleschi painted two depictions (now lost), one of the octagonal Baptistery in the plaza of the Duomo, the other of the Palazzo Vecchio, both depictions reputed to have been so lifelike that onlookers were lost in amazement.

finance, land surveying, and eventually politics. As David Harvey explains, perspectivism offered a "cold rationality" capable of compressing social and geographical spaces:

> Objectivity in spatial representation became a valued attribute because accuracy of navigation, the determination of property rights in land ... political boundaries, rights of passage and of transportation, and the like, became economically as well as political imperative ... The connection with perspectivism lay in this: that in designing the grid in which to locate places, Ptolemy had imagined how the globe as a whole would look to a human eye looking at it from outside. A number of implications then follow. The first is an ability to see the globe as a knowable totality ... The second implication is that mathematical principles could be applied, as in optics, to the whole problem of representing the globe on a flat surface. As a result, it seemed as if space, though infinite, was conquerable and containable for purposes of human occupancy and action.[82]

This "total" view established a practice of *seeing* that still resonates in social, political, and economic life – and International Law is no exception. Yet, much like cargo, perspectivism's legacy in shaping the legal "eye" is relatively underexamined. In fact, few international lawyers would be familiar with linear perspectivism's profound legacy in structuring how the legal world is *seen* today.[83] That void especially curious with recurring debates on International Law's universality, formalism, uncertainty, pluralism, constitutionalism, and, more recently, anthropocentrism, Eurocentrism, and decolonization. Discussions that – to a greater or lesser extent – have engaged perspectivism's *fil rouge* and underlying premise: "the world" can be authoritatively represented from a fixed viewpoint.[84] In sum, perspectivism

82 Harvey, *Condition of Postmodernity*, 245–47.

83 Samuel Y. Edgerton, *The Mirror, the Window, and the Telescope: How Renaissance Linear Perspective Changed Our Vision of the Universe* (Ithaca: Cornell University Press, 2009), 6: "the geometric-optical perspective method Brunelleschi first introduced ... managed ... to change the very way people, especially those in Westernized societies, visually verify the phenomenal world in their acculturated mind's eye. In other words, Brunelleschi's perspective not only altered how we represent what we see but how we actually see a priori."

84 See Stuart Clark, *Vanities of the Eye: Vision in Early Modern European Culture* (Oxford: Oxford University Press, 2007), 83:

> The adoption of geometric or linear perspective by European artists ranks as such an epochal event in the history of seeing ... Among the multitude of claims made for linear perspective the relevant ones here are not just that it

privileged the European "seeing eye" and, by implication, that hubris informed Europe's later founding of disciplinary International Law.[85]

Here Kenneth Burke's concept of "circumferential logic" from Chapter 2 becomes relevant. It speaks directly to our question: How did imperial maps travel from the confines of courtly archives to the realm of common social knowledge? Burke's *circumference of vision* captures the idea of a "fixed viewpoint" – a consistent gaze – which determines the scope and scale of what the legal "eye" perceives in any given spatial or temporal context.[86] The globe as pictured in International Law embodies this "totalizing" ideal, elaborated over centuries through Ptolemaic charts, imperial planispheres, and cartographic maps reproduced literally billions of times. The iconic World Map of states amounting to a culmination of both modern and Ptolemaic virtues, because its image became deemed to portray the natural "totality" of the planet, allegedly free of theoretical, teleological, or political distortions.

Yet *totality* is an elusive term, because its meaning is precise or vague – all depending on your social expectation. For instance, the generic meaning of totality – total – and the Latin root *totalis* is: entire, sum, or aggregate. What that means concretely has a lot to do with – in Burke's words – "the circumference" of what one expects to *see* as total or entire. My point in the abstract does not say much substantively, until one appreciates that imperial Europe's history of mapping – and especially today's World Map of states – reified a given vision, model, and meaning of what global "totality" *is* and *should* look like. It privileges some forms of spatial representation

because 'the naturalized visual culture of [a] new artistic order, or that it led to a wholly different way of seeing the world, but that it ... rests on the ultimate visual paradox: complete deception in the service of utter veracity.

85 See Antony Anghie, *Imperialism, Sovereignty, and the Making of International Law* (Cambridge: Cambridge University Press, 2012).

86 See Agnew, *Geopolitics*, 21:

> This a consistent reading of a building or a painting is made possible by imposing an orderly vision by means of an external point of viewing from which an object always appears in the same light. This conception of the consistent gaze as the key to understanding was not restricted to the pictorial arts ... The language of knowing – perspective, view, vision, world-view – was expressed in overwhelmingly visual terms. The world was an object separated from the viewing subject, and could be understood adequately only if seen as a whole.

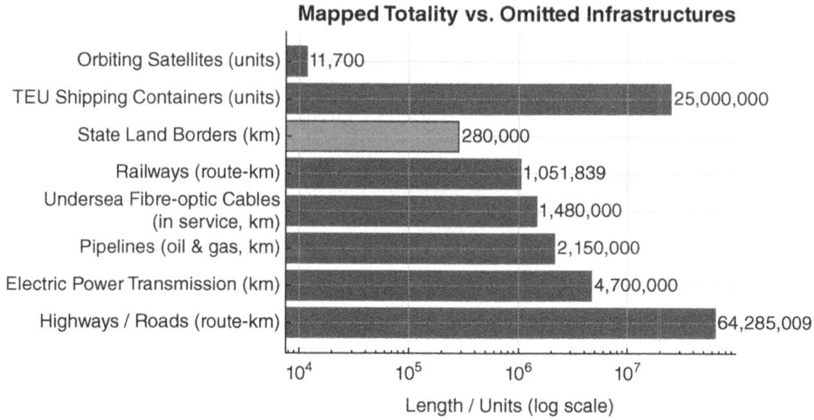

Figure 5.2 Comparison of state land borders (typically mapped) versus other lines and/or boundaries of human-made infrastructure (typically unmapped).

while rendering others invisible. That mapped totality foregrounds roughly 280,000 kilometers of state borders (See Figure 5.2),[87] yet it obscures the material and legal salience of other global infrastructures: for example, the more than 4 million kilometers of high-voltage transmission lines that underpin electricity markets;[88] the vast mesh of approximately 11,700 satellites orbiting Earth that carry GPS, climate, and defense data;[89] the 1.48 million kilometers of undersea fibre-optic cables snaking across continents;[90] the 2.15 million kilometers of oil and gas pipelines that connect extraction zones to refineries;[91]

[87] Central Intelligence Agency, "Land Boundaries," *The World Factbook*, 2022 Archive. Accessed August 10, 2025. www.cia.gov/the-world-factbook/about/archives/2022/field/land-boundaries

[88] Gregor Kalt et al., "A Global Inventory of Electricity Infrastructures from 1980 to 2017: Country-Level Data on Power Plants, Grids and Transformers," *Scientific Data* 8 (2021). Accessed August 10, 2025. www.sciencedirect.com/science/article/pii/S2352340921006351

[89] Union of Concerned Scientists, *UCS Satellite Database*. Updated May 1, 2023. www.ucs.org/resources/satellite-database

[90] Bethany Halford, "As Telecom Demands Grow, Optical Fibers Will Need to Level Up," *Chemical & Engineering News*, March 16, 2020. Accessed August 10, 2025. https://pubs.acs.org/doi/10.1021/cen-09810-cover

[91] GlobalData, *Oil and Gas Pipelines Length and Capital Expenditure (CapEx) – Market Analysis*, April 17, 2023. Accessed August 10, 2025. www.globaldata.com/store/report/oil-and-gas-pipelines-length-and-capital-expenditure-market-analysis/

1.05 million kilometers of railways, nearly 25 million TEU shipping containers in circulation, and the lattice of humanitarian and refugee corridors that emerge during crises. These omissions matter because they sustain legal realities just as profoundly as state border lines do – shaping jurisdictional claims, trade disputes, environmental regulation, and security regimes.

For international lawyers, the problem is that we continue to rely on this inherited, imperial cartographic frame to *see* and *know* global legal geography. But such dependence confronts the Achilles' heel of any totalized worldview: how inherent geophysical and historical changes ultimately depart from the ideal totality. As Bruno Latour illustrates succinctly:

> CO_2 is not spatialized in the same way as urban transport systems; aquifers are not local in the same sense as bird flu; antibiotics globalize the world in a way quite different from that of Islamic terrorists; cities do not form the same spaces as states ... an economy based on coal ... does not shape the same struggles as an economy based on oil. And so on.[92]

Latour's examples point to the enduring dilemma of assuming that one mapped "totality" can faithfully capture geographic reality. That ambition – initiated by the *Casas* to serve imperial appropriation and cargo-seeking – made it possible for the European "eye" to *see* and *seize* any quantum of the non-European world. This entwining of imperial teleology, mapped totality, and the physical world provided the normative rootstock from which legal concepts such as territory, jurisdiction, and property would grow as scions.[93] It also enabled cartographic metrics to naturalize a system of spherical coordinates,

92 Latour, *Down to Earth*, 93–94.

93 The intertwine between imperial teleology and the cartography medium summarized concisely by Matthew H. Edney, "The Irony of Imperial Mapping," in *The Imperial Map: Cartography and the Mastery of Empire*, ed. James R. Akerman (Chicago: University of Chicago Press, 2009), 13:

> Europeans have in the modern era idealized their own mapping practices as being thoroughly scientific and objective, in opposition to the mapping practices of non-Europeans (the unknowing Other). In this respect, the modern, empiricist paradigm of modern cartography is itself an imperial formation. We might therefore conclude that an empire is an empire not because it possesses certain formal attributes but because it has been discursively mapped as an empire ...while the modern concept of a map is the produce of the same imperial discourses.

embedding Cartesian space into the infrastructure of legal ordering – from property and income taxation to forest management, military strategy, and the spatial architecture of organizations such as the United Nations, NATO, and the European Union. All of this flowed from the core belief that a single geographic reality could be captured in a mapped totality – fulfilling, in modern form, Ptolemy's dream of universal geographic knowledge.

5.1.2.4 Pointillism, the Global Grid, and the Decline of Cartographic Rule

This belief was sustainable only so long as this mapped totality dominated geographic knowledge and, crucially, social perceptions. However, centuries of dominance now confront real-time decline versus a *pointillistic* worldview crafted by a newer mega-project and imperial patron. Specifically, a "global grid" defined not by mapped representation or cartographic states, but a trans-territorial coordinate system generated with electronic signals, dot-to-dot world-making, and computerized positioning systems. A coordinate system that has engendered a novel medium of pointillistic rule and, arguably, conquest.

Pointillism – in its initial connotation – emerged from a pictorial movement in late nineteenth-century Paris, driven by the science of optics and the visual effects of art tapestry. *Peinture au point* – in French – involved a dot-to-dot technique that painted countless tiny dots onto a surface, which would assume a visual whole once the viewer reached an adequate distance (see Figure 5.3).[94] Félix Fénéon described the pointillist experience as follows: "Take a few steps back, the technique … vanishes; the eye is no longer attracted by anything but that which is essentially painting."[95] Pointillism underlined how the interplay of dots can generate optical effects that define what a viewer's "eye" *sees* from a particular vantage point, that is, simply random points or homogeneous forms and social images.[96]

[94] Stephen Reyna, "Social Pointillism and Starry Nights: Making Points to Make Connections in the Sudanese Civil War," *Journal of Asian and African Studies* 51, no. 3 (2016): 358–79, at 358, 362.

[95] Félix Fénéon, "The Impressionists in 1886," trans. Belinda Thomson, *Art in Translation* 6, no. 2 (2014): 271–88, at 278.

[96] Fénéon, "The Impressionists in 1886," 279–80.

Figure 5.3 Pointillistic depiction of a tree. *Monochrome Pointillist Exemplar.* Author's own illustration, created with AI-assisted design tool, August 12, 2025.

Beyond the visual arts, this dot-to-dot technique illustrated how perceived space could be ordered through seemingly disconnected dots, which was an alternative to the "fixed view" of mapped representation and its lines of *contiguous* geometry. That emphasis on dots and optical effects challenged the core premise of authoritative representation: a map could reflect physical reality in the most objective, total, and truthful perspective. However, pointillism's dot-to-dot technique revealed that any physical depiction was in fact virtual to some extent. As such, there could only be authoritative *presentation* rather than *representation*, in the sense of credible, reliable, and useful exposition rather than objective or "true" depiction.[97]

Pointillism leapt from pictorial logic to engineered geography in March 1942,[98] when the Royal Air Force (RAF) first activated a

[97] This reflects Plato's assertion in *Theaetetus* that sight is inextricable from insight, that is the point of view. As explained by Karen Lang in *Chaos and Cosmos: On the Image in Aesthetics and Art History* (Ithaca: Cornell University Press, 2006), 2: "seeing, representing, and knowing are all related to theory. Theory, whose Greek stem is *thea*, means to look, to view, to contemplate. Interestingly, an archaic use of the word implies 'a spectator at festival theater performances, athletic contests, and other public events.' *Thea* also connotes the contemplation of *theos*, the divine … Simply put, theory beings with looking."

[98] Sven Lindqvist, *A History of Bombing* (London: Granta, 2001), 195–202.

"coordinate-based area-navigation system"[99] over northwest Europe. It was codenamed *Gee*, and enabled the RAF to perform a night-time bombing raid successfully over Essen.[100] However, RAF bombers were guided not by mapped representation – which was unreliable or often unusable at night – but instead a grid of electronic coordinates transmitted over Nazi Germany by *Gee*'s system of antennae.[101] The coordinate grid enabled radio navigation by night, because the bomber's location and that of Essen were each made known by intersecting two numbers, which established respective coordinate positions.[102] Notably, the bomber navigator did not see the plane's geographic position over Germany using the "seeing eye" of cartographic *representation*, rather navigation had been performed with a novel dot-to-dot *presentation* of geographic reality. Yet, dot-warfare did not stop at night-time bombing, in subsequent years gridded coordinates also overtook cartographic maps to become a pervasive medium for radar systems and artillery targeting.[103]

With the onset of the Cold War, pointillism expanded further and achieved predominance because the globe itself became perceived as an imminent battlefield.[104] The dawn of trans-territorial weapons, such as nuclear arms and intercontinental missiles, radically compressed global space and thus blurred the relevance of geopolitical and geophysical spaces like national, international, and continental geography. As a result, a new geography of warfare emerged that required coordination, navigation, and targeting across one seamless transnational space, as opposed to a puzzle of cartographic grids that emphasized state boundaries. In 1947, the US Army devised its initial pointillistic response. Mathematicians at the US Army Maps Service engineered a "worldwide common grid," called the Universal Transverse Mercator (UTM). It divided the Earth mathematically into sixty north–south strips, with each strip divided into twenty

99 R. J. Dippy, "Gee: A Radio Navigational Aid," *Journal of the Institution of Electrical Engineers – Part IIIA: Radiolocation* 93, no. 3 (1946): 468–84.

100 Rankin, *After the Map*, 221.

101 Air Ministry (UK), "The GEE-7000 System," in *Introductory Survey of Radar, Part II: A Non-Technical Account of Selected Airborne Equipments*, Air Publication 1093D, vol. 1, 1st ed. (June 1946), 63–74.

102 Air Ministry (UK), "The GEE-7000 System," 70.

103 Rankin, *After the Map*, 167.

104 Matthew Farish, *The Contours of America's Cold War* (Minneapolis: University of Minnesota Press, 2010), 1–40.

rows of latitude (Grid Zones), and each Grid Zone then divided further into a grid of (fifty-four) 100-kilometer squares. The UTM assigned "every point on the earth an easy-to-use Euclidean coordinate, expressed in meters, that [could] be used ... for everything from transnational infrastructure projects to ... aiming intercontinental ballistic missiles."[105]

Decades later, the United States consolidated pointillistic world-making on an unprecedented scale. In 1989, after two decades of development, the US Department of Defense launched the Global Positioning System (GPS). Today, more than 8 billion GPS receivers – roughly one for every human being – are in circulation worldwide, with projections exceeding 10 billion by 2030. Yet everyday familiarity obscures the deeper itineraries and normative implications of GPS: how it has, "little by little," to borrow de Certeau's phrase, constructed and normalized a pointillistic worldview that differs fundamentally from the cartographic one International Law inherited and continues to privilege.

The GPS is a nonrepresentational space designed to simulate the Earth through a grid of electronic points. Like the *Gee* system, it refers to a superimposed coordinate world rather than direct geophysical depiction. Two features – one normative, one orbital – made this geography both possible and globally pervasive. First, the system employs a mathematical model of the Earth, WGS 84, developed by the US military to adjust for irregularities in the planet's shape and gravitational field. Second, this model enabled a constellation of twenty-seven satellites, each completing eight-hour orbits, to project a worldwide coordinate grid. Any GPS receiver can thereby locate "individual instances of phenomena" with specified scale and pinpoint accuracy. What pointillism had achieved through painted dots, GPS achieves through standardized pixels: uniform electronic units, infinitely reproducible and designed to be machine-readable across platforms. Unlike the painted dot, which required interpretation, the pixel enforces interoperability and standardization. It must be read identically everywhere, by every device and user. This compulsory uniformity elevates the pixel from an aesthetic device to a juridical fact: an infrastructural standard that binds heterogeneous actors into a shared spatial frame and silently compels compliance.

[105] Farish, *Contours of America's Cold War*, 163–64.

The immense productive and compulsory power this generated first became vivid during the 1991 Gulf War,[106] when the US military – in an operation named the "Left Hook"[107] – used GPS coordinates to guide a surprise and war-ending attack by over 200,000 US soldiers across the roadless and barren deserts of Kuwait and Iraq.[108] Effectively, GPS coordinates were used to displace cartographic representation and local way-finding, demonstrating how pointillistic geography provided capacity to guide a historic military intervention without maps – irrespective of physical or national boundaries – and with precision accuracy. The GPS in effect flattened the Earth's surface into one seamless "commons"[109] of pixels and coordinates, no longer centered exclusively on the "cartographic state" but rather the spatial needs and vision of anyone empowered by the GPS system, whether for example individual, military, electoral, nonstate, humanitarian, corporate, or conservationist. In sum, the Global Grid introduced a new pointillistic medium and grammar of territorial rule, displacing mapped representation as the dominant form of geographic knowledge and – echoing Schmitt's fundamental claim – dislodging the reign of cartographic lines as the absolute medium through which normative authority and power are extended upon the Earth today.

5.2 Connect-the-Dots: The Rise and Reign of Pointillistic Geographies

International Law has yet to absorb the implications of pixels and pointillistic world-making. The discipline's inherited background

106 Martin Coward, "Networks, Nodes and De-Territorialised Battlespace: The Scopic Regime of Rapid Dominance," in *From Above: War, Violence, and Verticality*, ed. Peter Adey (Oxford: Oxford University Press, 2013), 105.

107 See Lawrence Freedman and Efraim Karsh, *The Gulf Conflict, 1990–1991: Diplomacy and War in the New World Order* (Princeton: Princeton University Press, 1993), 393–99: "Some 235,000 troops and all their equipment, 95,000 trucks and other wheeled vehicles, 12,000 tanks and other armoured personnel vehicles and sixty days of stocks."

108 Michael Rip and James Hasik, *The Precision Revolution: GPS and the Future of Aerial Warfare* (Annapolis: Naval Institute Press, 2002), 126–31; see also Kenneth Pollack, *Arabs at War: Military Effectiveness, 1948–1991* (Lincoln: University of Nebraska Press, 2022), 239.

109 See Barry R. Posen, "Command of the Commons: The Military Foundation of U.S. Hegemony," *International Security* 28, no. 1 (2003): 5–46, at 12–14.

assumptions remain entwined with statist cartography and – further back – with the legacy of linear perspectivism.[110] There are notable ruptures – Fleur Johns' work on digital humanitarianism, for example, shows how nonstate actors mobilize digital data and pointillistic geographies to expose the limits of statist representations of, inter alia, strategic border regions and Indigenous territories.[111] Yet the field's operative ontology still defaults to *cartographic theory as practice*. The result is a persistent blind spot regarding the extent to which geographic pointillism animates today's geopolitical and geo-economic designs and practices.

Crucially, "geographic knowledge" is no longer synonymous with representational mapping. Since the late twentieth century, geodesy, electronic mapping, and Geographic Information Systems (GIS) have proliferated. More importantly, the epistemic monopoly of the representational map has fractured: State and nonstate actors can now assemble chains of moving electronic coordinates into operational *world-pictures* for political, economic, and social ends. In other words, real-time geographic action has pivoted away from the cartographic presumptions that long conditioned how international lawyers imagine geophysical, political, and legal space. As William Rankin underscores, the rise of the *electronic point* over the *contiguous area* is not a technical footnote but an enabling condition for new, trans-territorial forms of governance:

> Maps ... tended to reinforce an all-or-nothing relationship between territory and sovereignty ... But with the ... pointillistic logic of coordinates, there is no longer this tight relationship because geographic legibility and political authority. Electronic coordinates are explicitly designed to exceed the boundaries of individual states, and maintaining a virtual grid does not require any long-term geographic commitment or sustained control over a contiguous expanse of land. Not only does this make things like ultra-long-range bombardment possible as never before, but many of the activities that previously relied on detailed maps can now be pursued with a much lighter presence on the ground ... Both in design and in practice, electronic coordinates cut across the usual categories of the state ... Territory need

110 On the dialectic of the line, see Sean Cubitt, *The Practice of Light: A Genealogy of Visual Technologies from Prints to Pixels* (Cambridge: MIT Press, 2014), 70–71.

111 Fleur Johns, *#Help: Digital Humanitarianism and the Remaking of International Order* (Oxford: Oxford University Press, 2023), 67–69.

not be simply a cleanly bounded area of space – an inert "container" for the power of states or empires – but can be understood as itself a distinct form of power created through geographic knowledge. The kind of consolidated and explicitly jurisdictional territory reinforced by mapping is about making claims to exclusive political authority within a well-bounded area. The unbound, dispersed, and politically ambiguous territory of electronic coordinates ... is instead primarily about enabling quick intervention and creating a robust spatial framework – a way of thinking, acting and governing – independent from any such claims.[112]

That shift Rankin describes from cartographic to pointillistic geography is legally consequential, because it challenges a central trope for many international lawyers vis-à-vis a categorical distinction between network and territory. The former is framed as a chain of related entities that are allegedly *a-jurisdictional* due to their nonplanar and noncontiguous form. This distinction serving as a "paratext"[113] within the discipline, mimicking the quaint liberal dichotomy between *market* and *state*. Notably, both kinds of paratext have stayed opaque with help from centuries of cartographic inscription and world-making that made planar, volumetric, and contiguous lines essential to the imaginary of territorialization. Yet, a sizeable ontological gap emerges because pointillistic geographies enable salient forms of *networked* geopolitics[114] and geo-economics,[115] which operate via para-jurisdictions (i.e., juriscapes) constituted by nonplanar, noncontiguous, and mobile lines of authority and power. As Martin Coward explains:

The network is thus a trope that envisages ontology as a series of distinct entities related to one another without direct reference to the jurisdiction in which they may be situated. It is thus a trope that deterritorialises the classical perception of the globe as divided into a patchwork of mutually exclusive parcels of political jurisdiction (typically states). However, this is not to say that the trope of the network does not re-territorialise, or spatialise, in its own way ... While terrain may play a role ... it is simply

112 Rankin, *After the Map*, 4.

113 Nigel Thrift, *Non-Representational Theory* (London: Routledge, 2008), 91.

114 See Steve Niva, "Disappearing Violence: JSOC and the Pentagon's New Cartography of Networked Warfare," *Security Dialogue* 44, no. 3 (2013): 185–202.

115 See Deborah Cowen and Neil Smith, "After Geopolitics? From the Geopolitical Social to Geoeconomics," *Antipode* 41, no. 1 (2009): 22–48.

another element of an assemblage which is not distributed across a surface, but assembled in data flows ... Points are not related across defined distance but in terms of significance. Moreover, they are not spatially fixed, but shift in dynamic ways according to relationships ... [A] set of nodes that are constituted through their relations with one another. Force is projected within this network, rather than across the territory in which it might be notionally located.[116]

These nonplanar, noncontiguous lines already structure political, economic, and legal practices – from sanctions evasion and financial surveillance to drone operations, humanitarian access logistics, and content moderation architectures. International lawyers are often placed on the back foot because our signature concepts of territoriality and jurisdiction are keyed to a cartographic ontology of legal space – what Deborah Cowen calls: "a particular historical-geographical instantiation of territory organized through nation-states."[117]

The disciplinary implication is a very narrow *circumference* of what international lawyers are able to see vis-à-vis growing nonplanar and noncontiguous forms of legal rule. As such, by contrasting pointillistic versus cartographic world-making, the "geography" of International Law may be construed not as brute geology but a spatial ontology now undergoing pointillistic compression. That compression expands trans-territorial possibilities for configuring authority, appropriation, and rule – via coordinates, not contours; via networks, not nested containers. The task, then, is not to abandon territory but to reconceive its juridical life in an era where legibility, control, and intervention are produced dot by dot across a global grid.

5.2.1 Pointillization and the Logistics Revolution

The ontological problem that international lawyers will find increasingly difficult to evade is this: the mapped totality from which the discipline emerged was a cartographic scheme institutionally rooted in the imperial world of cargo first enacted by the *carraca*. Nonetheless, that cartographic form, imaginary, and purpose has long exceeded

[116] Coward, "Networks, Nodes and De-Territorialised Battlespace," 110–12.

[117] Deborah Cowen, *The Deadly Life of Logistics: Mapping Violence in Global Trade* (Minneapolis: University of Minnesota Press, 2014), 10.

mere institutional power (Chapter 3) to symbolically and socially structure, "how we write the [legal] world ... Like the set-up of the page, indexes, footnotes and the rest of paraphernalia of written thinking ... [as] a kind of epistemic wallpaper."[118]

Pointillistic world-making, however, has introduced new geographies of intelligibility – modes of *seeing* in real time across chains of discontinuous, distant entities (nodes) linked solely by salient relations rather than contiguous geography. This *pointillization* erodes the spatial imperative once monopolized by cartographic rule – possession and control of contiguous jurisdiction – and replaces it with a different imperative: dynamic influence over a constellation of discrete points, assembling (or disrupting) noncontiguous lines of space to delineate authoritative relations and bounding, without the costs of sustaining a volumetric domain.

This transformation has altered not only the conduct of warfare – from planar "front lines" to trans-territorial "kill chains"[119] – but also the very profit-consciousness, appropriation, and cargo-seeking that propelled the first *planispheres* of the sixteenth century. It has given rise to what can be described as a pointillistic planisphere, in which the "business of seeing" is reoriented toward a global geography of geo-logistical nodes – maritime chokepoints such as the Straits of Malacca and Hormuz, strategic canals like Suez and Panama, container megahubs such as the Port of Singapore, overland gateways like Khorgos on the China–Kazakhstan border, air cargo hubs including Dubai International and Memphis, and high-capacity data cable landing stations in Marseille and Mombasa. These nodes are linked by transversal and competing chains (i.e., noncontiguous lines) of trans-territorial authority and power.

[118] Thrift, *Non-Representational Theory*, 91.

[119] Derek Gregory, "From a View to a Kill: Drones and Late Modern War," *Theory, Culture & Society* 28, nos. 7–8 (2011): 188–215, at 188–189; Martin Coward, "Network-Centric Violence, Critical Infrastructure and the Urbanisation of Society," *Security Dialogue* 40, nos. 4–5 (2009): 399–418; Lilly Muller, "Cybersecurity in Practice: The Vigilant Logic of Kill Chains and Threat Construction," *European Journal of International Security* (published online 2024): 1–21, https://doi.org/10.1017/eis.2024.27; Judith Verweijen, "A Microdynamics Approach to Geographies of Violence: Mapping the Kill Chain in Militarized Conservation Areas," *Political Geography* 79 (2020): 102153, https://doi.org/10.1016/j.polgeo.2020.102153

Pointillistic renderings compress state territories into dotted, cellular spaces,[120] while data-processing capacities become essential to *en-vision* and govern the trans-territorial flows and circulations that traverse them. This reimagined logistical geography aligns political, economic, and legal authority not around contiguous volumes, but through the movement of goods, people, and information along relational lines. In doing so, it recasts the logistical imaginary of how rule is geographically organized today. As Deborah Cowen explains relative to the rising salience of trans-territorial corridors and gateways:

> [G]lobalized logistics has hardly featured in critical scholarly work … [and] represents much more than simply a geography of trade routes. While the business school professor is right to suggest that a corridor … offers the best map of economic integration, it also offers a powerful mapping of the forms of mobility and security that are actively reworking the geopolitical state. This network geography bounds the emerging political space of logistics. Dynamic debates on the rescaling of the state and the "new regionalism" have explored these themes, but they have largely focused on the enlarging of political territories – the rescaling of the region, for instance – rather than the reconfiguration of the relationship between space, politics, and economy. Recent work on "geo-economics" has come closest … exploring a different logic of spatiality … that … emphasizes the recalibration of international space … by a wholly different, non-state-centric identification.[121]

Notably, these scholarly omissions Cowen highlights derive from a semantic conflation made between logistics and applied connotations,

120 See Shoshana Zuboff, *The Age of Surveillance Capitalism: The Fight for a Human Future at the New Frontier of Power* (London: Profile Books, 2019), 234:

> The noun *rendition* derives from the verb *render*, a most unusual word whose double meanings describe a two-sided equation that perfectly captures what happens in the gap between human experience and behavioral data. On one side of the equation, the verb describes a process in which something is formed out of something else that is originally given. It designates the casual action of turning one thing into another, such as rendering oil from fat (extraction) or rendering an English text from the original Latin (translation) … On the other side of the equation, *render* also describes the way in which the thing that is changed gives itself over to this process: it *surrenders*. The verb *render* first appears in tenth-century French, meaning 'to give back, present, yield,' as in 'rendering an account.'"

121 Cowen, *Deadly Life of Logistics*, 64.

which have been removed from the concept's more generic etymology – something we shall revisit Section 5.3. Such applied connotations linked to the provision of moving armies (military logistics) and, later, globalized systems of production and trade (Business Logistics). The term, *logistics*, gained that applied aura via Napoleonic strategy and warfare, when the French Imperial Army (*Grand Armée*) used extensive calculation and supply of provisions to leverage advantage against battlefield adversaries.[122] With the later rise of industrial warfare, and its dependence on fossil fuels (petrol, oil, and lubricants), that semantic attachment tightened further between logistics and the applied importance of in-time material provision and supply.[123]

After the Second World War, the global organization of vast quantities of soldiers and matériel captured the interest of American corporations and business schools, leading to the rise of *Business Logistics* as a management science.[124] Inspired both by systems thinking[125] and the US military's wartime example,[126] Business Logistics succeeded traditional management by offering "a new logic for how, and … where, to do business."[127] As Smykay and LaLonde illustrate, it reconceptualized corporate and economic space by dissolving the long-held presumption that productive and distributive operations were detached and unrelated:

> In traditional orientations to business operations, the end of the production line, as they put it in the paper industry, is at the dry end of the machine. Physical distribution perspectives, however, throw entirely new light on the question, "Where does the production line end?" In the view of physical distribution managements, the end of the production line is at the point

[122] See Antoine-Henri Jomini, *The Art of War* (1836; Kington: Legacy Books, 2009).

[123] See Martin van Creveld, *Supplying War: Logistics from Wallenstein to Patton*, 2nd ed. (Cambridge: Cambridge University Press, 2009).

[124] Murray Geisler, "Logistics Research and Management Science," *Management Science* 6, no. 4 (1960): 444–54, at 453.

[125] Ludwig von Bertalanffy, *General System Theory: Foundations, Development, Applications* (Harmondsworth: Penguin, 1973), 46–48.

[126] See Thomas Birtchnell, "The Missing Mobility: Friction and Freedom in the Movement and Digitization of Cargo," *Applied Mobilities* 1, no. 1 (2016): 85–101, at 90: "The need to fortify multiple fronts across global theatres led to an incredibly energetic war machine capable of ferrying both people and objects strategically and securely across great distances."

[127] Cowen, *Deadly Life of Logistics*, 24.

where the consumer actually puts the product to use. The petroleum industry is a good case in point. Gasoline sold at the pump is really the end of the whole process of products and distribution.[128]

Business Logistics generated a new mapping whereby production and distribution were presented as one "total" circulatory system, which then offered opportunities to generate profit maximization or value added along the chain of integrated operations.[129] This systemic view redefined "the whole process of business"[130] beyond traditional images of a company town and a factory floor, enabling business operations to be envisioned in real-time with far greater spatial and temporal extension.[131] It marked the conceptual root of what we call now "global supply (or value) chains," which involved a process where planar firms – bound to a contiguous locality – became compressed and stretched into trans-territorial nodes of production and trade.

By the turn of the millennium, the firm had been reconceived as a pointillistic space operating transversally across multiple, discontinuous sites. The Logistics Revolution engineered – within a few decades – a radically different logic of accumulation, one defined by nonplanar, noncontiguous lines of geographic bounding.[132] It elevated global "circulations" of goods, information, and capital above the fixity of state border lines, subtly displacing the absoluteness of cartographic borders. In doing so, it redefined proprietary world-making:

[128] Edward Smykay and Bernard LaLonde, *Physical Distribution: The New and Profitable Science of Business Logistics* (Chicago: Dartnell, 1967), 17.

[129] Peter Drucker, "Physical Distribution: The Frontier of Modern Management," in *Readings in Physical Distribution Management*, ed. Jonathan Bowersox et al. (London: Collier-Macmillan, 1969), 8.

[130] John Mangan et al., *Global Logistics and Supply Chain Management* (Chichester: Wiley & Sons, 2008), 338.

[131] Russell Ackoff, "Towards a System of Systems Concepts," *Management Science* 17, no. 11 (1971): 661–71, at 662.

[132] For an example of nonplanar and non-volumetric bounding:

> Airbnb is a giant enterprise active in 119 countries, where it lists over 500,000 properties ranging from studio apartments to actual castles and has served over ten million guests … [T]he company was valued to at more than $10 billion – a level surpassed by only a handful of the world's greatest hotel chains. In less than a decade, Airbnb … siphoned off a growing segment of customers from the traditional hospitality industry – all without owning a single hotel room on its own.

Geoffrey G. Parker, Marshall W. Van Alstyne, and Sangeet Paul Choudary, *Platform Revolution* (New York: W. W. Norton & Company, 2016), 2.

Appropriation and profit-seeking now move through *just-in-time* nodes, enabling resilient flows of commodities, expertise, and finance across – and often irrespective of – statist boundaries.[133] In this geography, the map of International Law's inherited cartographic totality no longer matches the pointillistic schemes of global authority and power.

5.2.2 Theatrum Orbis [Logisticus]: *Cargo Containers and the Global Containerscape*

At this point, the etymology and generic meaning of *logistics* (*logisticus*) becomes pertinent: "skilled in calculating."[134] The applied connotations now attached to the term – whether military, combat,[135] or business[136] – have obscured this original meaning, along with its broader engagement in calculating lived relations and undertakings at every scale. In its root sense, *logisticus* was not limited to operational schemes but encompassed grander calculations of scope and scale, including the cosmos or "the world" itself. This semantic lineage

133 See Parag Khanna, *Connectography: Mapping the Global Network Revolution* (London: Weidenfeld & Nicolson, 2016), 43–44:

> 40 percent of global GDP (as well as 25 percent of global growth) depends on the flows of goods, services, and capital across borders, while knowledge-intensive flows such as digital capital services are already worth $13 trillion annually (about half the value of all flows) and rising rapidly … Rather than presume that one's closest economic relations are with neighbours, we can now toggle between geographic distance and functional proximity, highlighting industry-specific supply chain linkages that show, for example, how closely tied Bangalore's software industry is to America. Distance is not dead, but it is certainly compressed.

134 "Logistic (adj): from Greek *logistikos* 'skilled in calculating'; endued with reason, from *logistes* 'a calculator,' from *logos* 'calculation, proportion.'" Douglas Harper, "Etymology of logistic," *Online Etymology Dictionary*. Accessed August 23, 2025. www.etymonline.com/word/logistic.

135 Christopher Kinsey and Ronald Ti, "Combat Logistics in the Twenty-first Century," in Mikael Weissmann and Niklas Nilsson eds., *Advanced Land Warfare* (Oxford: Oxford University Press, 2023), 63–85.

136 W. Bruce Allen, "The Logistics Revolution and Transportation," *Annals of the American Academy of Political and Social Science* 553, no. 1 (1997): 106–16, at 116, defines business logistics as: "a multidisciplinary approach concerned with how to coordinate all purchasing, selling, and producing activities together in order to assemble and distribute the right products in the right amounts to the right locations in the right condition so as to maximize profits for the firm."

loops us back to the chapter's opening emphasis on cargo and imperial world-making, and specifically the material and ontological role of the imperial *carraca* in constituting what Ortelius would later title the *Theatrum Orbis Terrarum* (1570) – the "Theatre of the Lands of the World" (see Figure 5.4). It also hints at why this section's title altered that name, deliberately replacing *Terrarum* with *Logisticus*.

Modern and imperial world-making has always revolved around logistics, concerned with calculating, seeing, and seizing an appropriable globe. This ontological work was indispensable to scaling Europe's colonial conquests, settlements, and ventures beyond the Mediterranean basin. The founding planispheres of the sixteenth century – whether by Münster, Mercator, or Ortelius – were more than geophysical representations; they were logistical maps, instruments for realizing a transoceanic world of appropriation and profit. To gaze at any World Map is thus to confront a medium whose representational work was inseparable from its logistical mission: imperial in scope, planetary in scale, and cartographic in rule.

In this light, what appears as a bland technical noun – intermodal cargo – now assumes profound ontological significance for international lawyers. The intermodal cargo container displaced the *carraca*, and successive generations of cargo ships, as the nodal object of the *Theatrum Orbis Logisticus*. Its apparent mundanity owes much to the aesthetics of linear perspectivism and cartographic world-making, which embedded planar and contiguous presumptions into the discipline's vision of authority, power, and territorialization. The traces of those presumptions become visible, for instance, by asking an innocuous classroom question: Following the Second World War, what events shaped the ensuing international legal order? The question harvests an immense number of happenings with indubitable systemic and legal significance. To name only a few: The inauguration of the United Nations (1945), the Nuremberg Trials (1945–46), the founding of the GATT (1947), the Universal Declaration of Human Rights (1948), the Korean War (1950–53), the founding of NATO (1949) and later the Warsaw Pact (1955), the hydrogen bomb (1952), the Bandung Conference (1955),[137] the Suez Crisis (1956), the launch of

[137] See Luis Eslava et al., eds., *Bandung, Global History, and International Law: Critical Pasts and Pending Futures* (Cambridge: Cambridge University Press, 2018).

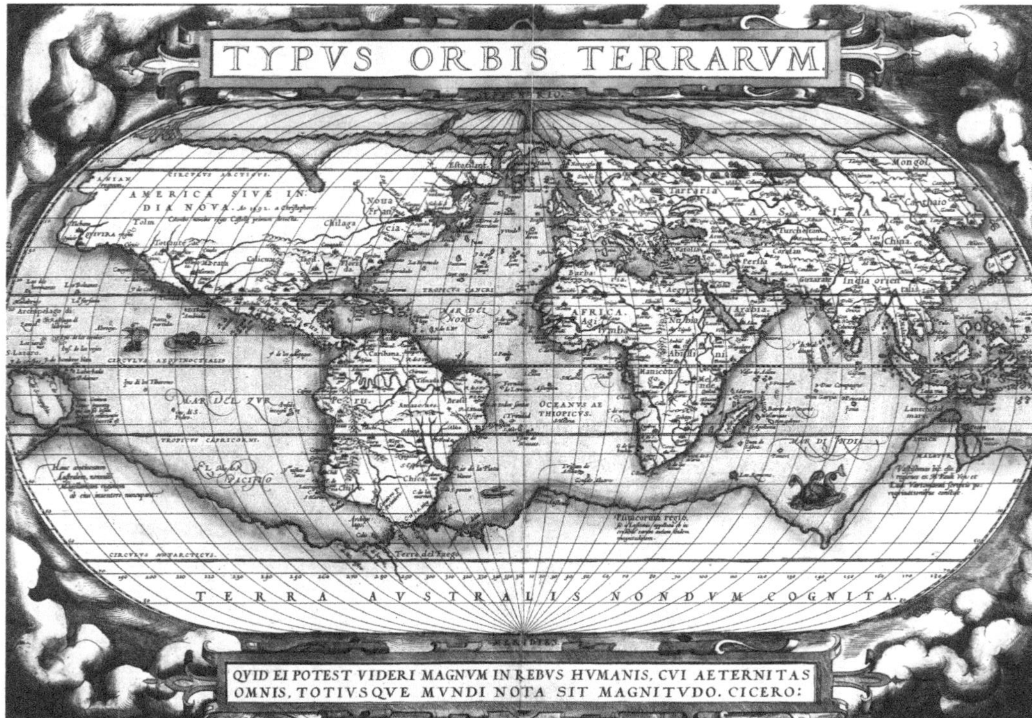

Figure 5.4 Abraham Ortelius' depiction of the globe "Typus Orbis Terrarum" (World Map) in *Theatrum Orbis Terrarum* (Antwerp: Gilles Coppens de Diest, 1570/72) (GL Archive / Alamy), www.alamy.com/ortelius-world-map-1570-by-abraham-ortelius-image499960542.html

Sputnik (1957), and the Cuban Revolution (1959). However, what you might notice is those typical examples share an interesting commonality: they trace a circumference of answers (i.e., vision) with events defined largely by their planar and cartographic implications.

For this reason, the 1958 patenting of the transoceanic steel cargo container[138] – or "intermodal container" in short – amounts to something of a lottery win if it ends up on an International Law dateline.[139] But to understand why, we need to grasp: What is the intermodal container, and what makes it significant in the aftermath of pointillization and the logistics revolution? Superficially, the intermodal container is just a big metal box. An alloy-sided cuboid that you have likely seen riding on grimy trailer trucks, lengthy train convoys, or stacked row upon row on the most immense ships ever built. However, such mundane appearances conceal how the intermodal container has become – literally and physically – the predominant medium for distributing commodities; via global networks of *standardized* trucks,[140] trains, ships, ports, gateways, routes, and distribution hubs.[141] Approximately 90 per cent of global production and trade now flows along a dotted world of 65 million intermodal containers that circulate over 2 billion metric tons of cargo annually.[142] Container ports worldwide currently process over 800 million containers a year, with the ports of Shanghai, Los Angeles, and Rotterdam each processing over 50, 10, and 8 million respectively.[143] The enormous scale and

138 Malcom McLean, *Apparatus for Shipping Freight*, U.S. Patent 2,853,968, filed August 26, 1954, and issued September 23, 1958.

139 But, notably, the shipping container is listed on the dateline of the US *Council on Foreign Relations*, see "Essential events since 1945": https://education.cfr.org/learn/timeline/essential-events-1945

140 See Karen Levy, *Data Driven: Truckers, Technology, and the New Workplace Surveillance* (Princeton, NJ: Princeton University Press, 2023).

141 See Daniel R. Quiroga-Villamarin, "Normalising Global Commerce: Containerisation, Materiality, and Transnational Regulation (1956–68)," *London Review of International Law* 8 (2020): 457–77.

142 "Container shipping – statistics & facts," Statista (online) www.statista.com/topics/1367/container-shipping/; Note that of the 65 million shipping containers, over 25 million are TEU sized containers: "The global shipping container fleet consists of millions of containers, with approximately 25 million TEUs (twenty-foot equivalent units) in circulation." *Containerlift*, May 22, 2024.

143 World Bank, "Container Port Traffic (TEU: 20-Foot Equivalent Units)," accessed August 23, 2025, https://data.worldbank.org/indicator/IS.SHP.GOOD.TU

impact of those container flows prompting – by analogy – the World Bank's label: "the physical internet."[144]

While all those empirics may seem impressive, the deeper significance of the intermodal container is actually ontological: It redefined a planisphere conceived around the *carraca* and, ultimately, an imperium centered on the cargo ship. That conceptual shift from the cargo ship to the container started when the American transportation mogul, Malcom McLean, invented a standardized container in the mid 1950s.[145] What made McLean's concept so profound was his emphasis on the principles of intermodality:[146] Cargo containers handled and moved rapidly from trucks, trains, and ships.[147] Today's version of the intermodal container, the "twenty-foot equivalent container" (TEU), embodies that original principle, measuring exactly 14.88m^2 in area, 33.3m^3 in cubic volume, and carrying up to 25 metric tons. Its modularity enabling the largest class of container ships – presently – to carry over 24,300 TEUs,[148] which amounts to approximately 233,000 metric tons – the rough equivalent of 2,330 *Santa Maria*-sized *carraca*.

Therefore, it might seem that conceptual significance resides only in the intermodal container's standardization as an essential unit of logistical calculation.[149] Yet, a more profound impact is visible when

144 World Bank, *Connecting to Compete: Trade Logistics in the Global Economy 2018*, accessed August 23, 2025, https://documents1.worldbank.org/curated/en/576061531492034646/pdf/Connecting-to-compete-2018-trade-logistics-in-the-global-economy-the-logistics-performance-index-and-its-indicators.pdf

145 See Marc Levinson, *The Box: How the Shipping Container Made the World Smaller and the World Economy Bigger*, 2nd ed. (Princeton: Princeton University Press, 2016), 47–71.

146 Craig Martin, *Shipping Container: Global Logistics and the Making of Modern Trade* (London: Bloomsbury Academic, 2016), 43: "Modular design is a system where individual parts can be linked together so that over a period of time parts can be added (or removed) as desired. For the designer of such a system the key factor is how different individual units can be joined together."

147 See Kingsley Haynes, "Intermodalism," *Journal of Transport Geography* 5 (1997): 21–34.

148 "MSC *Irina*," *VesselFinder*, accessed August 23, 2025, www.vesselfinder.com/vessels/details/9929429

149 See "Why Have Containers Boosted Trade So Much?" *The Economist*, May 21, 2013, www.economist.com/finance-and-economics/2013/05/21/why-have-containers-boosted-trade-so-much:

one looks closer at the term intermodality and, specifically, its root meaning of *modus*: "the way in which anything is done."[150] Within the span of several decades, the intermodal container physically remade *the way cargo has been done* by reengineering the geography of production and trade into – what Craig Martin has called – a *global containerscape*: "a unity of production and consumption … where the globe [becomes] envisioned as a vast logistical surface of containers being moved in huge container ships before being moved onto rail and road networks."[151]

Notably, the rise of intermodal containers has disentangled cargo not only from the hulls of cargo ships but also – most significantly – from cartographic placement at any singular port, warehouse, or state. The world-making significance being a novel planisphere recompressed and standardized by 65 million metal boxes, circulating across strategic corridors, gateways, seams, and hubs that compose a worldwide *containerscape*. Those millions of intermodal containers forming chains of "mobile mini-warehouses", which together enact the modularity that now reigns and remakes the *Theatrum Orbis Logisticus*. As Allan Sekula and Noel Burch highlight:

> As ships become more like buildings – the giant, floating warehouses of the "just-in-time" system of distribution – factories being to resemble ships, stealing away stealthily in the night, restlessly searching for ever cheaper labour. A garment factory in Los Angeles or Hong Kong closes' the work benches and sewing machines reappear in the suburbs of Guangzhou or Dacca. In the automobile industry, for example, the function of the ships is akin to that of conveyor systems within the old integrated car factory: parts span the world on their journey to the final assembly … What began in the

Between 1965 and 1970 the amount of capital locked up per tonne of inventory in transit between Hamburg and Sydney fell by half. Because containers were packed and sealed at the factory, losses to theft plummeted, which in turn drastically reduced insurance costs. More could also be loaded: in 1965 dock labour could move only 1.7 tonnes per hour on a cargo ship, five years later they could load 30 tonnes in an hour. As a consequence, ships could get bigger and more efficient while still spending less time in port. As containers made inland distribution by train and lorry easier, ports become bigger and fewer in number. (In 1965 there were 11 loading ports in Europe; by 1970 there were three.) This, along with increased productivity, meant fewer dockworkers were needed.

150 "Modus," *Online Etymology Dictionary*, accessed August 23, 2025, www.etymonline.com/search?q=modus

151 Craig Martin, *Shipping Container*, 62.

mid-1950s as a modest American improvement in cargo logistics has now taken on world-historic importance. The cargo container – a standardized metal box, easily transferred from ship to truck to train – has radically transformed the space and time of port cities and ocean passages.[152]

5.2.3 Pointillistic Empire(s), Perforation, and en-visioning Juriscapes

This brings us back to the immense salience of Business Logistics – not merely as a management discipline but as a powerful knowledge system that, by intent and effect, has reengineered the *Theatrum Orbis Logisticus* into a world of trans-territorial production, distribution, and profit-making. That claim is unremarkable should one appreciate that Business Logistics was always an ontological and material enterprise, which – by implication – engaged the full spectrum of productive, institutional, structural, and compulsory types of power (Chapter 3). Put another way, Business Logistics reconceptualized more than just the business firm, because its deeper purpose was to fundamentally redefine, standardize and, in turn, recalculate "the world" of transoceanic appropriation and accumulation. As Deborah Cowen explains:

> With logistics comes ... a new map of the world. For many, logistics may only register as a word on the side of the trucks that magically bring online orders only hours after purchase ... The entire network of infrastructures, technologies, spaces, workers, and violence that makes the circulation of stuff possible remains tucked out of sight ... Yet, alongside billions of commodities, the management of global supply chains ... relies on the calibration of an astonishing cast of characters, multiple circulations of capital, and complex movements across great distances ... Commodities today are manufactured *across logistics space* rather than in a singular place.[153]

Yet, International Law has strained to translate this geographic transformation due – in part – to what we discussed earlier on disciplinary world-making (Section 5.1). Business Logistics, as a prolific management discipline, has successfully yoked intermodal cargo as a subject

[152] Allan Sekula and Noël Burch, "A Film about the Sea: Notes on Allan Sekula and Noël Burch's *The Forgotten Space*," 17–18, https://cdn.dal.ca/content/dam/dalhousie/images/faculty/arts/centre-european-studies/Forgotten-Space.pdf

[153] Cowen, *Deadly Life of Logistics*, 1–2.

exclusive to its technical, "apolitical," and functional science.[154] This enabling a sterile framing of intermodal logistics via industrial idioms notably as "tertiary packaging": the thing used to transport other commodities worldwide.[155] Such vocabularies then narrowing the circumference of how the *global containerscape* is perceived and analyzed, stressing "real-time business" needs, such as transportation, warehousing, delivery times, total-cost, stock-keeping, data banks, inventory modelling, computation technologies, and – what is popularly known as – Supply Chain Risk Management.[156] However, as Thomas Birtchnell outlines, the ontological void is further explained by the material intricacies, technical orchestration, and para-jurisdictional character espoused by intermodal world-making:

> In part, the lacuna came about … due to the scale and complexity of this system alongside its secrecy, security, and circuitousness … First, there is the standardization of the steel transoceanic container so it is seamlessly moved from ports … Second, is the science of logistics involving a so-called bill of lading assigned to each container … [And] the superseding of paper by electronic tags [allowing] near-continuous tracking across borders alongside global positioning systems (GPS) and satellite shipping data so that clients and customers are always in control of … their freight. The third factor is security … container ships and ports all being legally protected zones … bound by … incredible cohesion and support through intra-national laws and policies.[157]

Intriguingly, what you may recall – from Section 5.1 – is that "secrecy, security, and circuitousness" defined similarly the world-making of the sixteenth-century *Casas* as they calculated, produced, and shrouded their inaugural planispheres of "the (imperial) world." That likeness might skip the eye should one read *Casa* superficially – merely as a physical house, while overlooking that the richer concept means an institution with a dedicated purpose. Such depth of meaning makes a

154 Martin Danyluk, "Capital's Logistical Fix: Accumulation, Globalization, and the Survival of Capitalism," *Environment and Planning D: Society and Space* 36, no. 4 (2018): 633.

155 Martin, *Shipping Container*, 8.

156 Charmaine Chua et al., "Turbulent Circulation: Building a Critical Engagement with Logistics," *Environment and Planning D: Society and Space* 36, no. 4 (2018): 617, 621–22; Joseph S. Szyliowicz, "Intermodalism, Supply Chains and U.S. Security," *Transport Reviews* 42, no. 6 (2022): 801–18.

157 Birtchnell, "The Missing Mobility," 85–86.

substantial difference in terms of grasping in practice what the *Casa da Mina* and the *Casa de la Contratación* represented as social institutions: just bureaucratic offices housed in the imperial boards of trade, or institutions in the "business of seeing" that were assigned an ontological and thus world-making mandate? The latter interpretation makes visible an underlying resemblance with what Business Logistics today has also embodied and enacted beyond merely its disciplinary form and commercial veneer.[158] In a nutshell, an influential social institution that has engineered a pointillistic globe of production, trade, and rule, which is spatially different from the planar and contiguous "world" the original *Casas* instigated and that international lawyers became accultured to see as an institutional state of nature.

This might explain the conviction Carl Schmitt expressed – in the chapter's opening – on how the "reproductive root" of normative ordering was tied to the inherent concreteness of planar and contiguous boundaries – that is, land appropriation. He displayed scant hesitation that such concreteness reflected less "the world" itself, and more a worldview engineered by a knowledge system launched by the imperial *Casas* and later refined by millions of planar, volumetric, and, ultimately, cartographic inscriptions. Put another way, Schmitt was partially correct in asserting that: "The constitutive process of a land-appropriation is found at the beginning of the history of every settled people … every empire." However, what he failed to acknowledge was this "constitutive process" began ontologically rather than with any immaculate history. It started with a system of knowledge intent on *en-visioning* a geography of imperial appropriation on a global scale, aided by iconography depicting a planar and contiguous "world." Once more, we loop back to our discussion in Chapter 4 regarding the *reification illusion*, and the extent to which *cartographic theory as practice* has structured and, arguably, ossified the perception of geographic and temporal ordering within the theoretical discipline.

The real-time consequence for international legal theory becomes detachment from how territorialization continues to unfold and mutate diachronically (Chapter 3). This implication accentuated

158 Allen, "The Logistics Revolution and Transportation," 116: "logistics is a multidisciplinary approach concerned with how to coordinate all purchasing, selling, and production activities together in order to assemble and distribute then right products in the right amounts to the right locations in the right condition so as to maximize profits for the firm."

because pointillism, pixels and Business Logistics have facilitated trans-territorial configurations of appropriation, violence, and rule, which now exceed the canonical discipline's cartographic imaginary. However, this does not suggest that statist cartography becomes obsolete or irrelevant for the field. Rather, like the metaphor of the rootstock and scion (Chapter 4), pointillistic geographies should be envisaged as recent outgrowths in a winding history of territorial rule, which remains entwined with its cartographic antecedent.

But where does this leave the incumbent World Map of states, and its planar and contiguous lines that Schmitt so privileged? What implication does the rise of pointillistic world-making have for the future of how international lawyers perceive and interrogate the globe's legal spacing? There have been varied attempts in recent years to theorize that transformation and many emanate from beyond the discipline, but with remarkable overlap and perceptiveness. For instance, numerous lawyers are familiar with Saskia Sassen's insight on: "transversally bordered spaces that not only cut across national borders but also generate new types of formal and informal jurisdictions ... deep inside national ... territory."[159] Much less known, however, is William Rankin's concept of pointillistic territories,[160] which specifies "transversal" spaces in terms of geographic nodes (such as cities, gateways, ports, hubs, extractive sites) that are connected and bound – transversally – via nonplanar and noncontiguous lines (corridors, routes, circuits, seams) of authority. More recently, Quinn Slobodian's notion of "perforation" has provided a piercing account of how the World Map of states has become altered by pointillistic world-making, both geographically and legally:

> [W]e make a mistake if we see the world only ... [as a] jigsaw of nations. In fact ... the modern world is pock-marked, perforated, tattered and jagged, ripped up and pinpricked. Inside the containers of nations are unusual legal spaces, anomalous territories, and peculiar jurisdictions. There are city-states, havens, enclaves, free ports, high-tech parks, duty-free districts, and innovation hubs. The world is riddled with *zones* – and they define the politics of the present in ways we are only starting to understand ... The zones are quasi-extraterritorial, both of the host state and distinct from it. Zones come in a bewildering range of varieties – at least eighty-two, by one

159 Sassen, "When Territory Deborders Territoriality," 23.
160 Rankin, *After the Map*, 203.

> official reckoning. Among the most prominent are the special economic zone, the export-processing zone, and the foreign-trade zone ... At one end of the socioeconomic spectrum, zones can be nodes in the networks of cross-border manufacturing. Often ringed by barbed wire, these are sites for low-wage production. At the other end, we can see a version of the zone in the tax havens where transnational corporations secrete away their earnings ... There are over 5,400 zones in the world ... Some are no bigger than a factory or a warehouse, a switch-point in the logistical circuitry of the global market, or a site for storing, assembling, or refining a product to avoid tariffs.[161]

Yet Slobodian's insight missed a deeper ontological implication, because he tied the concept of perforation to the metaphor of zone-making.[162] This narrow metaphor overlooks how the meaning of "perforation" is much richer and more profound: to bore, mine, hollow, or tunnel through a material. Perforation is, in fact, a term of landscaping par excellence, with zoning being only one of many particular legal metaphors that are applicable. This is not a pedantic observation, because perforation as a landscaping concept provides an ontological means to potentially untangle international legal theory from the grip of *cartographic theory as practice*. In other words, Slobodian's "zones" are more than cartographic pinpricks or "voids,"[163] they are vectors leveraging a new type of pointillistic geography and thus extension of territorial rule. When viewed with this wider circumference, what seem like extraterritorial dots in fact outline a novel circulatory geography that now predominates global production, trade and, ultimately, security.

[161] Quinn Slobodian, *Cracked-Up Capitalism: Market Radicals and the Dream of a World without Democracy* (London: Allen Lane, 2023), 2–3.

[162] On the intertwine between concepts and metaphors: see Onuf, *Making Sense, Making Worlds*, 40:

> Across many fields of study, scholars have turned to metaphors as a key to understanding some aspect of the human condition that has resisted or eluded their investigations ... We use metaphors as one of the many means to persuade others to accept or act on what we say. Representing the world, naming its contents, sorting things out: these are performative acts ... Some names for things that seem to alike (some concepts) fit better (as representations) and work better (as performances) than others; things change and so do conceptual vocabularies. Metaphors are concepts in the making; concepts are metaphors we no longer recognize as such.

[163] Slobodian, *Cracked-Up Capitalism*, 4.

For international lawyers, the implication is clear: to *en-vision* territorial rule today requires mapping these pointillistic perforations – geo-economic, geopolitical, and geo-legal – and tracing how they bore through cartographic jurisdictions. This is the work of identifying *juriscapes* (Chapter 4): conceptual spaces generated by pointillistic perforation and the re-engineering of the cartographic World Map. Juriscapes illuminate how authority now flows along nonplanar, noncontiguous lines, enabling forms of territorialization that are at once more mobile, more discrete, and more globally integrated than the statist template. In this sense, many practices of authority and power have navigated *off the map* of cartographic rule. Recognizing juriscapes not only recovers the centrality of cargo in the "business of seeing" the legal world – it also equips international lawyers to chart the evolving spatial grammar of power, authority, and appropriation that will preoccupy the discipline in the foreseeable future.

The challenge now is methodological as much as historical and ontological. It requires a willingness to interrogate the *Kartenpolitik* – the politics of mapping – that has long disciplined the field's imagination of space (see Chapter 4). The World Map of states remains an influential scaffold for disciplinary International Law, but it struggles to capture the pointillistic, perforated, and dynamically networked legal geographies of the present. Chapter 6 turns *off the map* to engage this problem directly. It considers how *Kartenpolitik* might be provincialized – how the inherited cartographic worldview can be placed in historical perspective, denaturalized, and reworked so as to reveal the juriscapes that organize trans-territorial authority today. Drawing on examples ranging from deep-sea resource regimes and digital jurisdiction to Arctic shipping corridors and outer space governance, the chapter probes the conceptual and visual tools needed to map spaces where legal authority travels along lines, cables, corridors, and orbital paths rather than neatly bounded territorialities. If the earlier chapters traced the imperial and logistical roots of International Law's spatial imagination, the final chapter shows how those roots are being overgrown, rerouted, and sometimes severed by circulatory geographies whose political and legal significance can no longer be read solely through the lines and volumes of the statist cartography.

6 *The Crisis of* Kartenpolitik

Wake up! We're heading into a perilous future without a map.

– *Gordon Brown*, "It's August 2024 – and Our World Is at a Turning Point. Here's What We Should Do Now," *The Guardian*

Somnium – the dream of rising above the Earth, like the sun, to behold the vivid totality of the world's surface – was never simply a poetic flourish. The cosmic dream originated in the Hellenic legend of Apollo's eye as the keeper of terrestrial harmony,[1] yet it has endured well beyond antiquity, living on through the visual and ontological projects of empires, states, corporations, and even satellites. Each has claimed this beatific gaze to present its own globalized image of the world as a natural picture of celestial reality. International lawyers have not been immune to this Apollonian lure; every "World Map" of states is bathed in the perpetual sunlight of an Apollo who, apparently, never sets.

Yet Gordon Brown's injunction jolts leaders, lawyers, and experts into confronting the peril that this beatific gaze is no longer available. The synoptic image – so fundamental to how Eurocentric rule was enacted and reproduced – has begun to lose its purchase among global elites and publics alike. Its fading grip provokes alarm at the prospect of a collapse in the very sense of global totality and harmony that the map once seemed to guarantee. This specter is illustrated by David Kennedy's reflections on a dissipating world order and its attendant dream:

> [W]hole regions of the world are coming unglued. Authoritarian rulers are newly empowered, flaunting their disregard ... If twenty years ago it could seem that rising powers were entering a global consensus, we can

[1] See Denis Cosgrove, *Apollo's Eye: A Cartographic Genealogy of the Earth in the Western Imagination* (Baltimore: Johns Hopkins University Press, 2001).

now see they rise with their own ideas, institutions and infrastructures ... Nationalism, populism, Brexit, Trump ... It's not clear what happened – whether the center began to wobble, other powers began to rise, the peripheries became more unstable – or people simply stopped believing. Perhaps all these, but no question, we've lost confidence and have started to describe the "postwar order" in the past tense. Looking back, it's easy to see what made that order so reassuring – although, with hindsight, it also looks too good to have been true. Indeed, it was always a dream – a dream which froze our imagination and stunted our powers of reinvention.[2]

The "dream" Kennedy describes was potent because it presented a singular vision of what the Earth *is* and *should look like* – geographically, politically, and legally. It produced a world in which legal authority appeared coextensive with geometric boundaries, privileging a narrow set of state-centric ideas and cartographic images to embody the iconic World Map of states. As earlier chapters have argued, what made the "dream" powerful – productively and structurally (see Chapter 3) – was precisely its portrayal of that iconic map as illuminating the *real* space of the terrestrial surface: a visual precursor that has conditioned how international lawyers have gazed upon and still see the legal globe. That conditioning, reinforced over recent centuries, has naturalized a planar, contiguous, and volumetric "world" in the discipline's imagination, even as Chapter 5 showed how pointillistic perforations are increasingly reconfiguring the spatial organization of global authority.

However, it is a *somnium* now in disarray, generating a level of political and legal angst that might even awaken Apollo to check on the sun. As Brown's warning implies, this is not merely a technical or political problem, but an unsettling conceptual one. First, there is the recognition that no single mapped totality can now reflect "the real globe" in a singular gaze – shaking the core presumption of universal space and time that underpinned the absolute and transhistorical presentation of the World Map of states. Second, there is the growing awareness that globalized images of the world are inseparable from geopolitical imaginaries, revealing that reigning visions of the globe have always been entwined with reveries of a singular terrestrial nature. As Bruno Latour reminds us:

[2] David Kennedy, "Law, Expertise and Global Political Economy," *Tilburg Law Review* 23, nos. 1–2 (2018): 110, https://doi.org/10.5334/tilr.130

> [W]hy it is that the *onus orbis terrarum* ... has become the only space for geopolitics to unfold. ... Because this image of the Globe is a highly complex and ... long history of mapping and of cartography, adding orbs after orbs, dome after dome, mixing many images of the *Orbis Terrarum* with that of the Blue Planet; all of those successive translations absorbed in some way inside the idea of the Globe of Nature.[3]

But how do such conceptual and visual reflections matter for lawyers and policymakers now facing the prospect of a world "coming unglued"? It is a fair question, for international lawyers are more likely to speak of *insomnia* in such a moment than of the pertinence of *somnium*. Yet belief in *somnium* has been omnipresent in globalized representations of the Earth, and the World Map of states has been a notable beneficiary of this Apollonian imaginary. For centuries, its sunlit projection has sought to capture the *Orbis Terrarum* in a single cartographic picture. Yes – that's right – international lawyers have been keen followers of the Apollonian dream.

The trouble is that few would ever admit such reverence. You are unlikely to hear an international lawyer profess: "this is my *somnium* of the legal globe." Yet, as the prior chapters have shown, the discipline has been so thoroughly entwined with a cartographic imaginary that it struggles to apprehend it *as* an imaginary. The present crisis, underscored by Brown's fear of a future without a map, is thus an ontological one – but not because the World Map of states has become irrelevant. Far from it.[4] Rather, the world the iconic map depicts is increasingly at odds with the pointillistic world rapidly reordering global authority and power – as traced in Chapter 5. The widening disconnect between cartographic and pointillistic orderings undermines the *somnium* the World Map once embodied. Put differently, the seeming certainty of terrestrial order rested less on any beatific gaze than on the deep assumptions of *cartographic theory as practice*.

[3] Latour, "*Onus Orbis Terrarum*," 308.

[4] See Wendy Brown, *Walled States, Waning Sovereignty* (Brooklyn: Zone Books, 2010), 36–37:

> sovereign nation-states no longer exclusively define the field of global political relations or monopolize many of the powers organizing that field, yet states remain significant actors in that field, as well as symbols of national identification ... Counterintuitively, perhaps, it is the weakening of state sovereignty, and more precisely, the detachment of sovereignty from the nation-state, that is generating much of the frenzy of nation-state wall building today.

This is why the term *Kartenpolitik* – first elaborated in Chapter 4 – is central to this closing chapter. My aim is not simply to provincialize the map in the Third World Approaches to International Law (TWAIL) sense, but to provincialize *the dream*:[5] the cartographic knowledge system behind the World Map of states, which made that global image appear absolutely *real* and essential in the Apollonian sense. *Kartenpolitik* targets that presentation of the World Map, because the legal globe is no longer exclusively cartographic, volumetric, or contiguous in its spatial constitution. Courtesy of pointillistic ordering, global extensions of authority and power have become increasingly noncontiguous, non-volumetric, and nonplanar. This prompts two questions that animate what follows: How may international lawyers see between and beyond *cartographic theory as practice*? And how can that be done when the discipline remains conceptually tied to a contiguous and volumetric cartography of authority and power?

6.1 Seeing between and beyond Cartographic "Reality"

Territorial rule has always required knowledge about the space it orders – whether the *Casas* charting imperial sea-lanes, nineteenth-century surveyors mapping colonial boundaries, or twenty-first-century GIS platforms tracking shipping corridors in real time. Geographic conceptions, images, and representations have been central to how authority is exercised because they establish a circumference of vision within which "the World" *is* and *should be* seen (see Chapter 2). This visual circumference, in turn, defines what counts as real space.

International Law is no different. As earlier chapters have shown, the discipline's inherited knowledge of the Earth derives from a narrow, cartographically mediated mode of representation – its lineage running from the imperial planispheres of the fifteenth century, through mercantile boards of trade, to the scientifically validated world atlases of the nineteenth century. From this lineage, international

5 See Dipesh Chakrabarty, *Provincializing Europe: Postcolonial Thought and Historical Difference*, new ed. (Princeton: Princeton University Press, 2008), 4: "The phenomenon of 'political modernity' – namely, the rule by modern institutions of the state, bureaucracy, and capitalist enterprise – is impossible to *think* of anywhere in the world without invoking certain categories and concepts, the genealogies of which go deep into the intellectual and even theological traditions of Europe."

lawyers absorbed a visual template that renders the globe as a contiguous, planimetric surface, divided into neatly bounded territorial compartments. This heritage laid the groundwork for key spatial concepts – territory, sovereignty, jurisdiction – by embedding them in a particular, and highly partial, *way of seeing*. In this respect, *cartographic theory as practice* has been a vivid example of productive and structural power (see Chapter 3): It has disciplined how international lawyers see the physical space of the legal globe, even as conditions of global authority have shifted toward pointillistic and pixellated geographies.

The difficulty, however, is that no cartographic reign could ever literally "mirror" the Earth – no spatial representation can achieve that Apollonian feat. Like any geographic likeness, the iconic World Map enacts an imaginary across the planet's surface. Yet international lawyers have long treated this imaginary as though it were the Earth itself: an institutionalized similitude of the *Orbis Terrarum* mistaken for "the real." This is not merely a matter of individual belief. Fundamental norms, terms, and debates within the field – borders, self-determination, territoriality, extraterritoriality – are framed and reproduced through this cartographic imaginary. That is why, even as authority now moves through noncontiguous circuits of ports, pipelines, data cables, financial hubs, and extractive sites (see Chapter 5), the mental image to which the discipline reflexively returns remains that of a bordered, contiguous globe. This enduring reflex is reinforced by what Chapter 4 described as the *reification illusion*, in which the cartographic image is mistaken for the territory itself, foreclosing recognition of alternative spatial grammars.

This reveals a latent vision embedded deep within international legal theory: an imperial and cartographic heritage that equates global "reality" with the geometry of a bounded sphere and the planimetric flattening of the globe into a legible surface. Stabilized by the epistemic authority of the *Casas* and their planispheres, and normalized later through centuries of juridical reliance on the cartographic image as the very condition for conceiving territory, jurisdiction, and sovereignty, this vision has proven remarkably durable. Yet sustaining it is increasingly strained in a world where the most pressing legal and political challenges – accelerating climate change, rising seas submerging low-lying states, mass displacement of populations, transnational resource extraction in the deep seabed, pandemic contagion traveling along flight routes and supply chains – are experienced at scales that are planetary, trans-territorial, and fundamentally noncontiguous.

The dilemma is stark: The cartographic world once furnished an apparently objective, Apollonian frame through which political, economic, and legal agency could be organized, but that frame now generates persistent blind spots, distorting how authority and obligation are spatially imagined and producing material consequences for both human and non-human life. More troubling still for certain entrenched political and economic interests, the "iconic world" of statist cartography no longer performs the discreet work it once did – of separating, and thereby politically insulating, the material consequences of industrialization, extraction, and security practices between European and non-European worlds. That insulation has been breached by the pointillistic and perforated geographies traced in Chapter 5: *juriscapes* of logistics, finance, data, and extraction, in which legal authority is exercised not across contiguous surfaces but through corridors, nodes, and flows. Maritime chokepoints such as Suez or Hormuz, for example, are not simply narrow seams on a map but dense legal spaces where registry suspensions, insurance warranties, and port denials can halt voyages irrespective of coordinates. Aviation terminals reveal a similar layering: Customs zones, security perimeters, slot allocations, and watchlists together create a palimpsest of authority that cannot be reduced to the footprint of a state polygon. In the digital domain, submarine cable landings, internet exchange points (IXPs), and cloud regions operate as infrastructural nodes where jurisdictional power is enacted through licenses, routing policies, and platform rules. In each case, what matters legally is less the boundary line on the atlas and more the gatekeeping decision at a corridor or node – the place where authority is assembled, responsibility attaches, and remedies must bite.

The deeper dilemma is less about terrestrial "reality" than about a reigning ontology – one that has conditioned the very terms on which international lawyers imagine, institutionalize, and legitimize global ordering. The cartographic world has so thoroughly shaped expectations of what global and international institutionalization *should look like* that it appears natural, even inevitable, in form. How, then, might one begin to see between and beyond those cartographic images? A first step is to reject the assumption that geographic knowledge functions as a kind of *prehistory* for the discipline, a store of brute material facts that exists ex ante and therefore needs no theoretical justification. As Chapter 4 emphasized, the conflation of the Earth with a cartographic world was always an *engineered* move – crafted to serve imperial purposes ranging from conquest and sovereign claim-making to the demarcation of trading monopolies and maritime corridors. A second step is to push decolonization in the discipline to a deeper ontological register, attentive to how the life of cartographic colonization has been both continuous and adaptive. The pointillistic perforations and logistical corridors mapped in Chapter 5 represent not rupture but transformation within that life. Yet this continuity has rarely been acknowledged, much less examined, in legal scholarship. As Sabarish Suresh reminds us:

> From the Treaty of Tordesillas to the Boundary Commission of India, from the Berlin Conference to the Irish Boundary line, it was a stroke on a parchment … that ultimately divided land, gradually distinguishing territories, and created jurisdictions. Although investigations of the role of cartography … in visually appropriating land as territory have burgeoned in the recent past, such examinations are yet to receive sustained attention in legal scholarship.[6]

What might be gained in pursuing those steps? First, the discipline cannot cancel or erase the cartographic world it has inherited and formalized: it has accrued centuries of institutional, material, and normative weight. This endurance is often weaponized – like a joker card – to defend the disciplinary status quo and discourage what is dismissed as wasteful "theoretical" reflection.[7] More striking, however, is the direct methodological implication: a cartographic imaginary has not simply been inherited but has reigned over the very conceptualization

[6] Sabarish Suresh, "The Cartojuridism of the British East India Company," *Law and History Review* 42, no. 3 (August 2024): 2.

[7] See Fuad Zarbiyev, "Of Theory and Reality, and Airplanes and Helicopters," *European Journal of International Law* 36, no. 1 (February 2025): 151–52:

> "Theory" versus "reality" is one of the most tired dichotomies in the discipline of international law. Yet this does not mean that we have a clear understanding of what "theory" or "reality" stand for. To start with the latter, most international lawyers tend to assume that "reality" needs no definition, treating it as a self-evident concept that requires no further explanation … It is not surprising that calls to be sensitive to reality often come from political conservative forces that conveniently overlook the fact that "at any given point reality equals status quo plus attempts at, or ideas about changing it."

Figure 6.1 *Apollo 8* mission picture *Earthrise (AS08-14-2383)*. Photograph, December 24, 1968. Gateway to Astronaut Photography of Earth, Public domain image courtesy of the Earth Science and Remote Sensing Unit, NASA Johnson Space Center https://eol.jsc.nasa.gov/SearchPhotos/photo.pl?frame=2383&mission=AS08&roll=14

of geographic space. This is precisely the disciplinary "freezing" and "stunting" Kennedy warned of – a structural incapacity for reinvention when the inherited imaginary no longer captures the most consequential geographies of authority and power.

The juxtaposition is telling: For two centuries, the World Map of states has been the dominant portrayal of the Earth in legal and political discourse, yet the first widely seen celestial "picture" of the planet – *Earthrise* (see Figure 6.1), taken by NASA's *Apollo 8* in 1968 – presented something profoundly different.[8] This nominally Apollonian image showed the Earth partially sunlit, cloud-shrouded, geologically opaque, and, in Brown's words, lacking any evident map!

How, then, can such divergent images of the same planet be reconciled? The answer leads back to a familiar and heavily loaded term – *reality* – that the discipline has long mobilized to sustain the authority of the World Map of states. The trouble is that reality here has no fixed, theory-neutral meaning. Its etymology offers little clarity: "real

[8] Cosgrove, *Apollo's Eye*, 257: "*Earthrise* comes from *Apollo 8*, launched on 21 December 1968 and splashing into the Pacific on 27 December. The first space mission to escape Earth's orbit, coast to the Moon, orbit, and return safely, its public impact was enhanced by spanning the Christmas period. A huge television audience saw the image on screen."

existence, what is real, the aggregate of all that is real," with "real" itself meaning "actually existing, having physical existence."[9] The circularity is striking.[10] Within disciplinary International Law, this vagueness has been filled, quietly but decisively, by *cartographic theory as practice*, which steps in to supply the visual referent. The result is an unexamined equation of reality with a preexisting, theory-free World Map of states – a supposedly material thing that requires no further explanation.

As Chapters 4 and 5 showed, however, nothing about the World Map of states was ever preexisting or geophysically inevitable. It was, and remains, a graphic, normative, and social construction – one that predates the discipline itself but became central to its self-image. Its apparent self-evidence is only plausible if cartographic world-making is pushed into the discipline's *prehistory*, where it can be imagined as a terrestrial precondition or an Apollonian superstructure. Yet *Earthrise* exposes the contingency of that conceit. It does not display the World Map geophysically; what it does display are the geophysical features of the planet – oceans, continents, clouds – without the legal partitions that international lawyers instinctively project onto it. This is why *Earthrise* is such a disruptive image: It interrupts the *somnium* and the beatific gaze by showing the planet from a genuinely celestial vantage point, unencumbered by the lines, colors, and projections of institutionalized cartography.

6.2 "To Write the Earth"

Houston, [do] we have a problem? Yes and no. The problem is less that the Earth itself has changed form, but that it is always apprehended through a reigning medium and ontology – one that conditions how "real space" is perceived in any particular presentation. This means that different visual media, grounded in different ontologies, can construct

9 "*Reality*: 'real existence, what is real, the aggregate of all that is real' is attested from the 1640s; the sense 'the real state (of something)' dates from the 1680s; in the 17th–18th centuries the word also sometimes meant 'sincerity'," *Online Etymology Dictionary*, accessed August 23, 2025, entry for "reality." www.etymonline.com/search?q=reality

10 "*Real*: 'actually existing, having physical existence (not imaginary)' (mid-15th c.); 'relating to things' (especially property), from Old French *reel* 'real, actual,' from Late Latin *realis* 'actual,' in Medieval Latin 'belonging to the thing itself'," *Online Etymology Dictionary*, accessed August 23, 2025, entry for "real." www.etymonline.com/word/real

markedly different spatial realities relative to the same referential body or thing.[11] For most scientists – and for litigation lawyers trained to deploy competing expert reports – this is hardly a radical proposition: Concepts, theories, and media are explicitly acknowledged as structuring perception, inquiry, and argument. Medicine offers a telling analogy. Like International Law, it orients itself to a single referential body – in this case, the human corpus. Yet physicians shift seamlessly between multiple, equally authoritative ways of envisioning the "fleshiness" of that one body, moving between what we might call "snapshot-stories": blood tests, X-ray plates, mammograms, nuclear imaging, ultrasound scans, magnetic resonance images.[12] Each visual regime isolates certain features, suppresses others, and tells a different but nonetheless valid story about the same body. The Earth Sciences adopt a similar multiplicity, conceptualizing the planet as a composite of interacting spheres – atmosphere, biosphere, cryosphere, hydrosphere, magnetosphere – each with its own methods of visualization and analysis.[13]

By contrast, International Law's perception of the Earth remains tethered to a singular imaging regime and an imputed unity: The geometric globe flattened into the contiguous, volumetric, and color-coded projections of the World Map of states. This attachment is less a matter of deliberate professional choice than the effect of long-running disciplinary capture by *cartographic theory as practice* – what Chapter 4 analyzed as *Kartenpolitik*'s reifying grip, and what Chapter 5 showed to be increasingly outpaced by the pointillistic and pixellated geographies organized through logistics, finance, data, and extraction. The discipline's *Houston-like* problem is that this cartographic ontology continues to operate as a tacit background assumption: rarely named, seldom interrogated, and therefore remarkably resilient.

Yet the lived realities of international legal practice already point elsewhere. Financial sanctions, for instance, often turn not on sovereign borders but on the moment when a correspondent bank's

[11] See Charlotte Epstein, *Birth of the State: The Place of the Body in Crafting Modern Politics* (Oxford: Oxford University Press, 2021).

[12] See Annemarie Mol, *The Body Multiple: Ontology in Medical Practice* (Durham and London: Duke University Press, 2002).

[13] See Elena E. Cirkovic and Danielle R. Wood, "Complex Earth–Outer Space Systems and New Spacetime for International Law," *International Journal of Law in Context* 21, no. 2 (June 2025): 300–13, https://doi.org/10.1017/S1744552325100086

screening algorithm halts a transfer. Drone operations depend less on the geometry of national airspace than on the orchestration of satellite tasking orders, base permissions, and telemetry logs.[14] Undersea cables and cloud regions, meanwhile, constitute decisive legal terrains where orders to service providers or IXPs can reroute, suspend, or terminate flows at scale.[15] These are not simply technical footnotes: they are the operative *juriscapes* in which rules are extended, responsibility attaches, and potential remedies become effective only when directed at normative and material infrastructures that enact global ordering.

Even critical interventions such as TWAIL, while incisively confronting the imperial histories of International Law, have tended to leave intact the imperial *imaging* of space that underpins how the legal globe is geographically envisioned. Specifically, the narrow mode of contiguous and volumetric cartography continues to occupy the ontological ground of international legal theory, enthroned optically because most lawyers still encounter that "picture" as a fixed material object rather than as an unfolding ontological artifice. In Kennedy's apt terms, the result is a discipline "frozen" and "stunted" in its capacity to register – let alone theorize – the contemporary practices of territorialization that now operate through noncontiguous circuits of ports, fiber-optic cables, shipping lanes, sanctions screens, and extractive sites. These practices steadily diverge from the cartographic imaginary that remains at the center of the legal globe.

However, there is something intriguing – almost disarming – about *cartography* as a noun: Its etymology carries none of the statist geometry or imperial legacy that now saturates the term in international legal usage. At its most basic, *cartography* simply denotes "to write the earth."[16] In this generic sense, it names a textual practice rather than a visual ideology, and this is what makes it a fitting hinge for the second half of my yes-and-no answer. For if cartography is a kind of

[14] See Katharine Hall Kindervater, "Drone Strikes, Ephemeral Sovereignty, and Changing Conceptions of Territory," *Territory, Politics, Governance* 5, no. 2 (2016): 207–21, 20–21. https://doi:10.1080/21622671.2016.1260493

[15] See Vili Lehdonvirta et al., "Weaponised Interdependence in a Bipolar World: How Economic Forces and Security Interests Shape the Global Reach of US and Chinese Cloud Data Centres," *Review of International Political Economy*, April 2025, 1–26. https://doi:10.1080/09692290.2025.2489077

[16] Nicole Reiz et al., "Exploring a Critical Legal Cartography: Law, Practice, and Complexities," *Geography Compass* 12, no. 5 (2018): 1–10, https://doi.org/10.1111/gec3.12368

writing, it is one that admits multiple genres, styles, and purposes. This textual quality is easily overlooked precisely because cartography is not a literary form; it belongs instead to the family of *nonbook* texts that includes architectural blueprints, engineering schematics, musical scores, programming languages,[17] and statistical charts. What distinguishes cartography within this family is that it constructs a highly simplified system of geographic representation – one that, over time, assumed unrivalled preeminence in depicting the legal globe.[18] That preeminence came at a cost: the cartographic image acquired such epistemic authority that it obscured its own status as a text, and with it the possibility of recognizing alternative ways of "writing" legal space. As Brian Harley reminds us:

> [W]e have to turn to the cartographic text itself. The word *text* is deliberately chosen. ... It has been said that "what constitutes a text is not the presence of linguistic elements but the act of construction" so that maps ... become texts. *Text* is certainly a better metaphor for maps than the mirror of nature ... Rather that working with a formal science of communication ... our concern is redirected to a history and anthropology of the image, and we learn to recognize the narrative qualities of cartographic representation as well as its claim to provide a synchronous picture of the world.[19]

Seen from this perspective, spatial "reality" acquires a different inflection. The World Map of states is less a neutral picture of the planet than a narrative text – one that enacts and continually reproduces a particular vision of "the World" and, by implication, a particular legal geography. This is the crucial difference between *cartography* and what I have called *cartographic theory as practice*. The former retains its generic, textual sense ("to write the earth") and describes a range of possible narrative framings of the legal globe. The latter goes further ontologically, teleologically and – even – ideologically: it takes that generic writing and folds it into a singular, totalizing "picture" of cartographic reality, embodied in the iconic World Map. In doing so, it defines *real* legal space through the prism of contiguous, volumetric, and planar lines of representation. In other words,

17 See Ethem Alpaydin, *Machine Learning*, 2nd ed. (Cambridge: MIT Press, 2016).

18 Chandra Mukerji, "Visual Language in Science and the Exercise of Power: The Case of Cartography in Early Modern Europe," *Studies in Visual Communication* 10, no. 3 (1984): 31–32.

19 Harley, "Deconstructing the Map," 5.

cartographic theory as practice has displaced the open-ended connotation of "writing the earth" with a tightly scripted *somnium* of the legal globe – an Apollonian projection that conditions what counts as *real* space and, correspondingly, what counts as a *real* boundary. As Jeppe Strandsbjerg underlines: "the way in which space is made real through cartographic… practices … conditions the way in which boundaries can be demarcated … [T]he … organisation of space is as much about defining a particular spatial reality as it is a question of enclosing, territorialising, controlling or otherwise partitioning space."[20]

6.3 Confronting International Law's Brute *Geo*-Politics

Earthrise displayed no cartographic "reality" in any terrestrial, celestial, or geophysical sense. What it presented was the planet stripped of the reigning ontology and imaginary that had, for centuries, structured geopolitical understanding. When it appeared in 1968, the photograph was largely consumed through the romanticized lens of the *space age* – an era steeped in Apollo missions, Cold War rivalry, and a *Star Trek* imaginary of boundless exploration. Few recognized that what made the image so striking was precisely its absence of the cartographic scaffolding that international lawyers and statesmen had long taken for granted. Even fewer grasped that the familiar World Map of states was not a passive reflection of geopolitical "reality" but an active narrative device – one that, since the imperial planispheres of the fifteenth century, had scripted the spatial grammar of global ordering in the contiguous, volumetric, and planar forms described in Chapter 4. This teleological conception of geography – treating "real" space as that which could be made to conform to the state-bound geometry of the World Map – remained intact, even as pointillistic circuits of authority and power (see Chapter 5) were already beginning to perforate that imagined totality.

Even today, few lawyers would think to see *Earthrise* as a "snapshot-story" of law's world – one among many possible – much less as an invitation to imagine others. Captured from beyond the planet's atmosphere, the photograph offered a non-cartographic,

[20] Jeppe Strandsbjerg, "Cartopolitics, Geopolitics and Boundaries in the Arctic," *Geopolitics* 17, no. 4 (October 2012): 827, https://doi.org/10.1080/14650045.2012.660581

celestial perspective that unsettled the universalizing map long upheld by the discipline. Where the iconic map had stabilized Eurocentrism's singular geopolitical vision – casting the globe as a jigsaw of sovereign containers – *Earthrise* revealed a planetary body without social borders, capitals, or lines of demarcation. Yet the absence of such demarcations has not loosened the grip of the cartographic imaginary: international legal education, scholarship, and practice continue to be trained on the bordered, planar world of statist cartography,[21] even as the spatial practices of law increasingly follow pointillistic supply chains, data corridors, financial flows, and resource concessions that move *off the map*.

To name geopolitics in this context is to risk controversy. For many international lawyers, the term is reflexively pigeonholed into a narrow doctrinal narrative: The expansionist ambitions of (European) great powers to extend control over vast territories, markets, and resources, regardless of sovereign boundaries or international legal obligations.[22] Yet, as the preceding chapters have shown, that account is itself framed by the very cartographic ontology whose brute geopolitics now needs to be confronted.

Geopolitics is far more than a rhetorical catchword; it is also a conceptual apparatus that shapes how international lawyers perceive and organize "the World."[23] The term is multifaceted,[24] carries a typology

[21] For example, see: Alain Pellet, *Le droit international à la lumière de la pratique: l'introuvable théorie de la réalité, Cours général de droit international public*, Recueil des cours de l'Académie de droit international de La Haye, vol. 414 (Leiden and Boston: Brill Nijhoff, 2021), at 9.

[22] Agnew, *Geopolitics*, 93–96.

[23] See Terrence W. Haverluk et al., "The Three Critical Flaws of Critical Geopolitics: Towards a Neo-Classical Geopolitics," *Geopolitics* 19, no. 1 (January 2014): 19–20, https://doi.org/10.1080/14650045.2013.803192: "A reinterpretation of geopolitics was necessary because from the 1890s to the 1990s geopolitics was imperialist, racist, environmentally deterministic, and worked closely with imperial state governments to achieve political goals … In moving 'beyond' classical geopolitics … other include popular geopolitics, formal geopolitics, and feminist geopolitics."

[24] See Terrence W. Haverluk et al., "The Three Critical Flaws of Critical Geopolitics," p. 5: "The term 'geopolitics' has long been used to refer to the study of the geographical representations, rhetoric and practices that underpin world politics. The word has in fact undergone something of a revival in recent years. The term is now freely used to refer to such phenomena as international boundary disputes, the structure of global finance, and geographical patterns of elections results." See also: Gearóid Ó Tuathail et al., *The Geopolitics Reader* (New York: Routledge, 2006).

of meanings. The most familiar to lawyers is bound to its nineteenth- and early twentieth-century militaristic idioms – *Weltpolitik* (imperial expansion beyond Europe) and *Machtpolitik* (the politics of force) – but its generic sense concerns how the spatial organization of power is perceived and acted upon at a global scale.[25] Significantly, the very word *geopolitics* only became thinkable once cartography had made it possible to envision the Earth as a single structural whole, over which political order could be imagined and administered. Imperial planispheres and, later, the contiguous geometry of the state-based World Map provided the textual and visual scaffolding for this conceptual leap, furnishing a taxonomy of global space in which lines on a map stood as the boundaries of the political universe.[26]

At its core, geopolitics is a practice of defining and inscribing real space, producing the boundaries through which political, legal, and economic order is enacted.[27] It has always been a struggle over spatial assumptions, strategic interests, graphic depictions, and competing imaginaries[28] – what Chapter 5 called the rival "grammars" of global rule, from imperial *Casas* to logistical *juriscapes*. While the term *geopolitics* was only coined in the early twentieth century, its ontological work long predates its semantics: The first imperial planispheres had already imposed *one-world* depictions of planetary life, shaping the frame within which law, commerce, and violence operated.[29]

25 John Bew, *Realpolitik: A History*, 2nd ed. (Oxford: Oxford University Press, 2016), 72–91.
26 Agnew, *Geopolitics*, 31.
27 Stefano Guzzini, "Which Geopolitics?" in *The Return of Geopolitics in Europe? Social Mechanisms and Foreign Policy Identity Crises*, ed. Stefano Guzzini (Cambridge: Cambridge University Press, 2013), 41:

> Whereas neoclassical geopolitics, "using geographic knowledge and representations to naturalise power, belongs to the realm of realist approaches," critical geopolitics, "problematising the fusion of geographical knowledge and power, belongs to the realm of constructivist approaches." This has important implications for how geopolitics is defined. "Geopolitics … should be critically re-conceptualized as a discursive practice by which intellectuals of statecraft 'spatialize' international politics in such a way as to represent it as a 'world' characterized by particular types of places, peoples and dramas." And, "the study of geopolitics in discursive terms … is the study of the socio-cultural resources and rules by which geographies of international politics get written."

28 See Meghan McConaughey et al., "Beyond Anarchy: Logics of Political Organization, Hierarchy, and International Structure," *International Theory* 10, no. 2 (July 2018): 181–218, https://doi.org/10.1017/S1752971918000040
29 Agnew, *Geopolitics*, 28–29.

What does this mean for disciplinary International Law? The prevailing assumption is that the discipline operates as an institutional counterweight to geopolitics, perhaps even as its legal constraint.[30] But this rests on a reductive reading of geopolitics as merely the great-power expansionism of European empires, divorced from the deeper processes of world-making. In reality, all institutional projects – whether imperial, corporate, or intergovernmental – are geopolitical in that they rest on spatial imaginaries that define, assemble, and organize geographic "reality."[31] International Law is no exception: Its *geo-* is envisioned through the iconic map, and its normative and institutional architecture works to reproduce that image as the authoritative depiction of the legal globe. This geopolitical dimension is often hidden behind the claim that the cartographic world map is *erga omnes* – a rational, objective, and universally equitable portrayal of "the World."[32]

That portrayal only works if the imperial histories and motivations that produced the *one-world* model are archived out of sight. Erasing or neutralizing those histories deflects critical inquiry into why the legal globe is taken to be contiguous, volumetric, and planar by default. This selectivity is the hallmark of the *geopolitics* International Law furthers – whether knowingly or not. It is also teleological: The *geo-* is predefined by a surface of mapped states, treated as a brute given rather than a contingent artefact. In this sense, the World Map of states sits at the productive, structural, and institutional core of modern geopolitics, its maintenance the implicit work of *cartographic theory as practice*.

This is why alternative spatial orders – such as noncontiguous legal geographies – are marginalized. If they do not match the cartographic form, they are treated as insufficiently *geo*, and thus *less real*. Here teleology intersects with the structural power of language (see Chapter 3), for the very categories by which reality is asserted

30 See Hersch Lauterpacht, *The Function of Law in the International Community*, ch. VII (Oxford: Clarendon Press, 1933; reissued Oxford: Oxford University Press, 2011), 147–73.

31 See Kennedy, *A World of Struggle*.

32 Or through acceptance in practice as a means of envisioning and enacting non-European self-determination, see Arnulf Becker Lorca, *Mestizo International Law: A Global Intellectual History 1842–1933* (Cambridge: Cambridge University Press, 2015).

depend on how we distinguish what John Searle calls *brute facts* from *institutional facts*:

We need to distinguish between *brute facts* such as the fact that the sun is ninety-three million miles from the earth and *institutional facts* such as the fact that [Trump] is president. Brute facts exist independently of any human institutions; institutional facts can exist only within human institutions. Brute facts require the institution of language in order that we can *state* the facts, but the brute facts *themselves* exist quite independently of language or of any other institution. Thus the statement that the sun is ninety-three million miles from the earth requires an institution of language and an institution of measuring distance ... but the fact *stated*, the fact there is a certain distance between the earth and the sun, exists independently of any institution ... Institutional facts, on the other hand, require special human institutions for their very existence. Language is one such institution; indeed, it is a whole set of such institutions.[33]

Disciplinary International Law is distinctive in that it systematically blurs the boundary between brute and institutional facticity when it comes to legal space. This is the result of a 500-year process of *cartographization* – in which the raw, physical Earth was reconstituted as a cartographic planet, both conceptually and institutionally. Through repeated inscription, the World Map of states acquired a majesty of self-evidence, appearing materially inherent in an Apollonian sense. That majesty stems from the way the cartographic text has come to dominate how real legal space is perceived: the map is treated not as one representation among others but as *the* representation. The effect is to fuse the reigning imaginary and the terrestrial into a single, seemingly immutable picture. This fusion offers a form of ontological security – an image of legal reality so naturalized as to be almost sacrosanct.[34] Yet, as Rob Kitchin and Martin Dodge remind us, such security is illusory:

Maps are ... brought into being through practices (embodied, social, technical), always remade every time they are engaged with; mapping is a process of constant reterritorialization. As such, maps are transitory and fleeting, being contingent, relational and context-dependent. *Maps are practices* – they are

[33] Searle, *The Construction of Social Reality*, 27. On institutional facts in IR, see also Kratochwil, *Rules, Norms and Decision*, 25–28.

[34] See also Jeremy W. Crampton, *The Political Mapping of Cyberspace* (Chicago: University of Chicago Press, 2003).

always *mappings*; spatial practices enacted to solve relational problems ... A map is never a map with ontological security assumed; it is brought into the world and made to do work through practices such as recognizing, interpreting, translating, communicating, and so on ... It does not re-present the world or make the world (by shaping how we think about the world) ... it is a production that is constantly in motion, always seeking to appear ontologically secure.[35]

6.4 "Wake Up"?

Where does this leave a cartographic text, imaginary, and teleology that has so profoundly shaped how international lawyers conceptualize and imagine the Earth? As Chapters 4 and 5 have shown, there is a historical irony in the fact that the blurring of brute and institutional space enabled the naturalization of the World Map of states. What began as an artefact of imperial mapping – produced through the selective inscription of planispheres, projection choices, and cadastral grids – has been sedimented into the discipline's very ontology. This map served not merely as a visual representation but as the primary organizing schema through which international legal theory, doctrine, and institutional practice structured the legal globe. In doing so, it legitimated a specific, state-centric horizon of legal possibility, one calibrated to the geometric and contiguous logics of Westphalian sovereignty and colonial partition. Yet it is precisely this reified cartographic vision – once generative of global legal order – that now "freezes" and "stunts" international legal thought. Despite its enduring appearance of stability, the spatial history underpinning global legal relations – its legal geographies, institutional arrangements, and constructed spatial "realities" – remains, as Kitchin and Dodge remind us, dynamic, contested, and continually *in motion*.

The World Map of states emerged from a historically contingent constellation of cartographic assumptions, imaginaries, and techniques that were later universalized through the spread of European treaty practices, colonial surveys, and nineteenth-century international conferences. This universalization of cartographic space is what underpins International Law's Eurocentrism to this day, reinforcing a singular, monolithic vision of global space, territorial

[35] Kitchin and Dodge, "Rethinking Maps," 334–35.

boundaries, and legal order. The cartographic text has shaped the discipline's spatial imaginary by privileging an ontology and grammar grounded in planar, contiguous, and volumetric geometries – seen most clearly in its doctrinal reliance on territorial integrity, jurisdictional exclusivity, and the bounding of maritime and aerial zones into fixed units. As Chapter 5 demonstrated in the context of pointillistic ordering, this spatial vision now blinds the discipline to emergent geographies that defy the geometric logics prescribed by *cartographic theory as practice* – geographies composed of logistics corridors, offshore finance hubs, and extractive frontiers, which operate as discontinuous yet legally consequential sites of global governance.

This critique is particularly significant because the iconic map was never a neutral or objective representation of terrestrial reality, despite its authoritative appearance. From the outset, it functioned as a normative project – a way of seeing and organizing "the World" that asserted cartographic authority while encoding specific legal and political hierarchies. Recognizing this becomes timely, as the cartographic world once embodied by the iconic map is losing its legal purchase as a *real-time* geography. It is becoming increasingly evident that new spatial possibilities are being constructed and constituted – both geopolitically and legally – through other kinds of authoritative texts, beyond the cartographic. As Gail Lythgoe illustrates:

> International lawyers can usually only see states and their spaces ... Some GVCs [global value chains] ... can bring "together hundreds if not thousands of suppliers in decentralized networks administered through contract governance. The semiconductor chip manufacturer Intel, for example, uses no less than 19,000 suppliers in over 100 countries ...." The contract is increasingly the "principle infrastructure of social ordering", and the chain of contracts [binds] a multitude of actors and [spans] the globe. Yet ... contracts ... are spaces ... they are practices with spatialities that can disrupt or perpetuate existing spaces, but the main point is that they are relations constitutive of the spatial all on their own.[36]

The institutional consequences become evident with legal problems and practices operating at scales that strain the spatial logic of

[36] Gail Lythgoe, "Contracts: Reterritorialising the (Global) Exercise of Authority," *International Journal of Law in Context*1 (2025): 2–3., https://doi.org/10.1017/S1744552325100050

cartographic rationality. Trans-territorial phenomena such as climate change, biodiversity loss, and environmental degradation unfold across ecosystems and atmospheric systems, rendering contiguous or volumetric models of geographic responsibility inadequate. Similarly, the sharp rise in extraterritorial legal claims – especially in contemporary conflict and security contexts – highlights how the one-time exception to state-centric geography increasingly appears like a novel rule.[37] The *Universal Jurisdiction Annual Review 2025* records ninety-five active extraterritorial and universal-jurisdiction cases across sixteen countries in 2024, with thirty-six new investigations – nearly double the number initiated in 2023.[38] No domain illustrates this geopolitical-legal shift more clearly than "shadow warfare."[39] US drone strikes have been deployed in at least eight countries outside formal theaters of war – such as Yemen, Somalia, Pakistan, and Libya – generating acute questions of jurisdiction, accountability, and legal authority.[40] Between 2004 and 2018, there were over 413 drone strikes in Pakistan alone, killing an estimated 2,366–3,702 individuals, of whom between 245 and 303 were civilians.[41] These operations are typically justified by broad interpretations of self-defense or consent – yet their increasing frequency and alleged normalcy raise fundamental questions about the ontological "reality" and security of cartographic boundaries.[42]

37 See Marko Milanović, *Extraterritorial Application of Human Rights Treaties: Law, Principles, and Policy* (Oxford: Oxford University Press, 2011).

38 Trial International, *Universal Jurisdiction Annual Review 2025*, accessed August 23, 2025, www.ecchr.eu/en/publication/universal-jurisdiction-annual-review-2025/. "This eleventh edition of the UJAR testifies to the enduring role of extraterritorial and universal jurisdiction as a central pillar of the global fight against impunity," including the opening of thirty-six new cases and twenty-seven convictions in 2024.

39 Niva, "Disappearing Violence," 185–86.

40 Neta C. Crawford, *The Costs of War: U.S. Counterterrorism Operations and Civilian Harm* (Providence, RI: Watson Institute for International and Public Affairs, Brown University, 2021), 6–10.

41 The Bureau of Investigative Journalism, *Drone Warfare: Pakistan*, accessed June 2025, www.thebureauinvestigates.com/projects/drone-war/pakistan

42 See Oona A. Hathaway and Scott J. Shapiro, *The Internationalists: How a Radical Plan to Outlaw War Remade the World* (New York: Simon & Schuster, 2017); see also Nick Turse, *The Changing Face of Empire: Special Ops, Drones, Spies, Proxy Fighters, Secret Bases, and Cyberwarfare* (Chicago: Haymarket Books, 2012).

There are also contemporary political slogans such as "Take Back Control" or "Make America Great Again," which reflect anxiety over the erosion of the ontological security once provided by cartographic world-making. For much of the modern era, the visual and legal grammar of the World Map of states – constituted by a grid of contiguous states – offered a beatific and reassuring vision through which International Law could imagine and govern law on a global scale. This cartographic ideal promised spatial universality, geometric coherence, and terrestrial control: a geopolitical tableau in which identity, authority, and geography aligned seamlessly. As that vision is increasingly overwritten by mass migration, ecological crises, Artificial Intelligence,[43] and the containerization of trade and production, the spatial certainty that cartographic boundaries once offered becomes exposed as contingent and institutionally limited. In this context, such slogans express a desire to restore the geometric stability of the receding spatial order, a longing for the ontological security that *cartographic theory as practice* once seemed to guarantee. Yet such a spatial imaginary was never absolute, although it was projected to appear as Apollonian. The World Map of states was forged through imperial and racialized projects that rendered the Earth appropriable through logics of enclosure, seizure, and exclusion.[44] Efforts that seek to restore this mapped imaginary obscure its contested and contingent origins, and in doing so, reaffirm a spatial ontology that disciplinary International Law must now critically confront – and ultimately move beyond.

However, the call to "move beyond" the cartographic imaginary confronts structural and institutional constraint: the embedding of cartographic ordering within both legal architectures and the cartographic grammar of International Law. The World Map of states remains a foundational and beatific image for the UN system, treaty-making, jurisdictional delineation, and the very organization of legal personality.[45] The task is not necessarily to cancel or replace this incumbent order wholesale, but to trace how its core concepts and

[43] See Samuel Greengard, *The Internet of Things* (Cambridge: MIT Press, 2015); Nick Srnicek, *Platform Capitalism* (Cambridge: Polity, 2017).

[44] See Lindahl, *Fault Lines of Globalization.*

[45] See Negar Mansouri and Daniel R. Quiroga-Villamarín (eds.), *Ways of Seeing International Organisations: New Perspectives for International Institutional Law* (Cambridge: Cambridge University Press, 2025).

institutions – sovereignty, territory, jurisdiction – are increasingly intersected and mutated by noncontiguous, pointillistic geographies.[46] Like scions grafted onto an old rootstock (see Chapter 4), emergent spatial practices – digital sovereignty, supply-chain governance,[47] climate-displacement regimes – reshape the operation of cartographic institutions from within, generating hybrid legal forms that international lawyers must learn to recognize and theorize.

Juriscapes offer one such analytical lens. Unlike the cartographic framework that presumes continuous, state-bound areal jurisdiction, *juriscapes* foreground the relational and networked dimensions of authority and power as they are exercised across diverse landscapes of legal spacing. They enable international lawyers to trace how military power, global trade,[48] and trans-territorial production are juridically organized through dispersed nodes of regulation, infrastructure, and control – sites often obscured from the contiguous grammar of state territory.[49] These are not merely anomalies to be catalogued as exceptions but constitutive forms of legal ordering.

Juriscapes in operation illustrate how such analysis works in practice. Consider maritime chokepoints and logistics corridors: ports, canals, and shipping lanes form not simply lines on a map but multi-layered legal corridors,[50] where customs regimes, sanctions enforcement, insurance requirements, and private security rules converge. Authority here is not reducible to the coastline; it is performed along lines of infrastructures that sustain trans-territorial circulations. Digital overlays – platform rules, data-localization mandates, interconnection exchanges – compose another kind of spatial inscription, perforating

46 See Brown, *Walled States*, 36:

> Rather than iterations of nation-state sovereignty, the new nation-state walls are part of an ad hoc global landscape of flows and barriers both inside nation-states and in the surrounding postnational constellations, flows and barriers divide richer from poorer parts of the globe. This landscape signifies the ungovernability by law and politics of many powers unleashed by globalization and late modern colonialization.

47 See Kate MacDonald, *The Politics of Global Supply Chains: Power and Governance beyond the State* (Cambridge: Polity, 2014).

48 Laleh Khalili, *Sinews of War and Trade: Shipping and Capitalism in the Arabian Peninsula* (London and New York: Verso Books, 2021).

49 Sassen, "When Territory Deborders Territoriality," 21–22.

50 See Bruce D. Jones, *To Rule the Waves: How Control of the World's Oceans Shapes the Fate of the Superpowers* (New York: Scribner, 2021).

states and thus jurisdictions.[51] In the security domain, forward basing, contractor compounds, satellite ground stations, and telemetry links knit together operational sites that do not map neatly onto contiguous areas,[52] yet whose legal salience emerges when their connective infrastructure is traced. At resource frontiers – deep-sea mining concessions, undersea cable routes, fisheries – United Nations Convention on the Law of the Sea's cartographic rootstock intersects with licensing chains, exclusion zones, and insurer-mandated corridors that delimit lawful action. Across these sites, *juriscape* literacy enables sharper identification of where obligations attach, how responsibility is allocated, and through what infrastructures remedies may travel.

Such literacy does not abandon statist cartography, but supplements it by clarifying how territorialization today is enacted not only at contiguous borders but also through compliance screens, routing protocols, inspection regimes, and licenses. It reorients the lawyer's gaze toward the infrastructural sites where responsibility crystallizes, where machine-generated logs and ledgers provide probative evidence, and where remedies must be directed if they are to be effective. In this sense, territorialization increasingly appears less as the drawing of geometric lines on a map than as a practice of gatekeeping – of opening, closing, or redirecting the corridors through which authority and power flows.

The anxiety that "we are heading into a perilous future without a map" is better understood as the exhaustion of a monopoly rather than the loss of an image. Once maps are recognized as nonbook texts – revisable media of world-making – the crisis of *Kartenpolitik* becomes an opportunity to reequip the discipline with the means of reinvention. The world has not "come unglued"; our habits of seeing have. *Juriscape* literacy keeps the dream and its ungluing in the same frame, enabling the discipline to navigate – normatively and institutionally – a world increasingly made, and unmade, *off the map*.

This is not a call for iconoclasm, but for a form of disciplinary revision that denaturalizes contiguity by recognizing it as a historically

51 See Mark Graham and Martin Dittus, *Geographies of Digital Exclusion: Data and Inequality* (London: Pluto Press, 2022).

52 Militaries often create and operate forward logistics hubs in remote theatres – often beyond state borders. See Lasse Elvemo, "Supply Chain Resilience in Military Operations: A Case Study Exploring Command and Control," *Scandinavian Journal of Military Studies* 8, no. 1 (2025): 184–85, https://doi.org/10.31374/sjms.356

successful, but partial, solution to the problem of legal extension; normalizing the coexistence of multiple spatial texts; tracing how new scions modify the cartographic rootstock; and placing the politics of mapping, logistics, digital networks, and remote sensing at the center of legal scholarship and pedagogy. If the cartographic imaginary once promised ontological security, *juriscape* literacy offers a different assurance – not the fixity of geometric lines, but the competence to navigate their shifting relations.

To "Wake Up" in this sense is not to discard the map but to see it in its rightful proportions: one spatial text among many, powerful but partial, authoritative yet revisable. The future of the legal globe will not be drawn along a single projection. It will be composed through overlapping inscriptions – infrastructural, ecological, digital, corporate – each performing its own vision of space, each demanding its own critical literacy. In this respect, the discipline's task resembles the cultivation of a complex graft: tending the old rootstock while learning the growth patterns of the new scions, so that the composite may continue to bear fruit. And, like a sequence of "snapshot-stories," these spatial forms must be read in concert, allowing disciplinary International Law to recognize the simultaneity of its dreams and its disruptions – and to keep arguing the legal Earth into being.

Bibliography

Aalberts, Tanja, and Thomas Gammeltoft-Hansen. "Sovereignty at Sea: The Law and Politics of Saving Lives in Mare Liberum." *Journal of International Relations and Development* 17 (2014): 439–68.

Abbott, Andrew. *The System of Professions: An Essay on the Division of Expert Labour*. Chicago: University of Chicago Press, 1988.

"Things of Boundaries." *Social Research* 62, no. 4 (1995): 857–82.

Chaos of Disciplines. Chicago: University of Chicago Press, 2001.

"The Context of Disciplines." In *Chaos of Disciplines*, 123–25. Chicago: University of Chicago Press, 2001.

Abbott, Kenneth W., and Duncan Snidal. "Hard and Soft Law in International Governance." *International Organization* 54, no. 3 (2000): 421–56.

Ackoff, Russell. "Towards a System of Systems Concepts." *Management Science* 17, no. 11 (1971): 661–71.

Adler, Emanuel. "Seizing the Middle Ground: Constructivism in World Politics." *European Journal of International Relations* 3, no. 3 (1997): 319–63.

Adler, Emanuel, and Vincent Pouliot, eds. *International Practices*. Cambridge: Cambridge University Press, 2011.

Agnew, John. "Sovereignty Regimes: Territoriality and State Authority in Contemporary World Politics." *Annals of the Association of American Geographers* 95, no. 2 (2005): 437–61.

"The Territorial Trap: The Geographical Assumptions of International Relations Theory." *Review of International Political Economy* 1, no. 1 (1994): 53–80.

Geopolitics: Re-Visioning World Politics. 2nd ed. London: Routledge, 2003.

Air Ministry (UK). "The GEE-7000 System." In *Introductory Survey of Radar*, Part II: A Non-Technical Account of Selected Airborne Equipments. Air Publication 1093D, vol. 1, 1st ed. June 1946.

Akkerman, Abraham. "Urban Planning in the Founding of Cartesian Thought." *Philosophy and Geography* 4, no. 2 (2001): 141–67.

Alexander, Jeffrey C. *Performance and Power*. Cambridge: Polity, 2011.

Allan, Bentley B. *Scientific Cosmology and International Orders*. Cambridge: Cambridge University Press, 2018.

Allen, W. Bruce. "The Logistics Revolution and Transportation." *Annals of the American Academy of Political and Social Science* 553, no. 1 (1997): 106–16.

Allott, Philip. "Review of Books." *British Yearbook of International Law* 80, no. 1 (2009): 409–25.

Alpaydin, Ethem. *Machine Learning*, 2nd ed. Cambridge: MIT Press, 2016.

Amell, Amaya. *Francisco de Vitoria and the Evolution of International Law*. Lanham: Lexington Books, 2021.

Amoore, Louise. "Algorithmic War: Everyday Geographies of the War on Terror." *Antipode* 41, no. 1 (2009): 49–69.

"Cloud Geographies: Computing, Data, and Sovereignty." *Progress in Human Geography* 42, no. 1 (2018): 4–24. https://doi.org/10.1177/0309132516662147

Anderson, Benedict. *Imagined Communities: Reflections on the Origin and Spread of Nationalism*. London: Verso, 1991.

Andreas, Peter. "Redrawing the Line: Borders and Security in the Twenty-First Century." *International Security* 28, no. 2 (2003): 78–111.

Anghie, Antony. *Imperialism, Sovereignty and the Making of International Law*. Cambridge: Cambridge University Press, 2005.

Appadurai, Arjun. *Modernity at Large: Cultural Dimensions of Globalization*. Minneapolis: University of Minnesota Press, 1996.

The Future as Cultural Fact: Essays on the Global Condition. London: Verso, 2013.

Aristotle. *Nicomachean Ethics*. Translated by Terence Irwin. 2nd ed. Indianapolis: Hackett, 1999.

Ashley, Richard K. "The Poverty of Neorealism." *International Organization* 38, no. 2 (1984): 225–86.

Ashley, Richard K., and R. B. J. Walker. "Introduction: Speaking the Language of Exile—Dissident Thought in International Studies." *International Studies Quarterly* 34, no. 3 (1990): 259–68.

Avant, Deborah D., Martha Finnemore, and Susan K. Sell, eds. *Who Governs the Globe?* Cambridge: Cambridge University Press, 2010.

Baldwin, David A. *Power and International Relations: A Conceptual Approach*. Princeton: Princeton University Press, 2016.

Balibar, Étienne. *Politics and the Other Scene*, 79, translated by Christine Jones, James Swenson, and Chris Turner. London: Verso, 2002.

Barnett, Michael, and Raymond Duvall. "Power in International Politics." *International Organization* 59, no. 1 (2005): 39–75.

Barney, Darin. *The Network Society*. Cambridge: Polity, 2004.

Bartelson, Jens. "The Social Construction of Globality." *International Political Sociology* 4, no. 3 (2010): 219–35.

Becoming International. Cambridge: Cambridge University Press, 2023.

Barton, David, and Sharon McCulloch. "Negotiating Tensions around New Forms of Academic Writing." *Discourse, Context & Media* 24 (2018): 8–15.

Beck, Ulrich. *Cosmopolitan Vision*. Cambridge: Polity, 2006.

Belcher, Wendy Laura. *Writing Your Journal Article in Twelve Weeks: A Guide to Academic Publishing Success*. Chicago: University of Chicago Press, 2019.

Bellanova, Rocco, and Marieke de Goede. "The Algorithmic Regulation of Security: An Infrastructural Perspective." *Regulation & Governance* 16, no. 1 (2022): 102–18, https://doi.org/10.1111/rego.12338.

Bendersky, Joseph W. *Carl Schmitt: Theorist for the Reich*. Princeton: Princeton University Press, 1983.

"Carl Schmitt at Nuremberg." *Telos* 72 (Summer 1987): 91–96.

Bennett, Jane. *Vibrant Matter: A Political Ecology of Things*. Durham: Duke University Press, 2010.

Benton, Lauren. "Anomalies of Empire." In *A Search for Sovereignty: Law and Geography in European Empires, 1400–1900*, 1–39. Cambridge: Cambridge University Press, 2010.

A Search for Sovereignty: Law and Geography in European Empires, 1400–1900. Cambridge: Cambridge University Press, 2010.

Berg, Maggie, and Barbara K. Seeber. *The Slow Professor: Challenging the Culture of Speed in the Academy*. Toronto: University of Toronto Press, 2016.

Berger, John. *Ways of Seeing*, 16. London: BBC Books, 1972.

Berman, Paul Schiff. *Global Legal Pluralism: A Jurisprudence of Law beyond Borders*. Cambridge: Cambridge University Press, 2012.

Bethlehem, Sir Daniel. "The End of Geography: The Changing Nature of the International System and the Challenge for International Law." *European Journal of International Law* 25, no. 1 (2014): 9–24.

Bew, John. *Realpolitik: A History*. 2nd ed. Oxford: Oxford University Press, 2016.

Bigo, Didier. "Security, Borders, and the State." In *Borders and Border Politics in a Globalizing World*, eds Paul Ganster, Alan Sweedler, James Scott and Wolf Dieter-Eberwein, 81–104. San Diego State University Press, 1997.

Birtchnell, Thomas. "The Missing Mobility: Friction and Freedom in the Movement and Digitization of Cargo." *Applied Mobilities* 1, no. 1 (2016): 85–101.

Black, Jeremy. *Maps and History: Constructing Images of the Past*. New Haven: Yale University Press, 1997.

Blomley, Nicholas. *Law, Space, and the Geographies of Power*. New York: Guilford Press, 1994.

Unsettling the City: Urban Land and the Politics of Property. New York: Routledge, 2004.

"The Spaces of Critical Geography." *Progress in Human Geography* 32, no. 3 (2008): 285–93.

Rights of Passage: Sidewalks and the Regulation of Public Flow. London: Routledge, 2011.

"Precarious Territory: Property Law, Housing, and the Socio-Spatial Order." *Antipode* 52, no. 1 (2020): 36–57.

Bodin, Jean. *Method for the Easy Comprehension of History*. New York: W. W. Norton, 1969.

Borrows, John. *Canada's Indigenous Constitution*. Toronto: University of Toronto Press, 2010.

Börzel, Tanja A. "Multilevel Governance or Multilevel Government?" *The British Journal of Politics and International Relations* 22, no. 4 (2020): 776–83.

Branch, Jordan. *The Cartographic State: Maps, Territory, and the Origins of Sovereignty*. Cambridge: Cambridge University Press, 2014.

"Mapping the Territorial State." In *The Cartographic State: Maps, Territory, and the Origins of Sovereignty*, 68–71. Cambridge: Cambridge University Press, 2014.

Bratton, Benjamin H. *The Stack: On Software and Sovereignty*. Cambridge: MIT Press, 2016.

Brenner, Neil. "Beyond State-Centrism? Space, Territoriality, and Geographical Scale in Globalization Studies." *Theory and Society* 28, no. 1 (1999): 39–78.

Brenner, Neil, and Stuart Elden. "Henri Lefebvre on State, Space, Territory." *International Political Sociology* 3, no. 4 (2009): 353–77.

Brighenti, Andrea M. "Lines, Barred Lines: Movement, Territory and the Law." *International Journal of Law in Context* 6, no. 3 (2010): 217–27.

Brotton, Jerry. *Trading Territories: Mapping the Early Modern World*. London: Reaktion Books, 1997.

A History of the World in Twelve Maps. London: Allen Lane, 2012.

Brown, Chris. *Understanding International Relations*. 5th ed. London: Macmillan International Higher Education, 2019.

Brown, Gordon. "It's August 2024 – and Our World Is at a Turning Point. Here's What We Should Do Now." *The Guardian*, August 24, 2024. www.theguardian.com/commentisfree/article/2024/aug/24/august-2024-world-turning-point-political-environmental-threats-urgent

Brown, Wendy. *Walled States, Waning Sovereignty*. New York: Zone Books, 2010.

Burke, Kenneth. *A Grammar of Motives*. Berkeley and Los Angeles: University of California Press, 1969.

Camille, Michael. "Signs of the City: Place, Power, and Public Fantasy in Medieval Paris." In *Medieval Practices of Space*, edited by Barbara A. Hanawalt and Michal Kobialka, 1–36. Minneapolis: University of Minnesota Press, 2000.

Carr, E. H. *The Twenty Years' Crisis, 1919–1939: An Introduction to the Study of International Relations*. 2nd ed. London: Macmillan, 1974.

Carraro, Valentina. "The C-word: How Critical Cartography, Critical GIS and Critical Data Studies Can Repoliticise Disaster-Related Maps." *Disaster Prevention and Management* 32 (2023): 1–14.

Cassidy, Michael, Anders Sandberg, and Lara Mani. "The Ethics of Volcano Geoengineering." *Earth's Future* 11, no. 10 (2023), 1–17. www.repository.cam.ac.uk/handle/1810/358375

Castells, Manuel. *The Rise of the Network Society*. Oxford: Blackwell, 1996.

Central Intelligence Agency. "Roadways—World (2023)." *The World Factbook*. Accessed August 10, 2025. www.cia.gov/the-world-factbook/about/archives/2023/field/roadways/

"Land Boundaries." *The World Factbook*. Accessed August 10, 2025. www.cia.gov/the-world-factbook/about/archives/2022/field/land-boundaries

Chakrabarty, Dipesh. *Provincializing Europe: Postcolonial Thought and Historical Difference*. New edition. Princeton: Princeton University Press, 2008.

Chamayou, Grégoire. *A Theory of the Drone*. Translated by Janet Lloyd. New York: The New Press, 2015.

Chambers, Samuel N., and Gabriella Soto. "The Geography of Intent: The Bodily Implications of Border Surveillance Technologies." *Political Geography* 120 (2025): 103332. https://doi.org/10.1016/j.polgeo.2025.103332

Chih, Sarah M., and Mikael Rask Madsen. "Legal Diplomacy: Law, Politics, and the Genesis of Postwar European Human Rights." *Law and Contemporary Problems* 82, no. 1 (2019): 137–61.

Chua, Charmaine, Martin Danyluk, Deborah Cowen, and Laleh Khalili. "Turbulent Circulation: Building a Critical Engagement with Logistics." *Environment and Planning D: Society and Space* 36, no. 4 (2018): 617–39.

Cirkovic, Elena, and Danielle R. Wood. "Complex Earth–Outer Space Systems and New Spacetime for International Law." *International Journal of Law in Context* 21, no. 2 (2025): 300–13. https://doi.org/10.1017/S1744552325100086

Clark, Ian, Sebastian Kaempf, Christian Reus-Smit, and Emily Tannock. "Crisis in the Laws of War? Beyond Compliance and Effectiveness." *European Journal of International Relations* 24 (2018): 319–43.

Clark, Stuart. *Vanities of the Eye: Vision in Early Modern European Culture*. Oxford: Oxford University Press, 2007.

Cohen, Felix S. "Transcendental Nonsense and the Functional Approach." *Columbia Law Review* 35, no. 6 (1935): 809–49.

Collini, Stefano. *What Are Universities For?* London: Penguin, 2012.

Collins English Dictionary. s. v. "off the map." Accessed June 18, 2025. www.collinsdictionary.com/dictionary/english/off-the-map

Cosgrove, Denis. *Apollo's Eye: A Cartographic Genealogy of the Earth in the Western Imagination*. Baltimore: Johns Hopkins University Press, 2001.

Coward, Martin. "Network-Centric Violence, Critical Infrastructure and the Urbanisation of Society." *Security Dialogue* 40, nos. 4–5 (2009): 399–418.

Cowen, Deborah. *The Deadly Life of Logistics: Mapping Violence in Global Trade*. Minneapolis: University of Minnesota Press, 2014.

Cowen, Deborah, and Neil Smith, "After Geopolitics? From the Geopolitical Social to Geoeconomics." *Antipode* 41, no. 1 (2009): 22–48.

Crampton, Jeremy W. *The Political Mapping of Cyberspace*. Chicago: University of Chicago Press, 2003.

"Cartography: Maps 2.0." *Progress in Human Geography* 33, no. 1 (2009): 91–100.

Crampton, Jeremy and John Krygier. "An Introduction to Critical Cartography." *ACME: An International Journal for Critical Geographies* 4, no. 1 (2006): 12.

Crawford, James. "International Law as a Discipline and Profession." *Proceedings of the American Society of International Law* 106 (2012): 471–85.

Crawford, Neta C. *The Costs of War: U.S. Counterterrorism Operations and Civilian Harm*, 6–10. Providence, RI: Watson Institute for International and Public Affairs, Brown University, 2021.

Crutcher, Michael, and Matthew Zook. "Placemarks and Waterlines: Racialized Cyberspaces in Post-Katrina Google Earth." *Geoforum* 40, no. 4 (2009): 523–34.

Cubitt, Sean. *The Practice of Light: A Genealogy of Visual Technologies from Prints to Pixels*. Cambridge: MIT Press, 2014.

Cutler, A. Claire and Thomas Dietz, eds., *The Politics of Private Transnational Governance by Contract*. London: Routledge, 2017.

Darvill, Timothy. *The Concise Oxford Dictionary of Archaeology*. 3rd ed. Oxford: Oxford University Press, 2021.

Davis, James W. *Terms of Inquiry: On the Theory and Practice of Political Science*, 10–60. Baltimore: Johns Hopkins University Press, 2005.

Davies, Robertson. *Tempest-Tost*. Salterton Trilogy, book 1. Toronto: Clarke, Irwin & Company, 1951.

De Certeau, Michel. *The Practice of Everyday Life*. Translated by Steven Rendall. Berkeley: University of California Press, 1984.

De Goede, Marieke. "Blacklisting and the Ban: Contesting Targeted Sanctions in Europe." *Security Dialogue* 42, no. 6 (2011): 499–515.

De Gregorio, Giovanni. "The Law of the Platforms." In *Digital Constitutionalism in Europe: Reframing Rights and Powers in the Algorithmic Society*, Giovanni De Gregorio, 80–122. Cambridge Studies in European Law and Policy. Cambridge: Cambridge University Press, 2022.

de Rijcke, Sarah, Paul F. Wouters, Alex D. Rushforth, Thomas P. Franssen, and Björn Hammarfelt. "Evaluation Practices and Effects of Indicator Use—A Literature Review." *Research Evaluation* 25, no. 2 (2016): 161–69.

Deias, Dalia. "A Vanished Curiosity from the Observatoire of Louis XIV: The Parterre Géographique, a Tool Both of Precision and of Representation." *Archives Internationales d'Histoire des Sciences* 72, no. 196 (2022): 74–96.

Delaney, David. *The Spatial, the Legal and the Pragmatics of World-Making: Nomospheric Investigations*. New York: Routledge, 2010.

Deleuze, Gilles, and Félix Guattari. *A Thousand Plateaus: Capitalism and Schizophrenia*. Translated by Brian Massumi. Minneapolis: University of Minnesota Press, 1987.

Della Porta, Donatella, and Michael Keating, eds. *Approaches and Methodologies in the Social Sciences: A Pluralist Perspective*. Cambridge: Cambridge University Press, 2008.

Descartes, René. *Oeuvres de Descartes*. Edited by Charles Adam and Paul Tannery, vol. 7. Paris: J. Vrin, 1964.

Dietz, Thomas. "Relational Contracts 2.0: Efficiency and Power." In *The Politics of Private Transnational Governance by Contract*, edited by A. Claire Cutler and Thomas Dietz, 115–30. Abingdon: Routledge, 2017.

Diffie, Bailey W. "Foreigners in Portugal and the 'Policy of Silence'." *Terrae Incognitae* 1, no. 1 (1960): 23–32.

Dijstelbloem, Huub, Rogier van Reekum, and Willem Schinkel. "Surveillance at Sea: The Transactional Politics of Border Control in the Aegean." *Security Dialogue* 48, no. 3 (2017): 224–40.

Dippy, R. J. "Gee: A Radio Navigational Aid." *Journal of the Institution of Electrical Engineers – Part IIIA: Radiolocation* 93, no. 3 (1946): 468–84.

Dodge, Martin and Chris Perkins, "Reflecting on J. B. Harley's Influence and What He Missed in 'Deconstructing the Map'." *Cartographica* 50, no. 1 (2015): 37–50.

Domingues, Francisco Contente, and Luís Filipe Barreto. "The Recovery of Ptolemy's Geography in Renaissance Italy and Its Impact in Spain and Portugal in the Period of the Discoveries." In *Geography, Cartography and Nautical Science in the Renaissance*, edited by W. G. L. Randles, 145–61. Aldershot: Ashgate, 2000.

Drucker, Peter. "Physical Distribution: The Frontier of Modern Management." In *Readings in Physical Distribution Management*, edited by Jonathan Bowersox, Bernard LaLonde, and Edward Smykay, 3–12. London: Collier-Macmillan, 1969.

d'Aspremont, Jean. *Formalism and the Sources of International Law: A Theory of the Ascertainment of Legal Rules*. Oxford: Oxford University Press, 2011.

d'Orsi, Cristiano, and Gino J. Naldi. "Climate-Induced Displacement in the Sahel: A Question of Classification." *International Review of the Red Cross* 103 (2021): 1029–65.

Easterling, Keller. *Extrastatecraft: The Power of Infrastructure Space*. London: Verso, 2014.

Edgerton, Samuel Y. *The Mirror, the Window, and the Telescope: How Renaissance Linear Perspective Changed Our Vision of the Universe*. Ithaca: Cornell University Press, 2009.

The Renaissance Rediscovery of Linear Perspective. New York: Basic Books, 1975.

Edney, Matthew H. "The Irony of Imperial Mapping." In *The Imperial Map: Cartography and the Mastery of Empire*, edited by James R. Akerman, 11–45. Chicago: University of Chicago Press, 2009.

"Cartography and Its Discontents." *Cartographica* 50, no. 1 (2015): 9–13.

"Historical Geography and the Cartographic Illusion of Exceptionalism." *Journal of Historical Geography* 88 (2025): 27–38.

Edwards, Jeffrey. "The Unity of All Places on the Face of the Earth." In *Reading Kant's Geography*, edited by Stuart Elden and Eduardo Mendieta, 233–63. Albany: SUNY Press, 2011.

Elden, Stuart. "Missing the Point: Globalization, Deterritorialization and the Space of the World." *Transactions of the Institute of British Geographers* 30, no. 1 (2005): 8–19.

The Birth of Territory. Chicago: University of Chicago Press, 2013.

Elvemo, Lasse. "Supply Chain Resilience in Military Operations: A Case Study Exploring Command and Control." *Scandinavian Journal of Military Studies* 8, no. 1 (2025): 184–202. https://doi.org/10.31374/sjms.356

Epstein, Charlotte. *Birth of the State: The Place of the Body in Crafting Modern Politics*. Oxford: Oxford University Press, 2021.

Escobar, Arturo. "Exploration, Cartography and the Modernization of State Power." In *State/Space: A Reader*, edited by Neil Brenner, Bob Jessop, Martin Jones, and Gordon Macleod, 35–147. Oxford: Blackwell Publishing, 2003.

Eslava, Luis, Michael Fakhri, and Vasuki Nesiah, eds. *Bandung, Global History, and International Law: Critical Pasts and Pending Futures*. Cambridge: Cambridge University Press, 2018.

Etymology Online. "Logistic." Accessed August 23, 2025. www.etymonline.com/word/logistic

"Modus." Accessed August 23, 2025. www.etymonline.com/search?q=modus

"Reality." Accessed August 23, 2025. www.etymonline.com/search?q=reality

Farish, Matthew. *The Contours of America's Cold War*. Minneapolis: University of Minnesota Press, 2010.

Fassbender, Bardo. "Stories of War and Peace: On Writing the History of International Law in the 'Third Reich' and After." *European Journal of International Law* 13, no. 2 (2002): 479–512.

Fénéon, Félix. "The Impressionists in 1886." Translated by Belinda Thomson. *Art in Translation* 6, no. 2 (2014): 271–88.

Ferguson, Yale H., and Richard W. Mansbach. *Remapping Global Politics: History's Revenge and Future Shock*. Cambridge: Cambridge University Press, 2004.

Ferretti, Federico. "From the Drought to the Mud: Rediscovering Geopoetics and Cultural Hybridity from the Global South." *Cultural Geographies* 27, no. 4 (2020): 597–613.

Fisher-Lescano, Andreas, and Gunther Teubner. "Regime-Collisions: The Vain Search for Legal Unity in the Fragmentation of Global Law." *Michigan Journal of International Law* 25 (2004): 999–1046.

Fitzpatrick, Kathleen. *Planned Obsolescence: Publishing, Technology, and the Future of the Academy*. New York: NYU Press, 2011.

Fleurke, Floor M., Han Somsen, Hans Lindahl, Marie-Catherine Petersmann, Michael C. Leach, and Phillip Paiement. "Constitutionalizing in the Anthropocene." *Journal of Human Rights and the Environment* 15, no. 1 (2024): 4–22.

Ford, Richard T. "Law's Territory (A History of Jurisdiction)." *Michigan Law Review* 97, no. 4 (1999): 843–930.

Foucault, Michel. *The Order of Things: An Archaeology of the Human Sciences*. New York: Vintage Books, 1994.

Security, Territory, Population: Lectures at the Collège de France, 1977–78. Edited by Michel Senellart. Translated by Graham Burchell. Basingstoke: Palgrave Macmillan, 2007.

Freedman, Lawrence, and Efraim Karsh. *The Gulf Conflict, 1990–1991: Diplomacy and War in the New World Order*. Princeton: Princeton University Press, 1993.

Freistein, Katja, and Philip Liste. "Introduction: Fragmented Territoriality." *Journal of International Relations and Development* 19, no. 2 (2016): 193–98.

Frodeman, Robert. *Sustainable Knowledge: A Theory of Interdisciplinarity*. Basingstoke: Palgrave Macmillan, 2014.

Gallie, W. B. "Essentially Contested Concepts." *Proceedings of the Aristotelian Society* 56 (1956): 167–98.

Garcia, Denise. "Algorithms and Decision-Making in Military Artificial Intelligence." *Global Society* 38, no. 1 (2024): 24–33.

Gaspar, Joaquim Alves. "Blunders, Errors and Entanglements: Scrutinizing the Cantino Planisphere with a Cartometric Eye." *Imago Mundi* 64, no. 2 (2012): 181–200.

Geisler, Murray. "Logistics Research and Management Science." *Management Science* 6, no. 4 (1960): 444–54.

George, Jim. *Discourses of Global Politics: A Critical (Re)Introduction to International Relations*. Boulder: Lynne Rienner Publishers, 1994.

"International Relations and the Search for Thinking Space: Another View of the Third Debate." *International Studies Quarterly* 33, no. 3 (1989): 269–79.

Germano, William. *Getting It Published: A Guide for Scholars and Anyone Else Serious about Serious Books*. 3rd ed. Chicago: University of Chicago Press, 2016.

Giddens, Anthony. *A Contemporary Critique of Historical Materialism*. Berkeley: University of California Press, 1981.

Ginsberg, Benjamin. *The Fall of the Faculty: The Rise of the All-Administrative University and Why It Matters*. New York: Oxford University Press, 2011.

Gjesvik, Lars, and Johann Ole Willers. "Beyond Control? The Political Economy of Private Interception, Intrusion, and Surveillance Markets." *Review of International Political Economy* 31, no. 6 (2024): 1840–64.

GlobalData. "Oil and Gas Pipelines Length and Capital Expenditure (CapEx)—Market Analysis," Product page. April 17, 2023. Accessed August 10, 2025. www.globaldata.com/store/report/oil-and-gas-pipelines-length-and-capital-expenditure-market-analysis/

Goodale, Mark. "After International Law: Anthropology beyond the 'Age of Human Rights'." *AJIL Unbound* 115 (2021): 289–93.
Gottmann, Jean. "The Evolution of the Concept of Territory." *Social Science Information* 14, no. 3 (1975): 29–47.
Graham, Mark, and Martin Dittus. *Geographies of Digital Exclusion: Data and Inequality*. London: Pluto Press, 2022.
Greene, Graham. *Journey without Maps*. London: Penguin, 1980.
Greengard, Samuel. *The Internet of Things*. Cambridge: MIT Press, 2015.
Gregory, Derek. *Geographical Imaginations*. Oxford: Blackwell, 1998.
"From a View to a Kill: Drones and Late Modern War." *Theory, Culture & Society* 28, nos. 7–8 (2011): 188–215.
"Networks, Nodes and De-Territorialised Battlespace: The Scopic Regime of Rapid Dominance." In *From Above: War, Violence, and Verticality*, edited by Peter Adey, 105–23. Oxford: Oxford University Press, 2013.
Grindsted, Thomas Skou. "Algorithmic Finance: Algorithmic Trading across Speculative Time-Spaces." *Annals of the American Association of Geographers* 112, no. 5 (2022): 1390–402. https://doi.org/10.1080/24694452.2021.1963658
Guilfoyle, Douglas. "Reading *The City and the City* as an International Lawyer: Reflections on Territoriality, Jurisdiction and Transnationality." *London Review of International Law* 4, no. 1 (2016): 195–207.
Guillaume, Gilbert. "The Future of International Judicial Institutions." *International and Comparative Law Quarterly* 44, no. 4 (1995): 849–72.
Guzzini, Stefano. "Structural Power: The Limits of Neorealist Power Analysis." *International Organization* 47, no. 3 (1993): 443–78.
"Which Geopolitics?" In *The Return of Geopolitics in Europe? Social Mechanisms and Foreign Policy Identity Crises*, edited by Stefano Guzzini, 41. Cambridge: Cambridge University Press, 2013.
Halford, Bethany. "As Telecom Demands Grow, Optical Fibers Will Need to Level Up." *Chemical & Engineering News*, March 16, 2020. Accessed August 10, 2025. https://pubs.acs.org/doi/10.1021/cen-09810-cover
Handl, Gunther. "Extra-Territoriality and Transnational Legal Authority." In *Beyond Territoriality: Transnational Legal Authority in the Age of Globalization*, edited by Gunther Handl, Joachim Zekoll, and Peer Zumbansen, 3–34. Leiden: Martinus Nijhoff Publishers, 2012.
Harley, J. B. "Deconstructing the Map." *Cartographica* 26, no. 2 (1989): 1–20.
"Historical Geography and the Cartographic Illusion." *Journal of Historical Geography* 15, no. 1 (1989): 80–91.
"Maps, Knowledge, and Power." In *The New Nature of Maps: Essays in the History of Cartography*, edited by Paul Laxton, 51–81. Baltimore: Johns Hopkins University Press, 2001.

Harper, Douglas. "Etymology of Logistic." Online Etymology Dictionary. Accessed August 23, 2025. www.etymonline.com/word/logistic

Hart, H. L. A. *The Concept of Law*. 2nd ed. Oxford: Clarendon Press, 1997.

Harvey, David. *The Condition of Postmodernity*. Oxford: Blackwell, 1990.

Hathaway, Oona A., and Scott J. Shapiro. *The Internationalists: How a Radical Plan to Outlaw War Remade the World*. New York: Simon & Schuster, 2017.

Haverluk, Terrence W., Kevin M. Beauchemin, and Brandon A. Mueller. "The Three Critical Flaws of Critical Geopolitics: Towards a Neo Classical Geopolitics." *Geopolitics* 19, no. 1 (2014): 19–46. https://doi.org/10.1080/14650045.2013.803192

Hayek, Friedrich A. *Law, Legislation and Liberty: A New Statement of the Liberal Principles of Justice and Political Economy*. London: Routledge & Kegan Paul, 1982.

Law, Legislation and Liberty, 485. London: Routledge, 1990.

Haynes, Kingsley. "Intermodalism." *Journal of Transport Geography* 5, no. 1 (1997): 21–22.

Hell, Julia. "Katechon: Carl Schmitt's Imperial Theology and the Ruins of the Future." *The Germanic Review: Literature, Culture, Theory* 84, no. 4 (2009): 283–326.

Herz, John. "Rise and Demise of the Territorial State." *World Politics* 9 (1957): 473–93.

Hillebrandt, Maarten, and Michael Huber. "Quantifying Higher Education: Governing Universities and Academics by Numbers." *Politics and Governance* 8, no. 2 (2020): 1–5.

Hinks, A. R. "The International One-in-a-Million Map of the World." *Royal Engineers Journal* 17 (1913): 77–86.

Hobson, John M. "What's at Stake in 'Bringing Historical Sociology Back into International Relations'? Transcending 'Chronofetishism' and 'Tempocentrism' in International Relations." In *Historical Sociology of International Relations*, edited by Stephen Hobden and John M. Hobson, 6–8. Cambridge: Cambridge University Press, 2002.

Hooker, William. *Carl Schmitt's International Thought: Order and Orientation*. New York: Cambridge University Press, 2009.

Horowitz, Morton J. *The Transformation of American Law: The Crisis of Legal Orthodoxy, 1870–1960*. Oxford: Oxford University Press, 1992.

Hu, Tung-Hui. *A Prehistory of the Cloud*, 7–8. Cambridge: MIT Press, 2015.

Jackson, Peter. *Maps of Meaning: An Introduction to Cultural Geography*, 185–86. London: Unwin Hyman, 1989.

Jacob, Christian. *The Sovereign Map: Theoretical Approaches in Cartography throughout History*. Translated by Tom Conley. Chicago: University of Chicago Press, 2006.

Jasanoff, Sheila. "Subjects of Reason: Goods, Markets, and Competing Imaginaries of Global Governance." *London Review of International Law* 4, no. 2 (2016): 361–91.

Jay, Martin. *Downcast Eyes: The Denigration of Vision in Twentieth-Century French Thought*. Berkeley: University of California Press, 1993.

Jennings, Robert Y. "The Role of the International Court of Justice." *British Yearbook of International Law* 68 (1997): 60–75.

Johns, Fleur. "Global Governance through the Pairing of List and Algorithm." *Environment and Planning D: Society and Space* 34, no. 1 (2016): 126–49.

#Help: Digital Humanitarianism and the Remaking of International Order. Oxford: Oxford University Press, 2023.

Johnson, Benjamin. "Sensing the Arctic: Situational Awareness and the Future of Northern Security." *International Journal* 76, no. 3 (2021): 404–26.

Johnson, Donald S. *Phantom Islands of the Atlantic: The Legends of Seven Lands That Never Were*. Fredericton: Goose Lane Editions, 1994.

Jomini, Antoine-Henri. *The Art of War*. 1836. Reprint, Kington: Legacy Books, 2009.

Jones, Bruce D. *To Rule the Waves: How Control of the World's Oceans Shapes the Fate of the Superpowers*. New York: Scribner, 2021.

Kalt, Gregor, Philipp Thunshirn, and Helmut Haberl "A Global Inventory of Electricity Infrastructures from 1980 to 2017: Country-Level Data on Power Plants, Grids and Transformers." *Scientific Data* 8 (2021). Accessed August 10, 2025. www.sciencedirect.com/science/article/pii/S2352340921006351

Kant, Immanuel. "On the Impossibility of a Sceptical Satisfaction of Pure Reason That Is Divided against Itself." In *Critique of Pure Reason*, translated by Paul Guyer and Allen Wood. Cambridge: Cambridge University Press, 1998.

Kennedy, David, "The 'Rule of Law,' Political Choices, and Development Common Sense." In *The New Law and Economic Development: A Critical Appraisal*, edited by David M. Trubek, and Alvaro Santos, 95–173. Cambridge: Cambridge University Press, 2006

A World of Struggle: How Power, Law, and Expertise Shape Global Political Economy. Princeton: Princeton University Press, 2016.

"Law, Expertise and Global Political Economy." *Tilburg Law Review* 23, nos. 1–2 (2018): 110–23. https://doi.org/10.5334/tilr.130

Kessler, Oliver. "So Close Yet So Far Away? International Law in International Political Sociology." *International Political Sociology* 4 (2010): 303–26.

Khalili, Laleh. *Sinews of War and Trade: Shipping and Capitalism in the Arabian Peninsula*. London: Verso Books, 2021.

Khanna, Parag. *Connectography: Mapping the Global Network Revolution*. New York: Random House, 2016.

Kim, Rakhyun E. "Is Global Governance Fragmented, Polycentric, or Complex? The State of the Art of the Network Approach." *International Studies Review* 22, no. 4 (2020): 903–31.

Kindervater, Katharine Hall. "The Emergence of Lethal Surveillance: Watching and Killing in the History of Drone Technology." *Security Dialogue* 47, no. 3 (2016): 223–38.

"Drone Strikes, Ephemeral Sovereignty, and Changing Conceptions of Territory." *Territory, Politics, Governance* 5, no. 2 (2016): 207–21. https://doi.org/10.1080/21622671.2016.1260493

King, Geoff. *Mapping Reality: An Exploration of Cultural Cartographies*. New York: St. Martin's Press, 1996.

Kingsbury, Benedict. "The Concept of 'Law' in Global Administrative Law." *European Journal of International Law* 20, no. 1 (2009): 23–57.

"Infrastructure and InfraReg: On Rousing the International Law 'Wizards of Is'." *Cambridge International Law Journal* 8, no. 2 (2019): 171–94.

Kingsbury, Benedict, Nico Krisch, and Richard B. Stewart. "The Emergence of Global Administrative Law." *Law and Contemporary Problems* 68, no. 3/4 (2005): 15–61.

Kingsbury, Benedict, and Nahuel Maisley. "Infrastructures and Laws: Publics and Publicness." *Annual Review of Law and Social Science* 17 (2021): 353–73.

Kingsbury, Philip, and John Paul Jones. "Walter Benjamin's Dionysian Adventures on Google Earth." *Geoforum* 40, no. 4 (2009): 502–13.

Kinsey, Christopher, and Ronald Ti. "Combat Logistics in the Twenty-First Century." In *Advanced Land Warfare*, edited by Mikael Weissmann and Niklas Nilsson, 63–85. Oxford: Oxford University Press, 2023.

Kitchin, Rob, Justin Gleeson, and Martin Dodge. "Unfolding Mapping Practices: A New Epistemology for Cartography." *Transactions of the Institute of British Geographers* 38, no. 3 (2013): 480–96.

Kitchin, Rob, and Martin Dodge. "Rethinking Maps." *Progress in Human Geography* 31, no. 3 (2007): 331–44.

Kitchin, Rob, and Oliver Dawkins. "Digital Twins and Deep Maps." *Transactions of the Institute of British Geographers* 50, no. 1 (2025): e12699. https://doi.org/10.1111/tran.12699

Kitchin, Rob, Juliette Davret, Carla Maria Kayanan, and Samuel Mutter. "Data Mobilities: Rethinking the Movement and Circulation of Digital Data." *Mobilities* 20, no. 5 (2025): 1–19. https://doi.org/10.1080/17450101.2025.2481309

Klabbers, Jan. "The Bridge Crack'd: A Critical Look at Interdisciplinary Relations." *International Relations* 23 (2009): 119–26.

Klinghoffer, Arthur Jay. *The Power of Projections: How Maps Reflect Global Politics and History*, 75. Westport: Praeger Publishers, 2006.

Knowles, Anne Kelly. "Why We Must Make Maps: Historical Geography as a Visual Craft." *Historical Geography* 42 (2014): 3–26.

Koinova, Maria. "Polycentric Governance of Transit Migration: A Relational Perspective from the Balkans and the Middle East." *Review of International Studies* 48, no. 3 (2022): 461–83.

Koller, David. "…and New York and the Hague and Tokyo and Geneva and Nuremberg and…: The Geographies of International Law." *European Journal of International Law* 23, no. 1 (2012): 97–119.

Koselleck, Reinhart. *The Practice of Conceptual History: Timing History, Spacing Concepts*. Stanford: Stanford University Press, 2002.

Koskenniemi, Martti. "Out of Europe: Carl Schmitt, Hans Morgenthau, and the Turn to 'International Relations'." In *The Gentle Civilizer of Nations: The Rise and Fall of International Law, 1870–1960*, 471. Cambridge: Cambridge University Press, 2001.

The Gentle Civilizer of Nations: The Rise and Fall of International Law, 1870–1960. Cambridge: Cambridge University Press, 2001.

From Apology to Utopia: The Structure of International Legal Argument. Cambridge: Cambridge University Press, 2006.

"The Fate of Public International Law: Between Technique and Politics," *Modern Law Review* 70, no. 1 (2007): 1–30.

"Miserable Comforters: International Relations as New Natural Law." *European Journal of International Relations* 15, no. 3 (2009): 395–422.

"The Politics of International Law – 20 Years Later," *European Journal of International Law* 20, no. 1 (2009): 24–26.

"Law, Teleology and International Relations: An Essay in Counterdisciplinarity." *International Relations* 26, no. 1 (2012): 3–34.

"Carl Schmitt and International Law." In *The Oxford Handbook of Carl Schmitt*, edited by Jens Meierhenrich and Oliver Simons, 593–612. New York: Oxford University Press, 2016.

To the Uttermost Parts of the Earth. Cambridge: Cambridge University Press, 2022.

"What Is International Law For?" In *International Law*, 6th ed., edited by Malcolm D. Evans, 41–43. Oxford: Oxford University Press, 2024.

Koskenniemi, Martti, and Päivi Leino. "Fragmentation of International Law: Postmodern Anxieties?" *Leiden Journal of International Law* 15 (2002): 553–79.

Koslowski, Rey, and Friedrich Kratochwil. "Understanding Change in International Politics: The Soviet Empire's Demise and the International System." *International Organization* 48, no. 2 (1994): 215–47.

Krasmann, Susanne, and Christine Hentschel. "'Situational Awareness': Rethinking Security in Times of Urban Terrorism." *Security Dialogue* 50, no. 2 (2019): 181–97.

Kratochwil, Friedrich. *Rules, Norms and Decisions: On the Conditions of Practical and Legal Reasoning in International Relations and Domestic Affairs*. Cambridge: Cambridge University Press, 1989.

"Sovereignty as Dominium: Is There a Right of Humanitarian Intervention?" In *Beyond Westphalia? State Sovereignty and International Intervention*, edited by Gene M. Lyons and Michael Mastanduno, 21–42. Baltimore: Johns Hopkins University Press, 1995.

"Constructivism: What It Is (Not) and How It Matters." In *Approaches and Methodologies in the Social Sciences: A Pluralist Perspective*, edited by Donatella Della Porta and Michael Keating, 80–98. Cambridge: Cambridge University Press, 2008.

"Of Maps, Law, and Politics: An Inquiry into the Changing Meaning of Territoriality." *DIIS Working Paper* 2011:03. Copenhagen: Danish Institute for International Studies, 2011, 8.

The Status of Law in World Society. Cambridge: Cambridge University Press, 2014.

Kratochwil, Friedrich, and John Gerard Ruggie. "International Organization: A State of the Art on an Art of the State." *International Organization* 40, no. 4 (1986): 753–75.

Krisch, Nico. "Introduction: Global Administrative Law in the International Legal Order." *European Journal of International Law* 17 (2006): 1–13.

Beyond Constitutionalism: The Pluralist Structure of Postnational Law. Oxford: Oxford University Press, 2010.

"Liquid Authority in Global Governance." *International Theory* 9 (2017): 237–60.

Krisch, Nico, and Benedict Kingsbury. "Introduction: Global Governance and Global Administrative Law in the International Legal Order," *European Journal of International Law* 17, no. 1 (2006): 1–13.

Kroll, Joshua A., Joanna Huey, Solon Barocas, et al. "Accountable Algorithms." *University of Pennsylvania Law Review* 165, no. 3 (2017): 633–705.

Kwan, Mei-Po. "Algorithmic Geographies: Big Data, Algorithmic Uncertainty, and the Production of Geographic Knowledge." *Annals of the American Association of Geographers* 106, no. 2 (2016): 274–82. https://doi.org/10.1080/00045608.2015.1117937

Kwan, Mei-Po, and Tim Schwanen. "Geographies of Mobility." *Annals of the American Association of Geographers* 106, no. 2 (2016): 243–56. https://doi.org/10.1080/24694452.2015.1123067

Kyriakou, Panagiotis A. "International Law Shaping and Digital Ecosystems: Between Sensationalism and Empowerment." *Asian Journal of International Law* 15, no. 1 (2025): 232–51. https://doi.org/10.1017/S2044251324000328

Lamont, Michèle. "On Disciplinary Cultures." In *How Professors Think: Inside the Curious World of Academic Judgment*, 53–57. Cambridge: Harvard University Press, 2009.

Lang, Karen. *Chaos and Cosmos: On the Image in Aesthetics and Art History*. Ithaca: Cornell University Press, 2006.

Lanham, Richard A. *The Economics of Attention: Style and Substance in the Age of Information*. Chicago: University of Chicago Press, 2006.

Lapid, Yosef. "The Third Debate: On the Prospects of International Theory in a Post-Positivist Era." *International Studies Quarterly* 33, no. 3 (1989): 235–54.

Last, Angela. "Fruit of the Cyclone: Undoing Geopolitics through Geopoetics." *Geoforum* 64 (2015): 56–64.

"We Are the World? Anthropocene Cultural Production between Geopoetics and Geopolitics." *Theory, Culture & Society* 34, nos. 2–3 (2017): 147–68.

Latour, Bruno. *Down to Earth: Politics in the New Climatic Regime*. Cambridge: Polity, 2018.

"*Onus Orbis Terrarum*: About a Possible Shift in the Definition of Sovereignty." *Millennium: Journal of International Studies* 44, no. 3 (2016): 305–20.

Politics of Nature: How to Bring the Sciences into Democracy. Translated by Catherine Porter. Cambridge: Harvard University Press, 2004.

Science in Action: How to Follow Scientists and Engineers through Society. Cambridge: Harvard University Press, 1987.

Lauterpacht, Hersch. "On Realism, Especially in International Relations." In *International Law, vol. 2: The Law of Peace, Part 1: International Law in General*, edited by Q. C. Elihu Lauterpacht, 57. Cambridge: Cambridge University Press, 2009.

The Function of Law in the International Community, ch. VII. Oxford: Clarendon Press, 1933; reissued Oxford University Press, 2011), 147–73.

Law, John. "On the Social Explanation of Technical Change: The Case of the Portuguese Maritime Expansion." *Technology and Culture* 28, no. 2 (1987): 227–52.

Lefebvre, Henri. *The Production of Space*. Translated by Donald Nicholson-Smith. Oxford: Blackwell, 1991.

Legg, Stephen, ed. *Spatiality, Sovereignty and Carl Schmitt: Geographies of the Nomos*. London: Routledge, 2011.

Lehdonvirta, Vili, Boxi Wú, and Zoe Hawkins. "Weaponised Interdependence in a Bipolar World: How Economic Forces and Security Interests Shape the Global Reach of US and Chinese Cloud Data Centres." *Review of International Political Economy* (2025): 1–26. https://doi.org/10.1080/09692290.2025.2489077

Leuenberger, Christine, and Izhak Schnell. *The Politics of Maps: Cartographic Constructions of Israel/Palestine*. Oxford: Oxford University Press, 2020.

Levinson, Marc. *The Box: How the Shipping Container Made the World Smaller and the World Economy Bigger*. 2nd ed. Princeton: Princeton University Press, 2016.

Levy, Karen. *Data Driven: Truckers, Technology, and the New Workplace Surveillance*. Princeton: Princeton University Press, 2023.

Li, Tania Murray. "What Is Land? Assembling a Resource for Global Investment." *Transactions of the Institute of British Geographers* 39, no. 4 (2014): 589–602.

Lindahl, Hans. *Fault Lines of Globalization: Legal Order and the Politics of A-Legality*. Oxford: Oxford University Press, 2013.

Lindqvist, Sven. *A History of Bombing*. London: Granta, 2001.

Liste, Philip. "Colliding Geographies: Space at Work in Global Governance." *Journal of International Relations and Development* 19, no. 2 (2016): 199–221.

"Geographical Knowledge at Work: Human Rights Litigation and Transnational Territoriality," *European Journal of International Relations* 22, no. 1 (2016): 217–39.

Locke, John. *Two Treatises of Government*. 1823. Accessed August 23, 2025. www.efm.bris.ac.uk/het/locke/government.pdf

Loiselle, Marie-Eve. *Building Walls, Constructing Identities: Legal Discourse and the Creation of National Borders*. Stanford: Stanford University Press, 2025.

Lorca, Arnulf Becker. *Mestizo International Law: A Global Intellectual History 1842–1933*. Cambridge: Cambridge University Press, 2015.

Lupton, Deborah. *The Quantified Self*. Cambridge: Polity, 2016.

Lythgoe, Gail. "A New Legal Geography for International Law." In *The Rebirth of Territory*, 249–58. Cambridge: Cambridge University Press, 2024.

"Contracts: Reterritorializing the (Global) Exercise of Authority." *International Journal of Law in Context* (2025): 1–19.

MacDonald, Kate. *The Politics of Global Supply Chains: Power and Governance beyond the State*. Cambridge: Polity Press, 2014.

MacKinnon, Danny. "Reconstructing Scale: Towards a New Scalar Politics." *Progress in Human Geography* 35 (2010): 21–36.
Malpas, Jeff, and Karsten Thiel. "Kant's Geography of Reason." In *Reading Kant's Geography*, edited by Stuart Elden and Eduardo Mendieta, 195–211. Albany: SUNY Press, 2011.
Mangan, John, Chandra Lalwani, and Tim Butcher. *Global Logistics and Supply Chain Management*. Chichester: Wiley & Sons, 2008.
Mann, Itamar. "Law and Politics from the Sea." *International Theory* 16, no. 1 (2024): 78–101.
Mansouri, Negar, and Daniel R. Quiroga Villamarín, eds. *Ways of Seeing International Organisations: New Perspectives for International Institutional Law*. Cambridge: Cambridge University Press, 2025. https://doi.org/10.1017/9781009552646
Markham, Beryl. *West with the Night*. New York: North Point Press, 1983.
Martin, Craig. *Shipping Container: Global Logistics and the Making of Modern Trade*. London: Bloomsbury Academic, 2016.
Marusek, Sarah. "Lavascape: Legal Spectacle at Kīlauea." *Social Semiotics* 29 (2019): 351–68.
Massicot, Dara. "What Russia Got Wrong: Can Moscow Learn from Its Failures in Ukraine?" *Foreign Affairs* 102, no. 1 (2023): 78–90.
McConaughey, Meghan, Paul Musgrave, and Daniel H. Nexon. "Beyond Anarchy: Logics of Political Organization, Hierarchy, and International Structure." *International Theory* 10, no. 2 (2018): 181–218. https://doi.org/10.1017/S1752971918000040
McCreary, Tyler, and Vanessa Lamb. "Reflections on a Political Ecology of Sovereignty." In *Locating Nature: Making and Unmaking International Law*, edited by Usha Natarajan and Julia Dehm, 134–55. Cambridge: Cambridge University Press, 2022.
McGraw-Hill Dictionary of Scientific and Technical Terms. 6th ed. New York: McGraw-Hill, 2003.
McLaren, Duncan, and Olaf Corry. "Clash of Geofutures and the Remaking of Planetary Order: Faultlines Underlying Conflicts over Geoengineering Governance." *Global Policy* 12, no. S1 (2021): 20–33.
McLuhan, Marshall. *Understanding Media: The Extensions of Man*. Cambridge: MIT Press, 1994.
Mearsheimer, John J. *The Tragedy of Great Power Politics*. New York: W. W. Norton, 2001.
Meierhenrich, Jens, and Oliver Simons, eds. *The Oxford Handbook of Carl Schmitt*. Oxford: Oxford University Press, 2017.
Merel, Ethan R. "Google's World: The Impact of 'Agnostic Cartographers' on the State-Dominated International Legal System." *Columbia Journal of Transnational Law* 54, no. 2 (2016): 424–72.

Merry, Sally Engle. *The Seductions of Quantification: Measuring Human Rights, Gender Violence, and Sex Trafficking*. Chicago: University of Chicago Press, 2016.

Mickelson, Karin. "The Maps of International Law: Perceptions of Nature in the Classification of Territory beyond the State." In *Locating Nature: Making and Unmaking International Law*, edited by Usha Natarajan and Julia Dehm, 159–78. Cambridge: Cambridge University Press, 2022.

"The Maps of International Law: Perceptions of Nature in the Classification of Territory." *Leiden Journal of International Law* 27, no. 3 (2014): 621–39.

Mignolo, Walter D. "Putting the Americas on the Map: Cartography and the Colonization of Space." In *The Darker Side of the Renaissance: Literacy, Territoriality, and Colonization*, 259–313. Ann Arbor: University of Michigan Press, 2003.

Milanović, Marko. *Extraterritorial Application of Human Rights Treaties: Law, Principles, and Policy*. Oxford: Oxford University Press, 2011.

Mitchell, Timothy. *Rule of Experts: Egypt, Techno-Politics, Modernity*. Berkeley: University of California Press, 2002.

Carbon Democracy: Political Power in the Age of Oil. New York: Verso, 2013.

Mol, Annemarie. *The Body Multiple: Ontology in Medical Practice*. Durham: Duke University Press, 2002.

Morgenthau, Hans J. *Politics among Nations: The Struggle for Power and Peace*. 6th ed. New York: Alfred A. Knopf, 1978.

Mukerji, Chandra. "Visual Language in Science and the Exercise of Power: The Case of Cartography in Early Modern Europe." *Studies in Visual Communication* 10, no. 3 (1984): 30–45.

"The Political Mobilization of Nature in Seventeenth-Century French Formal Gardens." *Theory and Society* 23, no. 5 (1994): 651–57.

Territorial Ambitions and the Gardens of Versailles. Cambridge: Cambridge University Press, 1997.

Müller, Jan-Werner. *A Dangerous Mind: Carl Schmitt in Post-War European Thought*. New Haven: Yale University Press, 2003.

Muller, Lilly. "Cybersecurity in Practice: The Vigilant Logic of Kill Chains and Threat Construction." *European Journal of International Security* (published online 2024): 1–21. https://doi.org/10.1017/eis.2024.27

Muscarà, Luca. "Maps, Complexity, and the Uncertainty of Power." In *Handbook on the Geographies of Power*, edited by Mat Coleman and John Agnew, 367–78. Cheltenham: Edward Elgar, 2018.

Mutua, Makau W. "Why Redraw the Map of Africa: A Moral and Legal Inquiry." *Michigan Journal of International Law* 16, no. 3 (1995): 1113–76.

Neep, Daniel. "State-Space beyond Territory: Wormholes, Gravitational Fields, and Entanglement." *Journal of Historical Sociology* 30, no. 3 (2017): 466–95.

Newitt, Malyn. *Navigations: The Portuguese Discoveries and the Renaissance*. London: Reaktion Books, 2023.

Niva, Steve. "Disappearing Violence: JSOC and the Pentagon's New Cartography of Networked Warfare." *Security Dialogue* 44, no. 3 (2013): 185–202.

Nye, Joseph S., Jr. "Soft Power." *Foreign Policy* 80 (1990): 153–71.

Ó Tuathail, Gearóid. *Critical Geopolitics: The Politics of Writing Global Space*. London: Routledge, 1996.

"Political Geography III: Dealing with Deterritorialization." *Progress in Human Geography* 22, no. 1 (1998): 81–94.

"Borderless Worlds? Problematizing Discourses of Deterritorialization," *Geopolitics* 4, no. 2 (1999): 139–54.

Ó Tuathail, Gearóid, Simon Dalby, and Paul Routledge. *The Geopolitics Reader*. New York: Routledge, 2006.

Oklopčić, Zoran. *Beyond the People: Social Imaginary and Constituent Imagination*. Oxford: Oxford University Press, 2018.

"The Nomos and the Gaze: Beyond Self-Determination (II)." In *Beyond the People: Social Imaginary and Constituent Imagination*, 193–230. Oxford: Oxford University Press, 2018.

Onuf, Nicholas. *World of Our Making: Rules and Rule in Social Theory and International Relations*. Columbia: University of South Carolina Press, 1989, reprinted London: Routledge, 2003.

International Legal Theory: Essays and Engagements, 1966–2006. London: Routledge, 2008.

Making Sense, Making Worlds: Constructivism in Social Theory and International Relations. London: Routledge, 2013.

"Worlds of Our Making." In *Making Sense, Making Worlds: Constructivism in Social Theory and International Relations*, 21–40. London: Routledge, 2013.

Onuf, Nicholas Greenwood. *The Mightie Frame: Epochal Change and the Modern World*, 1–11. Oxford: Oxford University Press, 2018.

Orford, Anne. "Regional Orders, Geopolitics, and the Future of International Law." *Current Legal Problems* 74, no. 1 (2021): 149–94.

"History and the Turn to the International." In *International Law and the Politics of History*, 70–104. Cambridge: Cambridge University Press, 2021.

Osiander, Andreas. "Sovereignty, International Relations, and the Westphalian Myth." *International Organization* 55, no. 2 (2001): 251–87.

Paasi, Anssi. "Bounded Spaces in a 'Borderless World': Border Studies, Power, and the Anatomy of Territory." *Journal of Power* 2, no. 2 (2009): 213–34.

Pahuja, Sundhya. *Decolonising International Law: Development, Economic Growth and the Politics of Universality*. Cambridge: Cambridge University Press, 2011.

Painter, Joe. "Prosaic Geographies of Statist Sovereignty." *Political Geography* 25, no. 7 (2006): 752–74.

Papastergiadis, Nikos. *The Turbulence of Migration: Globalisation, Deterritorialization and Hybridity*. Cambridge: Polity, 2000.

Parker, Geoffrey G., Marshall W. Van Alstyne, and Sangeet Paul Choudary. *Platform Revolution: How Networked Markets Are Transforming the Economy—and How to Make Them Work for You*. New York: W. W. Norton & Company, 2016.

Parker, Andy, Joshua B. Horton, and David W. Keith, "Stopping Solar Geoengineering through Technical Means: A Preliminary Assessment of Counter-Geoengineering," *Earth's Future* 6, no. 8 (2018): 1058–65, https://doi.org/10.1029/2018EF000864

Pastor Bodmer, Beatriz. *The Armature of Conquest: Spanish Accounts of the Discovery of America, 1492–1589*. Stanford: Stanford University Press, 1992.

Pauwelyn, Joost, Ramses A. Wessel, and Jan Wouters, eds. *Informal International Lawmaking*. Oxford: Oxford University Press, 2012.

"When Structures Become Shackles: Stagnation and Dynamics in International Lawmaking." *European Journal of International Law* 25, no. 3 (2014): 733–63.

Pearson, Alastair W., and Michael Heffernan. "Globalizing Cartography? The International Map of the World, the International Geographical Union, and the United Nations." *Imago Mundi* 67, no. 1 (2015): 58–80.

Pellet, Alain. "Le droit international à la lumière de la pratique: l'introuvable théorie de la réalité." *Recueil des cours* 414 (2021), doi .org/10.1163/1875-8096_pplrdc_A9789004465473_01

Penck, Albrecht. "The Construction of a Map of the World on a Scale of 1:1,000,000." *The Geographical Journal* 1, no. 3 (1893): 253–61.

Petersmann, Ernst-Ulrich. "Strengthening Multilevel Governance of Public Goods through Democratic and Republican Constitutionalism." *Cambridge International Law Journal* 11, no. 2 (2022): 180–201.

Philippopoulos-Mihalopoulos, Andreas. *Spatial Justice: Body, Lawscape, Atmosphere*. London: Routledge, 2015.

Pickles, John. *A History of Spaces: Cartographic Reason, Mapping and the Geo-Coded World*. London: Routledge, 2004.

"What Do Maps Represent?" In *A History of Spaces: Cartographic Reason, Mapping and the Geo-Coded World*, 27–59. London: Routledge, 2004.

Poggi, Gianfranco. *Forms of Power*. Cambridge: Polity Press, 2001.

Pollack, Kenneth. *Arabs at War: Military Effectiveness, 1948–1991*. Lincoln: University of Nebraska Press, 2022.

Popvaitė, Virginija. "Navigating Maps in the Arctic: Tracing More-than-Human Interactions of Mapping Practices in Norwegian Rescue Services." *Polar Geography* 46 (2023): 190–209.

Posen, Barry R. "Command of the Commons: The Military Foundation of U.S. Hegemony." *International Security* 28, no. 1 (2003): 5–46.

Pugliese, Joseph Jonathan. *State Violence and the Execution of Law*. London: Routledge, 2014.

Putnam, Hilary. *Reason, Truth and History*. Cambridge: Cambridge University Press, 1981.

Quiroga-Villamarin, Daniel R. "Normalising Global Commerce: Containerisation, Materiality, and Transnational Regulation (1956–68)." *London Review of International Law* 8 (2020): 457–77.

Rajkovic, Nikolas M. "What Is the Global? Reassembling How International Lawyers See Space and Time." *International Journal of Law in Context* 21 (2025): 203.

"The European Union and Critical Legal Cartography: Old Geopolitics, Worn Geopoetry, and the Return of Geopower." *European Law Open* 1 (Spring 2022): 144.

"The Visual Conquest of International Law: Brute Boundaries, the Map, and the Legacy of Cartogenesis." *Leiden Journal of International Law* 31, no. 2 (2018): 267–88.

"International Law and the Ides of March: A Response to David Kennedy." *Tilburg Law Review* 23, no. 1–2 (2018): 121–24. https://doi.org/10.5334/tilr.131

"The Space between Us: International Law, Teleology and the New Orientalism of Counterdisciplinarity." In *The Law of International Lawyers: Critical Reflections on the Work of Martti Koskenniemi*, edited by Wouter Werner, Marieke de Hoon, and Alexis Galán. Cambridge: Cambridge University Press, 2017.

"Global Law and Governmentality: Reconceptualizing 'Rule of Law' as Rule 'Through' Law." *European Journal of International Relations* 18, no. 1 (2012): 29–52.

"On Fragments and Geometry: The International Legal Order as Metaphor and How It Matters." *Erasmus Law Review* 6, no. 1 (2013): 6–16. https://doi.org/10.5553/ELR/221026712013001003

Rankin, William. *After the Map: Cartography, Navigation, and the Transformation of Territory in the Twentieth Century*. Chicago: University of Chicago Press, 2016.

"Zombie Projects, Negative Networks, and Multigenerational Science: The Temporality of the International Map of the World." *Social Studies of Science* 47, no. 3 (2017): 353–75.

Raz, Joseph. *The Authority of Law: Essays on Law and Morality*. Oxford: Clarendon Press, 1983.

Reiz, Nicole, Shannon O'Lear, and Dory Tuininga. "Exploring a Critical Legal Cartography: Law, Practice, and Complexities." *Geography Compass* 12, no. 5 (2018): 1–10. https://doi.org/10.1111/gec3.12368

Reyna, Stephen. "Social Pointillism and Starry Nights: Making Points to Make Connections in the Sudanese Civil War." *Journal of Asian and African Studies* 51, no. 3 (2016): 358–79.

Reynolds, Simon. *Retromania: Pop Culture's Addiction to Its Own Past*. London: Faber & Faber, 2011.

Riles, Annelise. *The Network Inside Out*. Ann Arbor: University of Michigan Press, 2000.

Collateral Knowledge: Legal Reasoning in the Global Financial Markets. Chicago: University of Chicago Press, 2011.

Rip, Michael, and James Hasik. *The Precision Revolution: GPS and the Future of Aerial Warfare*. Annapolis: Naval Institute Press, 2002.

Ripstein, Arthur. *Force and Freedom: Kant's Legal and Political Philosophy*. Cambridge: Harvard University Press, 2009.

Roberts, Stephen L., and Stefan Elbe. "Catching the Flu: Syndromic Surveillance, Algorithmic Governmentality and Global Health Security." *Security Dialogue* 48, no. 1 (2017): 46–62.

Rose, Carol M. "Property as Storytelling: Perspectives from Game Theory, Narrative Theory, Feminist Theory." *Yale Journal of Law & the Humanities* 2, no. 1 (1990): 37–57.

Property and Persuasion: Essays on the History, Theory, and Rhetoric of Ownership. Boulder: Westview Press, 1994.

Rose-Redwood, Reuben "Deconstructing the Map: 25 Years On – Introduction: The Limits to Deconstructing the Map." *Cartographica* 50, no. 1 (2015): 1–8

Rousseau, Jean-Jacques. *The Discourses and Other Early Political Writings*. Edited by Victor Gourevitch. Cambridge: Cambridge University Press, 1997.

"Discourse on the Origin and Foundation of Inequality." In *The Discourses and Other Early Political Writings*, edited by and translated by Victor Gourevitch. Cambridge: Cambridge University Press, 1997.

Ruggie, John Gerard. "Territoriality and beyond: Problematizing Modernity in International Relations." *International Organization* 47, no. 1 (1993): 139–74.

"What Makes the World Hang Together: Neo-Utilitarianism and the Social Constructivist Challenge." *International Organization* 52, no. 4 (1998): 855–85.

Rumford, Chris. "Theorizing Borders." *European Journal of Social Theory* 9, no. 2 (2006): 155–69.

Rush-Morgan, Rowan. "Geographies of Queer Economies." *Geography Compass* 17, no. 8 (2023): e12719. https://doi.org/10.1111/gec3.12719.

Ryngaert, Cedric. "Representations of the (Extra)Territorial: Theoretical and Visual Perspectives." *Utrecht Law Review* 13, no. 2 (2017): 1–23.

Sack, Robert D. *Human Territoriality: Its Theory and History*. Cambridge: Cambridge University Press, 1986.

Homo Geographicus: A Framework for Action, Awareness, and Moral Concern. Baltimore: Johns Hopkins University Press, 1997.

Salter, Mark B., ed. *Making Things International 2: Catalysts and Reactions*. Minneapolis: University of Minnesota Press, 2016.

"Introduction: Making Assemblages International." In *Making Things International 2: Catalysts and Reactions*, edited by Mark B. Salter, xvi. Minneapolis: University of Minnesota Press, 2016.

Santos, Boaventura de Sousa. "Law: A Map of Misreading. Toward a Postmodern Conception of Law." *Journal of Law and Society* 14, no. 3 (1987): 279–302.

Sartori, Giovanni. "Concept Misformation in Comparative Politics." *American Political Science Review* 64, no. 4 (1970): 1033–53.

Sassen, Saskia. *Territory, Authority, Rights: From Medieval to Global Assemblages*. Princeton: Princeton University Press, 2006.

"When Territory Deborders Territoriality." *Territory, Politics, Governance* 1, no. 1 (2013): 21–45.

"The New Global Market for Land." In *Expulsions: Brutality and Complexity in the Global Economy*, 80–116. Cambridge: Belknap Press of Harvard University Press, 2014.

Schabas, William A. "Synergy or Fragmentation? International Criminal Law and the European Convention on Human Rights." *Journal of International Criminal Justice* 9, no. 3 (2011): 609–32.

Schachter, Oscar. "The Role of Power in International Law." *Proceedings of the Annual Meeting (American Society of International Law)* 93 (1999): 200–05.

Schmitt, Carl. *Roman Catholicism and Political Form*. Translated by G. L. Ulmen. Westport: Greenwood Press, 1996.

The Concept of the Political. Translated by George Schwab. Chicago: University of Chicago Press, 1996.

The Nomos of the Earth in the International Law of the Jus Publicum Europaeum. Translated by G. L. Ulmen. New York: Telos Press, 2003.

"The Großraum Order of International Law with a Ban on Intervention for Spatially Foreign Powers (1939–41)." In *Writings on War*, edited by Timothy Nunan, 75–99. Cambridge: Polity Press, 2011.

In Space We Read Time: On the History of Civilization and Geopolitics. New York: Bard Graduate Center, 2016.

Schouten, Peer. "Security as Controversy: Reassembling Security at Amsterdam Airport." *Security Dialogue* 45 (2014): 23–42.

Scott, James C. *Seeing Like a State: How Certain Schemes to Improve the Human Condition Have Failed*. New Haven: Yale University Press, 1998.

Searle, John. *The Construction of Social Reality*. London: Penguin, 1995.

"Creating Institutional Facts." In *The Construction of Social Reality*, 31–58. New York: Free Press, 1995.

Sekula, Allan, and Noël Burch. "A Film About the Sea: Notes on Allan Sekula and Noël Burch's the Forgotten Space." 17–18. https://cdn.dal.ca/content/dam/dalhousie/images/faculty/arts/centre-european-studies/Forgotten-Space.pdf

Serres, Michel, and Bruno Latour. *Conversations on Science, Culture and Time*. Ann Arbor: University of Michigan Press, 1995.

Shah, Nisha. "The Territorial Trap of the Territorial Trap: Global Transformation and the Problem of the State's Two Territories." *International Political Sociology* 6, no. 1 (2012): 57–76.

Shim, David. "Remote Sensing Place: Satellite Images as Visual Spatial Imaginaries." *Geoforum* 51 (2014): 152–60.

Short, John Rennie. *Making Space: Revisioning the World, 1475–1600*. Syracuse: Syracuse University Press, 2004.

Simons, Oliver. "Carl Schmitt's Spatial Rhetoric." In *The Oxford Handbook of Carl Schmitt*, edited by Jens Meierhenrich and Oliver Simons, 776–802. Oxford: Oxford University Press, 2017.

Slobodian, Quinn. *Crack-Up Capitalism: Market Radicals and the Dream of a World without Democracy*. London: Allen Lane, 2023.

Sloterdijk, Peter. *Globes: Macrospherology: Spheres II*. Translated by Wieland Hoban. Cambridge: MIT Press, 2014.

"Geometry in the Colossal: The Project of Metaphysical Globalization." *Environment and Planning D: Society and Space* 27, no. 1 (2009): 29–40.

Skouteris, Thomas. "The Force of a Doctrine: Article 38 of the PCIJ Statute and the Sources of International Law." In *Events: The Force of International Law*, edited by Fleur Johns, Richard Joyce, and Sundhya Pahuja, 73–93. London: Routledge, 2011.

Smith, A. Mark. *From Sight to Light: The Passage from Ancient to Modern Optics*, 299. Chicago: University of Chicago Press, 2015.

Smykay, Edward, and Bernard LaLonde. *Physical Distribution: The New and Profitable Science of Business Logistics*. Chicago: Dartnell, 1967.

Snyder, John P. *Flattening the Earth: Two Thousand Years of Map Projections*. Chicago: University of Chicago Press, 1993.

Srnicek, Nick. *Platform Capitalism*. Cambridge: Polity Press, 2017.

Statista. "Container Shipping – Statistics & Facts." Accessed August 23, 2025. www.statista.com/topics/1367/container-shipping/

Steinberg, Philip E. "Sovereignty, Territory, and the Mapping of Mobility: A View from the Outside." *Annals of the Association of American Geographers* 99, no. 3 (2009): 467–95.

Stevenson, Edward L. "The Geographical Activities of the Casa de la Contratación." *Annals of the Association of American Geographers* 17, no. 1 (1927): 39–58.

Strandsbjerg, Jeppe. "Cartopolitics, Geopolitics and Boundaries in the Arctic." *Geopolitics* 17, no. 4 (2012): 817–36. https://doi.org/10.1080/14650045.2012.660581

Strange, Susan. *States and Markets*. London: Pinter Publishers, 1987.

Sullivan, Gavin. *The Law of the List: UN Counterterrorism Sanctions and the Politics of Global Security Law*. Cambridge: Cambridge University Press, 2020.

Suresh, Sabarish. "The Cartojuridism of the British East India Company." *Law and History Review* 42, no. 3 (2024): 1–25. https://doi.org/10.1017/S0738248024000051

Svantesson, Dan Jerker B. *Solving the Internet Jurisdiction Puzzle*. Oxford: Oxford University Press, 2017.

Szyliowicz, Joseph S. "Intermodalism, Supply Chains and U.S. Security." *Transport Reviews* 42, no. 6 (2022): 801–18.

TeleGeography. "Frequently Asked Questions about Undersea Submarine Cables." *TeleGeography Blog*. Accessed August 10, 2025. https://blog.telegeography.com/frequently-asked-questions-about-undersea-submarine-cables

Teschke, Benno. "Decisions and Indecisions: Political and Intellectual Receptions of Carl Schmitt." *New Left Review* 67 (2011): 61–95.

"Fatal Attraction: A Critique of Carl Schmitt's International Political and Legal Theory." *International Theory* 3, no. 2 (2011): 179–227.

Teubner, Gunther. *Constitutional Fragments: Societal Constitutionalism and Globalization*. Oxford: Oxford University Press, 2012.

Trachtman, Joel P. "The International Law of Financial Crisis: Spillovers, Subsidiarity, Fragmentation and Cooperation." *Journal of International Economic Law* 13, no. 3 (2010): 719–42.

The Bureau of Investigative Journalism, *Drone Warfare: Pakistan*, accessed June 2025, www.thebureauinvestigates.com/projects/drone-war/pakistan

The Economist. "Why Have Containers Boosted Trade So Much?" May 21, 2013. www.economist.com/finance-and-economics/2013/05/21/why-have-containers-boosted-trade-so-much

The New Oxford Dictionary of English. Edited by Judy Pearsall. Oxford: Oxford University Press, 1998.

Thrift, Nigel. *Non-Representational Theory*. London: Routledge, 2008.

Treaty of Tordesillas. June 7, 1494. In *The Avalon Project*, Yale Law School. Accessed August 23, 2025. https://avalon.law.yale.edu/15th_century/mod001.asp

Tsing, Anna Lowenhaupt. *Friction: An Ethnography of Global Connection*. Princeton: Princeton University Press, 2005.

Tully, James. *A Discourse on Property: John Locke and His Adversaries*, x. Cambridge: Cambridge University Press, 2009.

Tulumello, Simone, and Roberto Falanga. "Homeland as a Multi-Scalar Community: (Dis)Continuities in the U.S. Security/Safety Discourse and Practice." *Environment and Planning C: Politics and Space* 40 (2021): 143–64.

Turnbull, David. "Cartography and Science in Early Modern Europe: Mapping the Construction of Knowledge Spaces." *Imago Mundi* 48 (1996): 5–24.

Turse, Nick. *The Changing Face of Empire: Special Ops, Drones, Spies, Proxy Fighters, Secret Bases, and Cyberwarfare*. Chicago: Haymarket Books, 2012.

UCS (Union of Concerned Scientists). "UCS Satellite Database." Updated May 2025. www.ucsusa.org/resources/satellite-database

Unangst, Matthew David. "(De)Colonial Historical Geography and Historical GIS." *Journal of Historical Geography* 79 (2023): 76–86.

United Nations. *Status of Publication of IMW Sheets as at 31 December 1986*. U.N. Doc. ST/ESA/SER.D/17, Supp. 3. New York: United Nations, 1987.

Report of the Secretary-General: Termination of the International Map of the World Project. E/CONF.82/9. 1986.

United Nations. *LLDCs Global Report* (2017), table "Rail lines, total route (km)" (listing "World: 1,051,839"). Accessed August 10, 2025. https://sdgs.un.org/sites/default/files/2021-10/LLDCs-Globl-Report_11_25_2017_SPREAD_LowVersion.pdf.

United Nations Economic and Social Council. (1989) *Report of the Meeting of the United Nations Ad Hoc Group of Experts on the International Map of the World on the Millionth Scale (IMW), 9–11 December 1986: Papers Submitted by the United Nations Secretariat at the Fourth United Nations Regional Cartographic Conference for the Americas, 23–27 January 1989, Item 5(f) of the Provisional Agenda*. New York: United Nations, 1989.

Urry, John. *Offshoring*. Cambridge: Polity, 2014.

Vaai, Upolu Lumā. "Philosophical Vectors of Oceanic Diplomacy and Development: The Samoan Wisdom of Restraint Meets the Australian Indigenous Relationalist Ethos." *Australian Journal of International Affairs* 77 (2023): 677–81.

Valverde, Mariana. "Jurisdiction and Scale: Legal 'Technicalities' as Resources for Theory." *Social & Legal Studies* 18, no. 2 (2009): 139–57.

"Theorizing the Space and Time of Law." In *Chronotopes of Law: Jurisdiction, Scale and Governance*, Mariana Valverde, 30–53. New York: Routledge, 2015.

van Creveld, Martin. *Supplying War: Logistics from Wallenstein to Patton*, 2nd ed. Cambridge: Cambridge University Press, 2009.

Varadharajan, Vijay, and Neeraj Suri. "Security Challenges When Space Merges with Cyberspace." *Space Policy* 67 (2024): 1–8. https://doi.org/10.1016/j.spacepol.2023.101600

Venzke, Ingo. "Against Impact." *Leiden Journal of International Law* 37, no. 4 (2024): 757–62.

Verweijen, Judith. "A Microdynamics Approach to Geographies of Violence: Mapping the Kill Chain in Militarized Conservation Areas." *Political Geography* 79 (2020): 102153. https://doi.org/10.1016/j.polgeo.2020.102153

VesselFinder. "MSC *Irina*." Accessed August 23, 2025. www.vesselfinder.com/vessels/details/9929429

Virilio, Paul. *L'Insecurité du Territoire*. Paris: Stock, 1975.

Speed and Politics. New York: Semiotext(e), 2006.

Vitoria, Francisco de. *Political Writings*. Edited by Anthony Pagden and Jeremy Lawrance. Cambridge: Cambridge University Press, 1991.

Voigt, Rüdiger, ed. *Großraum-Denken: Carl Schmitts Kategorie der Großraumordnung*. Stuttgart: Franz Steiner Verlag, 2008.

von Bertalanffy, Ludwig. *General System Theory: Foundations, Development, Applications*, 46–48. Harmondsworth: Penguin, 1973.

Walker, R. B. J. *After the Globe, Before the World*. London: Routledge, 2010.

Inside/Outside: International Relations as Political Theory. Cambridge: Cambridge University Press, 1993.

Walters, William. "Aviation as Deportation Infrastructure: Airports, Planes, and Expulsion." *Journal of Ethnic and Migration Studies* 44 (2018): 2796–817.

Walzer, Michael. "On the Role of Symbolism in Political Thought." *Political Science Quarterly* 82 (1967): 191–204.

Weber, Max. *The Vocation Lectures*. Edited by David Owen and Tracy B. Strong. Translated by Rodney Livingstone. Indianapolis: Hackett, 2004.

Wendt, Alexander. "The Agent–Structure Problem in International Relations Theory." *International Organization* 41, no. 3 (1987): 335–70.

"Anarchy Is What States Make of It: The Social Construction of Power Politics." *International Organization* 46, no. 2 (1992): 391–425.

Quantum Mind and Social Science: Unifying Physical and Social Ontology. Cambridge: Cambridge University Press, 2015.

Westermeier, Carola. "From Flows towards Updates: Security Regimes and Changing Technologies for Financial Surveillance." *Review of International Studies* 49, no. 4 (2023): 615–36.

Wey Gómez, Nicolás. *The Tropics of Empire: Why Columbus Sailed South to the Indies*. Cambridge: MIT Press, 2008.

Wiener, Antje. "Enacting Meaning-in-Use: Qualitative Research on Norms and International Relations." *Review of International Studies* 35, no. 1 (2009): 175–93.

Winichakul, Thongchai. *Siam Mapped: A History of the Geo-Body of a Nation*. Honolulu: University of Hawai'i Press, 1994.

Wintour, Patrick. "World Inching Ever Closer to a Great Fracture." *The Guardian*, September 19, 2023. www.theguardian.com/world/2023/sep/19/world-inching-ever-closer-to-a-great-fracture-says-un-chief

Wood, Denis. *The Power of Maps*. New York: Guilford Press, 1992.

World Bank. "Rail Lines (Total Route-km)." *World Development Indicators (indicator IS.RRS.TOTL.KM; source: UIC Railisa)*. Accessed August 10, 2025. https://data.worldbank.org/indicator/IS.RRS.TOTL.KM

"Container Port Traffic (TEU: 20-Foot Equivalent Units)." Accessed August 23, 2025. https://data.worldbank.org/indicator/IS.SHP.GOOD.TU

Connecting to Compete: Trade Logistics in the Global Economy 2018. Accessed August 23, 2025. https://documents1.worldbank.org/curated/en/576061531492034646/pdf/Connecting-to-compete-2018-trade-logistics-in-the-global-economy-the-logistics-performance-index-and-its-indicators.pdf

Yeung, Karen. "Algorithmic Regulation: A Critical Interrogation." *Regulation & Governance* 12, no. 4 (2018): 505–23.

Young, Margaret A., ed. *Regime Interaction in International Law: Facing Fragmentation*. Cambridge: Cambridge University Press, 2012.

Zarbiyev, Fuad. "Of Theory and Reality, and Airplanes and Helicopters." *European Journal of International Law* 36, no. 1 (2025): 147–64.

Zhang, Chenchen, and Carwyn Morris. "Borders, Bordering and Sovereignty in Digital Space." *Territory, Politics, Governance* 11 (2023): 1051–58.

Zuboff, Shoshana. *The Age of Surveillance Capitalism*. New York: Public Affairs, 2019.

Zumbansen, Peer. "Defining the Space of Transnational Law: Legal Theory, Global Governance, and Legal Pluralism." In *Beyond Territoriality: Transnational Legal Authority in the Age of Globalization*, edited by Gunther Handl, Joachim Zekoll, and Peer Zumbansen, 53–86. Leiden: Brill, 2013.

"Transnational Legal Pluralism." *Transnational Legal Theory* 1, no. 2 (2010): 141–89.

"Transnational Law: Theories and Applications." In *The Oxford Handbook of Transnational Law*, edited by Peer Zumbansen, 3–30. Oxford: Oxford University Press, 2021.

Index

Printed in the United Kingdom by TJ Clays Ltd.